Studien zur europäischen Kinder- und Jugendliteratur (SEKL) | *Studies in European Children's and Young Adult Literature*

Herausgegeben von / *Edited by*
BETTINA KÜMMERLING-MEIBAUER
ANJA MÜLLER
ASTRID SURMATZ

Band 4

Studien zur europäischen Kinder- und Jugendliteratur/ Studies in European Children's and Young Adult Literature (SEKL)

Herausgegeben von / Edited by
BETTINA KÜMMERLING-MEIBAUER, ANJA MÜLLER, ASTRID SURMATZ

Ein zentrales Anliegen dieser Buchreihe besteht darin, literatur- und kulturtheoretisch anspruchsvolle Studien zur Geschichte und Theorie der Kinder- und Jugendliteratur (inklusive anderer Kindermedien) zu veröffentlichen. In ihrer Ausrichtung vertritt die Reihe dezidiert eine europäische Perspektive, d.h. sie versteht sich als Publikationsorgan für Forschung zu den Kinder- und Jugendliteraturen unterschiedlicher europäischer Sprachräume. Auch Studien, die sich mit dem Einfluss außereuropäischer Kinderliteraturen auf die europäische Kinder- und Jugendliteratur befassen, sind willkommen. Die Forschungsperspektive kann komparatistisch geprägt sein oder sich auf eine Einzelphilologie konzentrieren. In dieser Serie können sowohl deutsch- als auch englischsprachige Monographien und Sammelbände veröffentlicht werden. Eingereichte Buchprojekte und Manuskripte werden anonym von zwei ausgewiesenen Fachwissenschaftler/innen begutachtet.

The series aims to publish original studies on literature or media for children and young adults. It seeks to unite a variety of approaches from literary or cultural studies and welcomes historically or theoretically informed research. With its decidedly European perspective, the series understands itself as a platform for research in the children's literatures of different European regions and in different European languages. The series also seeks to include studies dealing with the influence of non-European literatures on European literature for children and young adults. While the languages of publication in the series are either English or German, the topics of the volumes can address children's literature in any other European language, as well. Comparative studies are particularly welcome. We invite submissions for monographs or essay collections. Proposals will be submitted to double blind peer review.

SANDRA STADLER

South African Young Adult Literature in English, 2000–2014

Universitätsverlag
WINTER
Heidelberg

Bibliografische Information der Deutschen Nationalbibliothek
Die Deutsche Nationalbibliothek verzeichnet diese Publikation in der Deutschen Nationalbibliografie; detaillierte bibliografische Daten sind im Internet über *http://dnb.d-nb.de* abrufbar.

Zugl.: Regensburg; Univ., Diss., 2015

ISBN 978-3-8253-6641-4

Imprimé en Allemagne · Printed in Germany
Umschlaggestaltung: Klaus Brecht GmbH, Heidelberg
Druck: Memminger MedienCentrum, 87700 Memmingen

Gedruckt auf umweltfreundlichem, chlorfrei gebleichtem und alterungsbeständigem Papier

Den Verlag erreichen Sie im Internet unter:
www.winter-verlag.de

Contents

Acknowledgements

It is a privilege to express my deepest gratitude to Jochen Petzold for his advice throughout this project and to acknowledge with great appreciation the untiring support I received throughout the project from my colleagues in Germany and abroad: Anne-Julia Zwierlein, Petra Kirchhoff, Bettina Kümmerling-Meibauer, and Betsie van der Westhuizen, thank you for your advice and mentoring at different stages of the project. My thanks also go to John Stephens, Elwyn Jenkins, and AbdouMaliq Simone for inspiring conversations in Potchefstroom and Chemnitz, to Crystal Warren, Thando Njovane, Robin Malan, and Russell Kaschula for helping me to deepen my understanding of South Africa and its youth, and to my dear colleagues and friends Heidi Weig, Katharina Boehm, Anna Farkas, and Martin Decker for their words of encouragement at different stages of this project. I also want to thank the anonymous reviewers of the series for their feedback, as well as the staff of the National English Literary Museum (NELM) for their assistance during my research visit in Grahamstown. I am indebted to the DAAD (German Academic Exchange Services) for providing me with a research grant, which allowed me to access sources which are archived at NELM. For the opportunity to complete this thesis, I am particularly indebted to the Gleichstellungsprogramm Bayern.

Last but not least, my warmest thanks to my parents, my sisters, and my partner for their unfailing support and love. This thesis is for you.

I Introduction

> "I wish we would more often read down – for the past, the allegorical, the metaphoric, the symptom, apartheid – but also across – the horizontal, the surface, the new – the place where paradoxically the fugitive meanings of the now might reside."
>
> (Sarah Nuttall, "The Way We Read Now," 2011a)

> "It's an interesting time to be a youth writer in South Africa. [...] Our writers have their fingers on the pulse."
>
> (Sally-Ann Partridge, "Youth lit in South Africa")

> "[I]t is not on this side or that, speaking on behalf of this group or that, espousing this ideology or that. It is on the new high that is South African lit, it plumbs the lows; it is also elusively, unclassifiably in-between."
>
> (Craig MacKenzie 2010, 6)

The year 2014 marked not only the twentieth anniversary of "the New South Africa",[1] but also the twentieth anniversary of new South African literature. Since 1994, the year in which Nelson Mandela was elected president of the newly founded government, the country's literature has diversified massively in terms of genre, content, form, and authorship. In fact, literary production has been so manifold that Leon de Kock has expressed fears that literary critics may no longer be able to cope with "the sheer profusion of new work" published every year (2009, abstract). And indeed, while developments in the country's adult literature have been reviewed and critically assessed internationally, other literary fields have not received the same amount of attention. In the field of children's and young adult literature, research lacunae are particularly evident, despite the cultural significance of these literary texts. As children's and youth literature often includes a didacticism which aims to guide readers in their development into full-fledged members of society, transformative processes in literary texts for young readers are particularly indicative of just such processes in a country that is currently in a phase of transition. According to Judith Inggs, a paradigm shift in written texts for and about the young people of South Africa becomes traceable particularly in novels published after the year 2000:

[1] The phrase was coined by F. W. de Klerk and has meanwhile become synonymous with post-1994 South Africa (cf. Jolly and Attridge 4).

> Towards the end of the 1990s, and at the beginning of this century, works for young adults reflected a shift away from the fundamental issues of power and powerlessness on racial grounds towards a greater focus on the adolescent characters' attempts to negotiate positions of power for themselves in relation to more varied sites of authority, such as school, religion, sex and identity. (2006, abstract)

To date, no comprehensive analysis or systematization of South African youth literature from this period has been undertaken. This age group is, however, uniquely representative of the present condition of South Africa, a country which is itself an adolescent nation. This is the age group that was born into an atmosphere of unprecedented hope when the apartheid regime finally came to an end in 1994, and this is the first generation to grow up in the new democratic Republic of South Africa. Moreover, the largest group of South Africa's population is comprised of young people: Nearly 40% of all citizens belong to the age group 15–34 ("Social Profile of Vulnerable Groups" ii)[2] and thus also account for the biggest group of potential book buyers.

Attempting to fill this research gap, the present study intends to offer new insights into literary developments in the field of South African English young adult literature of this early twenty-first century. More specifically, I examine novels written in English in the realist mode[3] between the years 2000 and 2013, drawing on both quantitative and qualitative methodology, more commonly known in literary studies as distant reading[4] and close reading, in order to be able to establish what I hope will be a literary social profile of contemporary South African narratives for young adults.

The present study is based on the results of a corpus analysis of 247 English-language novels which were written by South African authors and published in

[2] Contrary to the UN, which defines youth as aged 15–24 (cf. "Definition of Youth"), official reports and statistics by *Statistics South Africa* refer to youth as aged between 15–34 (cf. "Social Profile of Vulnerable Groups"). Adolescent literature is usually addressed to an audience roughly between the ages of 12 and 18 (cf. section "Young Adult Literature – Adult Literature – Children's Literature"). The protagonists in the texts selected for close readings in this thesis fall roughly into this latter age span.

[3] In this thesis, 'realist fictions' are understood as texts that depict post-apartheid South Africa realistically to the extent that the stories contain believable settings and that the character development in the fictional texts resembles that of real people. Historical novels, which are usually also categorized as realist fictions, are excluded in this paper's debate as the focal point of analysis lies on the literary discussion of the now, i.e. the years following 2000. For a further discussion of "Realism in South African English Youth Literature", see section II.

[4] This method of literary criticism was established by Franco Moretti (2013). For further information, see the upcoming section "Methodology/Corpus".

South Africa between the years 2000 and 2013.[5] The emergence of new topics in literature written after the democratic revolution – the majority of which are related to issues of space, gender, race and class, sociology, and politics – correlates with a wider climate of change in South Africa. The repeated inclusion of the thematic areas space, gender, and what can be summarized as 'social economics' in twenty-first century realist fiction does not come as a surprise as these are among the most controversial areas of social life in contemporary South Africa.

Thematically, twenty-first century young adult literature puts its focus on documenting processes of spatial segregation in the new South Africa (cf. chapter 1), on discussing the persistence of gender hierarchies and stereotypes (cf. chapter 2), and on the impact of socio-economic issues on young people's lives (cf. chapter 3). In my distant reading of 147 texts written in the realist mode, I came to the conclusion that the genre is heterogenic with a variety of life worlds being represented (cf. Stadler 2014, 2015). While this is a positive outcome, it is arguably not very specific. In order to substantiate my claim of heterogeneity, this thesis includes close readings of twenty-one novels[6] leading to more nuanced findings: Broadly speaking, the implementation of a democratic constitution in 1996 and the consequent transformation of South African space and economy have led to the emergence of new major issues of socio-economic and cultural dispossession affecting especially the nation's adolescents. Given the complex relationship between historical change, nation-making, and the young (cf. Levander) authors of post-transition South African adolescent literature have started to 'experiment' with narrative structure and different narrative techniques in order to write the story of their nation (cf. Inggs 2006). Their texts tackle the new hot spots of South African society, which are located in both the public sphere (education, youth unemployment, economic policies, etc.) and the private sphere (family, lack of adult role models, identity, sexually transmitted diseases, value

[5] The "Annotated Corpus" was first published in *Bookbird* (cf. Stadler 2015, 56–58). It is also included in the Appendix to this thesis.

[6] Chapter 1 includes close readings of K. Sello Duiker's *Thirteen Cents* (2000), Margie Orford's *Dancing Queen* (2004), Jayne Bauling's *E Eights* (2009), David Donald's *Call on the Wind* (2007), Gillian D'Achada's *Sharkey's Son* (2008), John van de Ruit's *Spud* (2005), Anoeschka von Meck's *My Name Is Vaselinetjie* (2011), and Fiona Snyckers's *Trinity Rising* (2009). Chapter 2 examines Russell H. Kaschula's *Take Me to the River* (2006), Thando Mgqolozana's *A Man Who Is Not a Man* (2010), Sifiso Mzobe's *Young Blood* (2010), Biron Alnam's *No Problem, Man!* (2003), Robin Malan's *My "Funny" Brother* (2012), Kagiso Lesego Molope's *This Book Betrays My Brother* (2012), and Kgebetli Moele's *Untitled: A Novel* (2013). Chapter 3 looks at Dianne Case and Yvonne Hart's *Katy of Sky Road* (2007), Sello Mahapeletsa's *Tears of an Angel* (2007), Jenny Robson's *Back to Villa Park* (2013), Willem 'Thembalethu' van der Walt's *Heist Wind* (2003), Jenny Robson's *Monday Evening, Thursday Afternoon* (2013), and Sally-Ann Partridge's *Dark Poppy's Demise* (2011).

orientation, importance of peer group, etc.), and put youth rights, juvenile participation, and membership in society up for discussion. Literary texts portray juvenile characters as significantly more open-minded than their adult counterparts, and a majority of realist fictions promote multiculturalism and diversity with the help of hopeful endings; yet these hopeful endings cannot hide the fact that established spatial, socio-economic, and gender hierarchies still remain pressing issues twenty years after the end of apartheid. Twenty-first century young adult novels address these hierarchies and reveal them as providing the basis for continued spatial, social, and mental segregation among South African people. While juvenile protagonists are depicted as eager to overcome these segregations, they are not always successful within a novel's pages. In the following, I will explore how literature for young adults represents the social impacts of spatial, economic, and political changes made after 1994 in stories about individualized and often excluded characters. My argumentation aligns with de Meyer and ten Kortenaar's statement that post-transition South African narratives "challenge our taboos about illness, our assumptions about community, our ideas about intimacy and sexuality, and the very future of [the country]" (21) and thus partake in the current literary project of developing a "new hybrid realism" (cf. Pearson and Reynolds 73).[7]

Period Investigated in the Project

The period investigated in this study comprises the years 2000 to 2013. This time frame provides particularly fertile ground for a study of the nexus between contemporary South African literary texts and theoretical, empirical, and commenting observations of scholars of neighbouring disciplines and for a consideration of their shared fascination with the struggle of the South African country to overcome its troubled past. Although the country is said to be in its post-transitional stage, "there are sharp disparities in income, gender and level of education [...] due to the implementation of public policies and programmes that often miserably fail to reduce poverty and/or improve quality of life" (Mapadimeng and Khan i). By 2014, the "democratic 'revolution' and its co-optation by late capitalism" were widely perceived as a "'failure' [...] rendering the much-desired rupture with the apartheid past itself an awkward fiction to deal with" (de Kock 2014). Although implemented on behalf of the people, many South Africans feel betrayed by the new government and the promise of democracy and concomitant ideals of equality, pluralism, and freedom. Consequently, a term such as 'post-apartheid' has become "problematic" (Chapman and Lenta viii; cf. Chapman 2011b), as

[7] The concept of this "new hybrid realism" will be explained in section II.

> a sociological analysis might question whether, in terms of economic consequences, apartheid has actually ended for many who, in a vastly unequal society, continue to live in poverty. However, in the subjective experimental terrain, the terrain of literary expression, *then* is distinct from its counterpart *now*. (Chapman and Lenta viii)

Thus, Chapman and Lenta recommend reducing the term 'post-apartheid' to its temporal dimension, hence as referring to the actual time that has passed since the end of apartheid. Chapman and Lenta do not take into account degrees of social and economic development, as this would wrongly indicate that with the end of apartheid its social structures and cultural conceptions also dissolved. In this study, the term 'post-apartheid' is used in Chapman and Lenta's temporal sense.

Under apartheid, South African literature was dominated by politics. The overrepresentation of this theme was not put up for discussion until 1989 when Albie Sachs argued that art should no longer be seen as "a weapon of struggle" (239). Initially, his appeal was picked to pieces. On hindsight however, it was highly inspiring to all literary genres (cf. Attridge and Jolly). For Chapman, "beyond 2000 begins to mark a quantitative and qualitative shift from the immediate 'post' years of the 1990s to another 'phase'" in which literary texts "tangential to heavy politics, or even to local interest, have begun to receive national recognition" (2011a, 1). Chapman and Lenta found that in opposition to the literary criticism of the 1990s, which was concerned with difference, critical observations beyond 2000 are interested in connections (cf. viii). This is certainly true for the genre of South African literature for young adults, which has developed into one of the most vibrant literary fields in South Africa. Today, English-language writers of youth fiction are no longer "preoccupied with issues of race and politics and ways in which their works might shape opposition to the apartheid system" (Inggs 2006, 22) as they were in the 1980s. Instead, Pucherová argues, the country's literature is marked by a "tendency to seek political direction for post-apartheid society in the private encounters" (131; cf. Inggs 2006). Arguably, post-millennial texts are thus closer to reality and more emancipated than earlier publications, in which "delicate socio-political situations, the many sensitive areas and explosive issues [within South African society] have been largely avoided by authors" (Davies 136). The quest for patterns and for (new) common grounds, which can serve as pillars for a new national narrative, has become characteristic of the post-apartheid era. Critics who want to take part in this search have to be aware that "the *now* requires its own gradations" (Chapman and Lenta viii).

Young Adult Literature – Adult Literature – Children's Literature

In 2014, the "Great Y.A. Debate" (Williams 2014) resurfaced across international public and social media, such as *Twitter*, *The Washington Post*, *The Guardian*, *Nerve*, *InsideHigherEd*, and *Slate*.[8] The loose age frame for young adult literature, ranging more or less between the twelfth and eighteenth years of age (cf. McCallum 214; Rauch 15), is the access point for recurring debates about its readership and whether fiction for young people is to be considered highbrow or lowbrow literature. Discussions concerning the worthiness of the genre are not new. What was new in 2014 was that the discussion happened simultaneously in different international media with academics, international bloggers, journalists, and general readers arguing vigorously for and against Y.A. literature. In a recent study, *Books for Children, Books for Adults: Age and the Novel from Defoe to James* (2014a), Teresa Michals shows how novels have come to be seen specifically as "for children" or "for adults" and that the precise distinction between the two is an invention of modernist authors such as James Joyce, Henry James, or D. H. Lawrence, who "were the first writers to rely on 'adult' as a synonym for 'good'" (Michals 2014b). The boundaries between adult and young adult literature have thus been an artificial construct. Thus, Michals's findings put recurring debates about 'good' or 'bad' literature, about the lack of quality in youth literature as opposed to its presence in adult literature, and about the validity of the discussion of teenage fiction in academia into perspective, revealing them to be outdated and in need of modernization. Interestingly, Michals's findings stand alongside a growing list of critical publications which try to shatter the invisible border between adult and young adult literature (cf. Clifton; Blume; Ewers; van Lierop-Debrauwer and Bastiaansen-Harks). In South Africa, the country's special history has played an active part in undermining the barriers between adult literature and literature for young people.[9] At least since the years of transition, a

[8] Y.A. stands for "young adult" and is in itself a rather ambiguous term concerning the exact definition of what age group, with the respective literature, should be classified as young adult. Robyn McCallum points out that literature for young adults fills "a more or less hypothetical space between junior fiction and adult fiction" (214). Patricia Meyer-Spacks's much quoted conceptualization of "[a]dolescence designat[ing] the time of life when the individual has developed full sexual capacity but has not yet assumed a full adult role in society" (7) has the clear advantage of not being age-restricted. Julia Kristeva, too, sees adolescence rather as "an open psychic structure" than "an age category: [...] The adolescent structure opens itself to the repressed at the same time that it initiates a psychic reorganization of the individual" (8).

[9] This is not to deny the persistent underrepresentation of children's literature in South African literary studies, nor to distract from the many research lacunae that characterize this area of literary criticism. For more information, see the upcoming sections on "Local Availability", "International Reception", and the "State of Research".

certain degree of didacticism, which is usually attributed only to children's and young adult literature, has also entered the country's literary works for adults, as Jochen Petzold's study shows (cf. 2002).[10] Moreover, more authors like Anoeschka von Meck, Margie Orford, or Marita van der Vyver are starting to write for both an adult and a younger audience; and the recurrent use of children's voices as narrators also in adult fiction speaks of a blurring of boundaries between adult and young adult literature (cf. Mann).[11]

Contrary to arguments fought concerning adult vs young adult or children's literature, the difference between literature for children and literature for youths has never been that heavily debated, although different approaches have been used to examine those areas of study. Whereas German scholars in the field usually do not insist on there being structural differences between children's literature and youth literature,[12] English and Scandinavian literary critics tend to do so (cf. Rauch 18). All of them agree that generally speaking, texts for youths "are informed by values and assumptions about adolescence that are dominant in the culture at the time of the texts' production" (McCallum 214; see also Weinkauff and von Glasenapp 118 quoted in Rauch 18), and that both the form and the themes of youth literature are of greater complexity than in narratives for children. Teenage fictions give more space of the narration to character reflection whereas children's fictions spend more time on the action (cf. Rauch 18). Moreover, literary texts for youths question the safety of home and express the gaps between the youth's and the adult generation which result from their different conceptions of how to live life (*ibid.*). In contrast, children's fictions treasure the "home–away–home" pattern (Nodelman 1992 quoted in Rauch 18).[13] According to Svenja Blume, a safe return to one's home after an educational adventure away is as significant in children's texts as the "home–away" pattern ("Heim–Aufbruch–Schema") is for youth novels (54). Texts for teenagers place the search for an individual identity at the centre of their stories and declare the striving for a new and better world an ideal which might never be attained (cf. Blume quoted in Rauch 19). As literature for young adults is a genre deeply intertwined with the time of its production, it reworks contemporary political, social, and economic discourses, hence

[10] In his final chapter, Petzold concludes that two of Brink's novels for adults, *On the Contrary* (1993) and *Imaginings of Sand* (1996), are "highly didactic in their project of constructing a new white identity that sees itself as part of a more comprehensive South Africa" (2002, 209).

[11] Examples of child narrators in literary texts for adults are Troy Blacklaws's *Karoo Boy* (2004), Michiel Heyns's *The Children's Day* (2009), Carolyn Slaughter's *Before the Knife* (2002), Mary Watson's *Moss* (2004), and Rachel Zadok's *Gem Squash Tokoloshe* (2005).

[12] An exception is, for instance, Svenja Blume's study *Texte ohne Grenzen für Leser jeden Alters* (2005).

[13] The home–away–home pattern is also typical for the medieval chivalric novel or, more generally, for adventure literature.

discourses which are located in the world of grown-ups (cf. Rauch 17). These discourses are, however, also deeply connected to their place of origin.

The spatial distinctiveness of a certain geographical location always influences the content of a narrative. The inclusion of a distinctly South African setting has been a staple in the country's literature for children and youths since its earliest beginnings (cf. Jenkins 1993; Carpenter, Hillel, and van der Walt). As the country "is the one thing that all South Africans share", it has been used by South African authors of children's literature since the "mid- to late 1990s" to foster a common cultural identity "as South Africans, rather than as Whites, Coloureds, Blacks or Indians" (Inggs 2000, 46, 47). In the early years of transition literary texts for adults, such as André Brink's *On the Contrary* (1993), also presented "the land itself" as "a possible nexus for a more comprehensive form of identity that would include all South Africans" (Petzold 2002, 85). Till today, the majority of South African texts for young people chose their own country as the setting of their texts (cf. Stadler 2015). However, since the turn of the century, the significance of the local in children's literature has stood in contrast to a turn towards transnational and non-local settings in English South African texts for adults by authors such as "[Zukiswa] Wanner [...], David Mitchell, Chimamanda Adichie, Teju Cole, [or] Amitav Ghosh" (de Kock 2014). De Kock argues that this new type of transnational literature "speaks to a loss of [a distinctly South African] plot that is both exhilarating and disorienting" (2014; cf. 2005). Ultimately, de Kock finds that in 2014 South African adult literature in English "has reached yet another moment of crisis, but this time it might just be a black hole" (*ibid.*). At the same time, the country's English literature for youths is experiencing a revival. The genre has adapted to the new socio-political contexts and writers have developed fresh modes, with which they imagine present-day South Africa.

Coming–of–Age Novels and the *Bildungsroman*

As we will hereafter be concerned with the study of coming–of–age stories of South African adolescents, the term *Bildungsroman* is not far – or could not be further away? Of course by definition the *Bildungsroman* itself spans a much larger time in a protagonist's life than the conventional coming–of–age novel (cf. Baldick 27). Its intended audience also differs as the *Bildungsroman*'s protagonist usually has already proceeded into adulthood. Furthermore, the *Bildungsroman* is first and foremost a European writing tradition. Drawing on Athol Fugard's *Tsotsi*, which he wrote around 1959, Rita Barnard has shown that a comparison between the affirmative *Bildungsroman* and its closest South African relative, the "Jim Comes To Joburg" story, which "dat[es], roughly, from the teens to the early seventies" and "concern[s] the journey of a black protagonist from the country to the city" (Barnard 547), is at best incongruous as the socio-political outline of the apartheid state had entirely different demands and effects on the individual's position and rights than the European nation-states on their citizens. In a 'Jim Comes To Joburg' story

> it is neither possible nor desirable (whether from the point of view of the individual or that of the colonial state) for the protagonist to become a fully developed 'person.' For to do so, for the process of *Bildung* to come to term, the protagonist must be capable of exercising the rights enabled by a particular sociopolitical formation and, at the same time, be willing to submit 'freely' to its norms. The movement toward modernity traced in the 'Jim Comes To Joburg' plot thus never really becomes a movement toward maturity; the African city never becomes a site of emancipation. (Barnard 547)

What has been called the European model of the affirmative *Bildungsroman* has thus never found an equivalent in South Africa. Even greater problems must thus appear when analysing contemporary fiction along the lines of the traditional *Bildungsroman.* In the same essay Barnard, but also Simone (1998) and Mbembe (1992) in their works, problematizes a new type of fiction written in the *Bildungsroman* convention which they believe is supposed to "serv[e] the standard 'feel-good' pedagogical function that such stories have come to serve in today's global cultural marketplace – that of developing the 'full humanity' of the international audience, who are treated to a *soupçon* of difference reassuringly tempered by the same" (Barnard 556). Closure, i.e. "the moment in which there should, notionally at least, be some accommodation between the protagonist and the social order" (Barnard 559), which is one of the principal aims of the *Bildungsroman*, becomes a particularly problematic tool in contemporary South African fiction especially when the harmonious ending of a novel is achieved with a "gesture of surrender" (Barnard 560) of the protagonist to the state or other social authorities. Even more so when in "the postcolonial (and specifically, the postapartheid) state [which] has found itself incapable of creating work opportunities for all its citizens and protect them from destitution" it is "usually [the] black and almost always male[s], who in urban space the world over have become threatening, if marginal, presences" (Comaroff and Comaroff quoted in Barnard 562). But not only black men in urban contexts have become the new anti-heroes of present-day South Africa. More generally, "youth or rather *youths* [have] come to stand for the grotesque inversion of the progressive project of modernity [...], a kind of counternation operating in a twilight zone between the local and the global and viewing themselves as 'ironic mutant citizens of a new world order'" (Barnard 562). The existence of such a counternation nurtures feelings of "concern" and "anxiety" which can only be "firmly set at rest at the conclusion, when [...] both the law and the normative nuclear family [...] reassert their power over the [...] threatening youths" (Barnard 563). Of course, it should be noted that both the law and the normative nuclear family remain highly flawed entities in the post-apartheid state, as the high level of state corruption and the comparatively low number of nuclear families actually living in present day South Africa imply.

Nevertheless, such concerns and anxieties have given rise to the development of new types of *Bildungsromane* and of coming–of–age stories in the South African context. Barnard sees especially the bourgeois nuclear family as "the new thing" in South Africa, as it symbolizes "a kind of postmodern telos of the upwardly mobile" into which "the aspiring individual [...] must be incorporated" (Barnard 563). Like Barnard, Jones arrives at the conclusion that the recent inclusion of nuclear families or of moments of closure, which are achieved by the return of the 'stray' child to the family's home, can be seen as "normative" (Jones 211) elements in narratives "suggest[ing] that the new South Africa [...] shares something of the generally punitive temper of contemporary states" (Barnard 563). According to Barnard, incorporating such elements as the nuclear family in contemporary South African fiction also points to the dubious desire of local texts to become part of "the contemporary canon":

> [I]n order to be welcomed into what we may call [...] the 'world republic of letters,' [the South African] quasi-mythic story must be rewritten in a significantly constrained way. It must surrender its modernist eccentricity, its irony, its dimension of protest and become more standardized, recognizable, upbeat. The outlaw, or the once-unpublished outlaw text, must become – well, more manageably different, just different enough for the consumer to feel satisfied that he or she, all of us, are virtuously on our way to a fuller humanity. (Barnard 569)

The effect these new types of *Bildungsroman* can have on the reader is either one of self-affirmation in the manner of "[y]ou start off watching a movie about people that are very different from yourself, but by the end of the movie you feel that, but for a different roll of the dice, that could have been your own life" (Hood quoted in Barnard 569), or it is an effect of self-delusion as one is being portrayed as "the selfsame figure that long ago struck Walter Benjamin as precisely the negation of continuous personal development and narrative potentiality" over and over again (Barnard 569–570). Either way, the inclusion of didactic moments is characteristic of these new types. Judith Inggs argues in her 2007 article that contemporary South African novels for adolescents such as *Welcome to the Martin Tudhope Show!* (2002) by Sarah Britten, *The Eighth Man* (2002) by Michael Williams, *Someone Called Lindiwe* (2003) by Gail Smith, *Flowers of the Nation* (2005) by Sandile Memela, and *The Mending Season* (2005) by Kagiso Lesego Molope are postmodern "*Entwicklungsromane*, in which the characters grow to some extent through their experiences, but do not reach maturity, as in a *Bildungsroman*" (Inggs 2007, 37–38). The didactic purpose usually ascribed to adolescent fiction only, i.e. the intention to infuse some sort of *Bildung* into the reader in order for him to become a full-fledged member of society, connects the coming–of–age story, i.e. the *Entwicklungsroman*, and its older brother, the *Bildungsroman*. Thus, across the borders of genre and intended audience, didactic moments permeate contemporary literary productions of South Africa. The upcoming analysis will examine the possible concessions that have come to affect local writings with respect to character development or the use of hopeful endings in young adult literature as more general and "normative conclusions" (Jones 211).

Methodology/Corpus

When conducting an analysis of the contemporary period an interdisciplinary approach is most suitable, as literary analyses profit highly from the inclusion of empirical data and critical findings from other disciplines, such as sociology, psychology, and pedagogy. Working with methodologies from experimental psychology, child pedagogy, sociology, and literary history, this project wants to bridge the gap between hermeneutic methods from the humanities and empirical methods from the social sciences. For this purpose, I draw on both distant and close reading strategies. In his groundbreaking study, Franco Moretti introduced *Distant Reading* (2013) as "*a condition of knowledge* [which] allows you to focus on units that are much smaller or much larger than the text: devices, themes, tropes – or genres and systems" (57; emphasis in the original). Distant reading is Moretti's response to the internationally established method of close reading. For Moretti "the trouble with close reading (in all its incarnations, from the new criticism to deconstruction) is that it necessarily depends on an extremely small canon. This may have become an unconscious and invisible premise by now, but it is an iron one nonetheless: you invest so much in individual texts only if you think that very few of them really matter" (Moretti 57). When conducting an analysis along the lines of distant reading, "the text itself disappears" "between the very small and the very large" (*ibid.*). However, Moretti reasons, "[i]f we want to understand the system in its entirety, we must accept losing something. We always pay a price for theoretical knowledge: reality is infinitely rich; concepts are abstract, are poor" (Moretti 57–58). While to Moretti "less is actually more" (58), I found that less was not enough in the particular case of this thesis. Inspired by South African literary critic Leon de Kock's argument that studies on the country's literature would benefit from distant reading – because, as he claims, if "you want to look beyond the canon, close reading will not do the job" (2011, 36) – I sought to understand both the concept and the text, to gain a distant overview of the genre as well as close insight into storylines. Only then, I felt, would I be able to do justice to the literary works and their time and place of production. Hence, based on the premise that literature is a cultural production, I approach contemporary literary texts for and about young people, which respond to the shifting social, political, and economic conditions of South Africa as what I call *witness documents*[14] of the contemporary period. In doing so, I place literature in dialogue with recent societal and cultural discourses.

[14] The term is inspired by the term 'eyewitness testimony' as it is used in psychology (cf. Wells and Olson) and by the term 'oral history', which describes the historian's method of questioning eyewitnesses of a time period to gain insights into the happenings of that period

Critical discourse analysis (cf. Fairclough), an approach developed in the field of cultural studies, serves as a general frame for the analysis. A bibliography compiled predominantly at the National English Literary Museum and with the help of Jay Heale's database SACBIP serves as the second cornerstone of the thesis. Previous to this project no comprehensive bibliography of published texts for young adults was available, which would have facilitated the process of selecting novels for a detailed literary analysis. Thereafter, the bibliography, which contains every novel that was found to be written by a South African author in English – or was translated into English – and published in South Africa between the years 2000 and 2013, was evaluated statistically. The data was analysed quantitatively and qualitatively according to predefined categories – namely, type of fiction, space, gender, social economics, and focalization – in the manner of Franco Moretti's distant reading. The evaluation was published separately in *Bookbird* (cf. Stadler 2015). Its findings are the third pillar of the present study and have influenced the structure of this thesis and its chapters decisively. The results of the statistical assessment are integrated into the different chapters. The findings were also consulted regarding the selection of texts for detailed analysis.

The main body of this thesis will discuss selected features of cultural categories, such as space, gender, race and class, sociology, and politics, in three self-contained chapters,[15] although of course the results of previous chapters always inform the readings of subsequent chapters. Such an approach allows one not only to analyse texts according to different thematic aspects, characters, or the type of focalization within the same thesis, but also to acknowledge the complexities of South African young adult novels and their contents, and to discuss certain texts in more than one chapter. Incorporating methodologies and relevant findings from experimental psychology (cf. Piaget et al.; Hickson and Kriegler; Swanson, Edwards, and Spencer), child pedagogy (cf. Schreckenberger and Brodbeck; Bort), sociology (cf. Lefebvre 1994; de Certeau 2002; Oldenburg), human geography (cf. Soja 1989, 1996, 2008, 2009a, 2009b; Foucault 1986), cultural studies (cf. Bhabha), gender studies (cf. Butler; De Beauvoir), postcolonial studies (cf. Said), and literary history (cf. Attwell and Attridge) has helped to conceptualize how notions of global and local spaces intersect in the literary imagination of the child, what the gender of the adolescent narrator tells us about plot structure and storyline, and how South African socio-economic issues correspond to global discourses and become noticeable particularly in the

and how they experienced it (cf. Henke-Bockschatz 187). The aim of the latter method is not to gain insights into facts and circumstances of the past, but to achieve an understanding of those mental and cultural mechanisms and structures that shape people's life experiences (cf. Henke-Bockschatz 187). In the process of sharing his/her experiences, creative deformations naturally occur in the eyewitness's account, as they do in literary texts.

[15] A more detailed outline of the individual chapters follows in the section "Scope of the Present Study".

country's literature for young adults. According to Jean and John Comaroff, as well as according to Achille Mbembe, who reviewed the Comaroffs' monograph *Theory from the South* (2012), "'to theorize' only makes sense if theory is part of a broader design: to make '*the history of the future different from the history of the present*'" (Mbembe 2012, 22; emphasis in the original). In the case of this study, the integration of abstract theories on space, gender, social ethics, and class and race have helped "to assess with some degree of plausibility various intuitions about what is going on, what is possible, and the odds against it" (*ibid.*), as will become apparent in the subsequent chapters. The examination of literary publications by Jayne Bauling, K. Sello Duiker, and Sally-Ann Partridge, amongst others, happens alongside the reading of influential studies of the abovementioned neighbouring disciplines. Ultimately, the thesis wants to provide an analysis of South African English literature for young adults by means of structuring the publications between 2000 and 2013 in categories which are topical in a 'glocal' cultural discourse.

Overview of the Young Adult Genre

Sara Nuttall's "wish [that] we would more often read [...] across [...] the new" (2011a) and Partridge's observation that "[o]ur writers have their fingers on the pulse" prefigure this introduction. Nuttall's and Partridge's notions are representative of the local and the global standing of South African literature for young adults and will serve as an opener for the discussion of the genre's development since the beginning of the twenty-first century. Sarah Nuttall is one of South Africa's foremost literary and cultural critics of the post-apartheid era. Her work is predominantly concerned with theorizing the present state of development in South Africa, its (spatial) entanglements with the past, and the resurfacing of these entanglements in general literature (cf. 2009, 2004). The above statement shows her discontent and scepticism with regard to traditional theoretical approaches and today's 'way' of reading in general, calling for their revision. According to Nuttall, a change of perspective is needed, one that is not content with superficiality and window dressing but goes deeper and is more encompassing. Only then, she posits, can the "now" be deciphered (Nuttall 2011a). Nuttall's statement alludes to the complexities surrounding critical analyses of the present and the finding of suitable frameworks for the discussion of contemporary literary representations. Together with Nuttall, Achille Mbembe (2008, 2012, 2014) as well as Jean and John Comaroff (2012) and Jennifer Robinson (2006) are at the forefront of theorizing South Africa's ever changing social reality. Sally-Ann Partridge, by contrast, has taken to the writing of young adult literature to dissect the present. Being amongst the country's most prolific young writers of youth literature, Partridge has already received numerous literary awards for her post-millennial fiction, but also informs us about trends in South Africa's young adult market on a more general basis on her blog on *BooksLive*. Taking a variety of post-millennial publications for young people into account, for example by John Coetzee, Gillian D'Achada, Judy Froman, Joane Hichens, Jenny Robson, Dumisani Sibiya, Marita van der Vyver, or Fanie Viljoen, her résumé of the current state of the genre is positive, if not excited, and she specifically points to diversity in contemporary literature for teenagers (cf. Partridge). If one were to draw a preliminary conclusion from these two quotes, it could be said that while South Africa's theorists, such as Sarah Nuttall, are still hesitant and struggle for words that can measure the new South Africa theoretically, the country's young writers, like Sally-Ann Partridge, are more self-confident and appear to have already found methods for writing 'good' fiction which resonate with the country's development. More precisely, the latter have started to negotiate sociological contents via realist fiction.

International Reception

While J. M. Coetzee, Zakes Mda, or Ivan Vladislavic have become synonymous with contemporary South Africa and its adult literature, today's authors of children's and youth literature like Helen Brain, Dianne Case, Robin Malan, Khulekani Magubane, or Kagiso Lesego Molope have generally lagged behind in achieving such fame both inside and outside the country. Traditionally, the local readership of South African literature for both adult and younger readers has been comparatively small (cf. Murray 2011, 83). Small print runs of usually 500 to 2000 copies have long mirrored the absence of a South African reading culture. Abroad, the reception of South African children's and young adult literature – but also of the country's adult literature – by the general public and the academic world has also only happened on a limited scale, often due to pragmatic reasons. South African publications have seldom been available in print outside the country.[16] Exceptions are of course those local authors who have turned to overseas publishing houses to have their books marketed there. This was a characteristic practice during the times of apartheid given the politics of censorship in that era, but also today, local authors continue to turn to foreign publishers. The reasons for this move are, however, no longer politically motivated. Since the end of

[16] Apparently, the same holds true for the reception of South African scholarly publications, as Elizabeth le Roux illustrates in her article on "The International Reception of South African Scholarly Texts" (2012). Her "examination of the circulation of academic texts shows that the dominant relationship is still one of a centre/periphery binary rather than of a transnational network. […] [T]he location of a publisher still does influence the reception of its texts, even in a globalised context – there are still borders to be crossed, even in a so-called borderless world. The physical distribution of books still takes place along the lines of power and authority established in the colonial and early postcolonial period. Moreover, the distribution of books remains expensive, bureaucratic and subject to prejudice and bias from potential buyers" (le Roux 83).

apartheid, local authors have used the trend of globalization to access new markets and audiences for the profits to be gained from an extended readership. Edyth Bulbring has republished her *Melly, Fatty and Me* Series (2010–2011) under a different title, the *April–May* Series (2013), with Hot Key Books in the United Kingdom, for instance. Bulbring also republished *The Summer of Toffie and Grummer* (2007) as *I Heart Beat* (2014) with Hot Key Books. Today, more and more novels which are successful locally also become available in translation in foreign countries. Examples are Kagiso Lesego Molope's *Dancing in the Dust* (2004), Lutz van Dijk's *Stronger than the Storm* (2000), or Linzi Glass's *The Year the Gypsies Came* (2006), which were translated into German, or John van de Ruit's *Spud* (2005), which was translated into Spanish and Italian, among others (cf. Stadler 2014). Lehman et al.'s compilation of "[p]rofiles of the work of twenty-nine authors and illustrators", which intends to "raise global knowledge of, interest in, and knowledge about the current status" of South African literature for the young, certainly aids in "stimulat[ing] greater use of the literature in South Africa, the U.S., and around the world" (7). In the past, the European reception of South African youth novels was limited, as the focus of the educational sector, the area of society where such literature is mostly promoted and read, was on the United States of America and the United Kingdom. Particularly since the beginning of the twenty-first century, due to canon revision and the reconsideration of curricula in both schools and universities, literary texts from previously neglected areas have become more visible in European bookshops and classrooms. Although this is an important development, the significance of the promotion of South African youth novels in more than one language lies not in their availability in foreign countries but in fostering this diversity in the country itself.

Local Availability

Since the implementation of the new Constitution of the Republic of South Africa in 1996, equality between and the maintenance of the diversity of the eleven official languages – Sepedi, Sesotho, Setswana, siSwati, Tshivenda, Xitsonga, Afrikaans, English, isiNdebele, isiXhosa, and isiZulu ("Constitution" Chapter 1.(6)) – has been a declared aim of the South African government. The rights to receive school education in one's mother tongue and to practice one's "[l]anguage and [c]ulture" are enshrined in Sections 29 and 30 of the Bill of Rights. To date, however, only a minority of texts exist in the indigenous languages although 8 out of 10 South Africans consider one of them their mother tongue (cf. Lehohla 2012a). I have previously elaborated on the contradictions and complexities surrounding language and South African youth literature in an article in *Bookbird*, stating that most children's and youth literature continues to be published in Afrikaans and this is also the sector where most profits are gained, namely R33.8 million in 2010 (cf. Struik and le Roux 80; Stadler 2015, forthcoming). In the same year, texts in all of the indigenous languages only accounted for a minority of publications. Interestingly, every text published in an indigenous language in 2010 was intended for a young audience (cf. Struik and le Roux 82; Stadler 2014). Publications in English and their sales ranked second according to the "Annual Book Industry Survey Report 2011" conducted by Willem Struik and Beth le Roux in 2012 (cf. Stadler 2015). Although only 9.6% named English as their home language, it has a unique status in South Africa: It is its lingua franca (cf. Lehohla 2012a, 24, 27). Today, the majority of the country's youths not only "perceive English as the ticket to success" (Rudwick 165; cf. Kapp), but use it automatically when asked to express themselves in writing: In 2014, Mxit Reach, a non-profit organization, conducted an essay competition in which the participants could chose the language of their liking to tell their stories (cf. Rudge). 90% of the participants were black, 7% were coloured, and isiZulu and isiXhosa were the predominant spoken languages; nevertheless, the majority of participants decided to write their stories in English (*ibid.*). Exemplary studies conducted by Kapp (2004) in the Western Cape and by Rudwick (2004) in a KwaZulu-Natal township have furthermore shown that while embracing the concept of English as their lingua franca, young people are also crucially aware that a preference for English goes hand in hand with a gradual abandonment of their African mother tongue (cf. McKinney). For these reasons, today's readership of literature written in English is potentially more heterogeneous than that of any of the other official languages, and these texts have the potential to reach a diversified audience, thus making the study of youth novels written in English particularly worthwhile.

Traditionally, local publishing houses and educational departments have played a most influential role in what kind of South African children's and youth literature is published. Jenkins found that during the time when Afrikaans publishers dominated the scene "[m]atters of translation, illustrations and format, and, of course, whether a book is to be published at all, [were] kept firmly out of the hands of authors" (1993, 5). Due to hypocritical language policies of publishers, only "perhaps a dozen" English books were published per year until the 1970s; afterwards this changed to "about a hundred" per year (Jenkins 1993, 1, 4). Till today, the "list of prescribed books" for schools is a powerful tool to influence what kinds of texts are written by authors. Due to small print runs only little profit can be gained from sales on the general market. Having your book prescribed by schools, which results in the printing of tens of thousands of copies, makes such an order most attractive despite the selection process being "extremely cautious" (Jenkins 1993, 5). Before the end of apartheid this meant that "very few South African books with post-World War II themes [were] approved" and "children's books on modern social themes were subjected to the ultimate sanction of being banned by the government" (Jenkins 1993, 5). Also twenty years after the end of apartheid, a list of prescribed books exists containing both classic texts and recent titles. In 2013 it included graded readers such as Charles Dickens's *Oliver Twist (Retold by Margareth Tarner)* (Grade 9, English home language, 2013) or

Robert Louis Stevenson's *Treasure Island (Retold by S. Colbourn)* (Grade 7, English home language, 2013) as well as recent local publications by Jayne Bauling (*E Eights*, Grade 9, first additional language, 2009), Glaydah Namukasa (*Voice of a Dream*, Grade 9, English home language, 2013), Dorothy Dyer (*Friends Forever*, Grade 9, first additional language, 2013), Diane Hofmeyr (*Oliver Strange and the Journey to the Swamps*, Grade 9, first additional language, 2012), and Janis Ford (*Drugs Are for Mugs*, Grade 8, English home language, 2003). Pan Macmillan and Oxford University Press are two of the major publishers who produce fictional and non-fictional texts for South African schools (cf. "Grade 7–9 Catalogue").[17] Independent publishers such as the recently founded Cover2Cover have traditionally contributed fewer titles to the list of prescribed books than the major publishers like Heinemann or Macmillan. For authors who do not primarily aim to write for the educational sector, prize competitions such as *The Sanlam Prize*, the *Percy Fitzgerald Prize*, or the *M.E.R Prize* have provided an incentive to create new stories since the 1970s. Of these, *The Sanlam Prize* is the most diverse as it awards medals for English, Afrikaans, and indigenous language novels.

State of Research, Eminent Critics

To date, comparatively few local and even fewer foreign critics have turned their attention to young adult literature despite South Africa having a long tradition of children's and youth literature and the country being "the most prolific publisher" (Lehman et al. 5) on the African continent. Elwyn Jenkins's article "Research into the Multilingual Children's Literature of South Africa" (2008) is the most comprehensive evaluation of local and international research conducted in the field since its formation. In his evaluation Jenkins does not exclusively concentrate on academic publications, but gives insight into local documentation practices and the gradual internationalization of the genre. He shows that despite the formation of local research centres in the form of the research unit "Research in [Afrikaans] Children's Literature" at the Potchefstroom University of Christian Higher Education or the "Children's Literature Research Unit" at the University of South Africa in Pretoria, the absence of "established university schools of children's literature, professional organizations, and specialist journals" has left many gaps in literary criticism (Jenkins 2008, 437). Moreover, he has found that "[a]s yet, research has concentrated on English and Afrikaans language literature, and much remains to be done to encourage black researchers to come forward and integrate

[17] More information on "Learner and Teacher Support Material" (2015) can be found on the website of a province's Department of Education, for instance at <http://www.kzneducation.gov.za/TextbookCatalogueInformation/LearnerTeacherSupportMaterialLTSM.aspx >. I am indebted to Mignon Hardie from The FunDza Literary Trust for making me aware of these sources.

South Africa with the rest of the African continent" (Jenkins 2008, 437). Systematic coverage of South African children's and youth literature ended with the closure of the magazine *Bookchat* in 1997 (cf. Hunt 2004b, 951). Until 2015, the journal's former editor, Jay Heale, maintained the eponymous webpage *Bookchat*, which included the database South African Children's Books in Print (SACBIP). Next to the archives of the National English Literary Museum in Grahamstown and Crystal Warren's complilations of the latest book publications in South Africa in *The Journal of Commonwealth Literature* (2003, 2004, 2005, 2006, 2007, 2008, 2012, 2014), Jay Heale's website was the most comprehensive address when looking for the latest publications and reviews. The Jay Heale Children's Books Collection, containing about 800 books, is now available at Enlighten Trust in Hermanus (cf. CBN).

Elwyn Jenkins is the leading authority in the field of English children's and young adult literature. He has published widely on the history of South African children's and youth literature, folk tales, oral narratives, and fictional paintings (1993, 2002, 2005, 2006, 2012). His studies, which examine the genre from its earliest beginnings up until the beginning of the twenty-first century, encompass detailed discussions of a variety of significant topics, such as nature (cf. Jenkins 2004), urban and rural space (cf. Jenkins 2006), and cross-cultural encounters (cf. Jenkins 2006), but also take into account the politics of publishing children's literature in South Africa and consider issues of language (cf. Jenkins 2008, 2012). Judith Inggs is the second local expert that needs to be menioned. She specializes in the field of South African teenage fiction in English. Her research focuses predominantly on South African youth novels of the 1990s. In her articles, she examines how "The English Language Youth Novel in South Africa" is "Grappling with Change" (Inggs 2002), but also investigates a variety of central topics in Y.A. literature, amongst them the formation of character and identity (Inggs 2000), issues of space and race (Inggs 2004), as well as the role of romance, power, and sexuality (Inggs 2009). Inggs's monograph *Transition and Transgression: English Young Adult Fiction in Post-Apartheid South Africa* (2016) is the first to focus exclusively on South African young adult literature. The book is comprised of an updated collection of her previously published essays covering a great variety of genres, including realist fiction and fantasy, and giving both an overview and analysis of selected works written from the 1980s through to the present. Apart from Jenkins's and Inggs's work, comparatively few critics have reviewed South Africa's youth novels since the end of apartheid (cf. Grünkemeier; Hillel and van der Walt; Hlongwane; Jacobs; Lundgren and Khau; Maddy and MacCann 1996, 1998; McGillis; Oike; Osa; Petzold 2005; Samuelson; van der Westhuizen). More unpublished material such as Jenna Williams's master thesis "A Changing Didacticism", or the dissertations by "C.W. du Plessis, M. du Plessis, and Greyling" (cf. Jenkins 2008, 434) can be found in the archives of South African universities, yet these sources are difficult to trace. Overall, companions, essay collections, or bibliographies of (South) African children's and youth literature like the ones by Jenkins (1993, 2006, 2012), Khorana (1994), Killam and Rowe (2000), Lehman et al. (2014), Odiase (1986), or Schmidt (1975; 1979) are still rare. Regarding the period investigated in this project, none of the above deals exclusively with English literature for children and teens published between 2000 and 2013. Regarding international encyclopedias, Jenkins lists the *Cambridge Guide to Children's Books in English* (2001) edited by Victor Watson and *The Oxford Encyclopedia of Children's Literature* (2006) in four volumes edited by Jack Zipes as giving accurate representations of South African children's literature (cf. Jenkins 2008, 432). Other volumes, such as the *International Companion Encyclopedia of Children's Literature* (Hunt 2004a, 2004b), do not list South African literature for young adults. The *Routledge Companion to International Children's Literature* (forthcoming) edited by John Stephens will be the first to have an entry on the country's twenty-first century youth novels (cf. Stadler forthcoming).

How delicate cross-cultural analyses can be is shown by the controversy arising after the publication of MacCann and Maddy's *Apartheid and Racism in South African Children's Literature 1985–1995* (2001). In "Cross-Cultural Misreadings" (2008) Elwyn Jenkins and Elizabeth Muther give a detailed account of the limitations of MacCann and Maddy's research, which wrongly accuses South Africa's contemporary texts for young adults of racism (cf. Jenkins 2008; van der Westhuizen 2008). Such misreadings show that more comparative analyses of South African literature written in the different languages as well as of "the connections between Afrikaans and European literature and between South African folktalkes and European fairy tales and fables" (Jenkins 2008, 437) need to be undertaken in order to arrive at a more global understanding of the nexus between local children's fiction. Carpenter, Hillel, and van der Walt's discussion of "The Dynamics of Local and Global in Australian, Canadian and South African Children's Literature" (2005) or Hillel and van der Walt's article on "Representations of Mothers and Mothering in Popular Australian and South African Books for Young Adults" (2009) are two examples of critical cross-cultural analysis.

Lastly, I want to briefly point out research conducted on children's and youth literature published in languages other than English. Gretel Wybenga and Maritha Snyman's essay collection *Van Patrys-hulle tot Hanne Hoekom: 'n Gids tot die Afrikaanse Kinder- en Jeugbook* [From Patrys-hulle to Hanne Hoekom: A Guide to the Afrikaans Children's and Youth Book] (2005) documents some of the most recent research conducted in Afrikaans children's literature. There is no comprehensive analysis of contemporary children's and youth literature available in print for any of the other indigenous languages. The lack of research in African-language children's books is congruent with the general lack of children's books in these languages, although the market has recently become more open and more books have been published in this sector since the turn of the century (cf. Jenkins 2008, 429; Stadler 2014). Given this amount of research lacunae concerning contemporary children's literature in the different languages, the circle of investigation of this study is restricted to the analysis of English literature for teenagers published between the years 2000 and 2013, and more exclusively to realist fiction, as a wider approach, regarding time frame, text format, or other languages would run the risk of superficiality and inaccuracy.

Scope of the Present Study

The upcoming analysis of English-language literary publications of the years 2000 to 2013 will provide an overview of the genre's latest developments and will thus serve as a basis for further discussions. The present study contributes to the field of literary studies on different levels. It adds to local research by exploring literary texts from a so far under-researched literary field in relation to current socio-political developments. Moreover, the present study establishes South African literature for young adults as a highly innovative player in the global project of developing new hybrid realism(s) (cf. Pearson and Reynolds). Put very generally, this study seeks to substantiate Bwesigye bwa Mwesigire's claim that "[t]here is such a thing as African contemporaneity that is not mimicry of European culture nor is it a re-imagination of an African past" (2014) through an examination of a selected set of texts which set their stories in the here and now and debate topics that relate to three hot spots of early twenty-first century South Africa, namely the nature and development of (social) spaces, the discussion of gender norms, and the impact of social economics on young people's lives. This is the reason why this book is entitled *South African Young Adult Literature in English*, although I am aware that such a title may be considered problematic due to the lack of "a single national identity" (cf. Inggs 2016, 2).

This brings me to the present study's limitations. As the project touches on numerous contested topics and due to the ongoing development of the young adult genre, only preliminary conclusions can be drawn for the examined field. The restriction of the discussion to spatial, gender, socio-political as well as socio-economic topics in realist fiction leaves gaps in other thematic areas and subgenres such as fantasy, science fiction, or non-fiction for teenagers. Although the corpus for this study includes those books that have been translated into English from Afrikaans – for instance, Anoeschka von Meck's *My Name Is Vaselinetjie* (2011) and Marita van der Vyver's *The Hidden Life of Hannah Why* (2007) – more comprehensive comparative analyses of the literary output of the other official South African languages are necessary. What is more, literary texts for younger children as well as picture books have been excluded from the analysis leaving a whole body of work open for further discussion.

All the chapters in this thesis are self-contained, however the results of preceding chapters inform subsequent readings. Each chapter contains close readings of a selected set of novels, discussed chronologically according to the date of publication of the novels in order to point to lines of development whenever possible. Therefore, chapter 1 explores literary representations of South Africa's (social) spaces, problematizing the notion that urban areas have become the new 'heartlands' of adolescent novels. Examining a range of urban, rural, and heterotopian school settings, the different subchapters support the notion of the impossibility of defining a unitary South African space and point to persisting spatial demarcations. Young adult characters are shown to struggle to adjust to pre-existing spatial concepts and to look for new ways of appropriating their surroundings, turning to alternative ways of living together whenever possible. All subchapters investigate the mapping processes of juvenile characters on a spatial and a social level. Twenty years after the end of apartheid, a person's right to his/her space and his/her integration into the social fabric remains a controversial topic throughout urban, rural, and heterotopian spaces.

The second chapter elaborates on issues related to gender identity formation. In three subchapters, this section of the thesis discusses how hegemonic masculine identities are deconstructed and upheld at the same time and how novels written in the realist mode are starting to include characters whose sexual orientation differs from heterosexuality, and illustrates the struggle of young females to make their stories known and their voices heard in communities in which silence remains the number one method of 'problem solving'. Representing multiple gendered identities, South African adolescent fiction comments on gendered behaviour and on communities' attitudes towards particular types of people, pointing to a generation gap. Close readings furthermore show that although young adult characters want to break up preconceived notions of gender roles, they, too, fall into the trap of gender stereotyping. The silence concerning topics like HIV/AIDS, gender violence, or rape is not only thematized but is shown to be a major reason for discomfort for the younger generation. Generally, literary texts speak out against patriarchal family or community structures by including a multitude of characters from different backgrounds and with different sexual orientations and belief systems in their narratives. Thus, there is no "single story" (Adichie) of South African youth, but a variety of his-, her-, their-, and our-stories.

In the final chapter, analyses of socio-economic hard data alongside literary hard and soft data come to the conclusion that literary texts represent the present socio-economic climate in South Africa to a surprisingly accurate extent. Novels by Jenny Robson or Willem van der Walt debate the effects that neoliberal market structures and globalization are having on the young and investigate the responsibility of such policies for persisting social segregation and inequalities. In many cases, fictional discussions of socio-economic issues are connected to questions of class, race, fairness, and social ethics. The second subchapter shows that literary texts transcend popular notions of popularizing ubuntu by demanding a reconceptualization of social ethics not only on a Euro-African, but also on a transnational, and a digital level.

II Realism and the English South African Youth Novel

Realism is dead, long live realist fiction? At least this appears to be the paradigm in this early twenty-first century. Conceptions of contemporary realism have become ambiguous, if not contradictory in recent years. Not too long ago, leading scholars such as Lucy Pearson and Kimberley Reynolds declared the "narrative mode [...] inadequate as a way of representing this age of cultural uncertainty" (73). Yet, within the same sentence, the scholars had to admit that ever since its emergence in the nineteenth century, "realism has been intensified and enlarged" (*ibid.*). In 2010, another scholar, David Shields, announced the end of classic realist fiction. In his manifesto, *Reality Hunger* (2010), Shields describes the individual as being driven between a constant urge to escape from this world and a simultaneous demand to experience reality as intensely as possible. In her article "Hungry for What?" South African critic Sarah Nuttall draws on Shield's concept of reality hunger and simultaneously invokes Baudrillard's idea of hyperreality when she says that

> [t]he reality phenomenon in its current phase is that which is taken to be reality – memoir, fabricated memoir, documentary, multiple forms of reality television, cable news, celebrity culture, Facebook pages – and which increasingly includes features of the unreal, the fictional, and that we are drawn to that melange of forms, live increasingly inside that paradox. (2011b)

In light of Nuttall's conceptualization and descriptions of contemporary South African media culture, the question arises whether the concept of a South African realist fiction has become obsolete. In order to clarify this question, we have to take a brief look at what "classic" realist fiction actually looked like.

Traditionally "[c]lassic realist texts" are, according to Catherine Belsey, defined as containing three features: They draw the reader into a world that resembles the world in which the reader lives most truthfully, "aligning [the reader's] views with those of a trustworthy voice and ensuring that no ambiguities complicate the ending" (quoted in Pearson and Reynolds 64). An ending which brings "[c]losure [...] is central to the way classic realist texts seek to efface the fact that they are works of fiction [...]. Through these [three] elements [...] classic realist texts make readers highly prone unconsciously to absorb books' ideological views" (Pearson and Reynolds 63). This three-fold definition makes us aware of the influential effects that mimesis and closure have on the reader. These are also the central concerns of John Stephens's most influential study, *Language and*

Ideology in Children's Fiction (1992). As Lucy Pearson and Kimberley Reynolds summarize, Stephens, but also Peter Hollindale (1988), "pointed out that because for the most part writing for children is concerned with teaching them about the world in which they live and shaping their attitudes, it reveals a great deal about the prevailing ideologies of a given period" (Pearson and Reynolds 64). John Stephens highlights that "a mode of reading which locates the reader only within the text is disabling, and leaves readers susceptible to gross forms of intellectual manipulation" (1992, 4). Georg Lukács prefigured Stephen's work when he said that "[i]t is the view of the world, the ideology or *weltanschauung* underlying a writer's work, that counts. And it is the writer's attempt to reproduce this view of the world which constitutes his 'intention' and is the formative principle underlying the style of a given piece of writing" (Lukács 19; also 71). The bond between the world and mankind, a concept once assumed as "natural", has since been disintegrated, leading to new modes of writing that disclose the precise bond as a "conscious, constructed unity" (Lukács 39). However, Lukács argues, such (fictive) "disintegration of the world of man – and consequently the disintegration of personality – coincides with the ideological intention" of modernist fiction (39). According to McCallum it was

> in the 1970s, 1980s, and 1990s, [that] what has become known as the 'new realist' novel for adolescents has emerged. This is typified by fictions by writers such as Robert Cormier, Melvin Burgess, and John Marsden. Like the problem novel, [which emerged in the 1960s and is representative of 'old' realism,] new realism deals with taboo subject matters, but also includes a socially critical and political dimension that is often pessimistic and cynical. (216)

Pat Pinsent aligns with McCallum's time frame, stating that "[i]t was not until the 1970s and the beginning of legislation dealing with issues of discrimination in [Western] society that significant numbers of children's authors began to take on board issues of equality. During this period there was an increased awareness of how literature could affect social attitudes" (2005a, 192). Pearson and Reynolds argue that, broadly speaking, this awareness was created

> in response to the educational philosophies of Friedrich Froebel, Jean Piaget, Maria Montessori and Rudolf Steiner, which mapped out models of children's physical, cognitive and emotional needs, and the popularization of Sigmund Freud's ideas about the inner world of the child and the importance of childhood experience in the formation of adult identity. (65)

McCallum's, Pinsent's, and Pearson and Reynolds's research is predominantly concerned with developments in American and British children's literature. These, however, have also been relevant for the South African context. Local authors like "Marguerite Poland and Jenny Seed, for example, openly acknowledged" the influence of "modern trends in [children's literature] overseas – especially in

Britain, the USA and Australia" (Jenkins 1993, 3). Nevertheless, South African authors have always understood themselves as chroniclers of South African history. While prior to the 1970s, "myth and fantasy" had been the dominant modes of writing and indeed "the only way for children's literature to subvert the reality of the racial and cultural divide in the country" (Inggs 2000, 46), stories written in the realist mode[18] have since been the preferred choice of South African authors of children's and young adult literature. However, the nature of realist writing in South Africa has changed over time and in relation to the dominant ideology, similar to the changing face of realist literature in Western contexts.[19] Drawing on Alex la Guma, Mbulelo Mzamane explains:

> The artist or cultural worker,[[20]] like the school teacher, is the vehicle for the expression and propagation of certain values, consciously or unwittingly. Whether an individual artist knows it or not, every artist is committed to such values long before sitting in front of a typewriter, stepping on a stage, or pulling out canvas(s) and paints; what the artist produced affirms or opposes certain dominant social relations. (Mzamane 1996, 346)

A change in the local political climate, the growing resistance to the apartheid government, and, most importantly, the Soweto Uprising influenced the "willingness [of authors] to explore new paradigms of human relations in South Africa" (Jenkins 1993, 2) in their fictions for teenagers. The Soweto Uprising took place on 16 June 1976 and was initiated by predominantly black school children who went to the streets in response to the apartheid government having made Afrikaans the second compulsory language in school education after English.[21]

[18] Attebery's distinction between mode and formula has been most helpful in defining contemporary South African realist literature for young adults. Instead of using a concrete formula of realism for structuring literary texts, South African authors draw on the concept of realism as "a stance, a position on the world as well as a means of portraying it" (Attebery 2). A "mode is a way of doing something", "a formula, on the other hand, can lead to an understanding of the structural basis of a related genre" (*ibid.*). In the country's literary texts the classic realist formula, as envisaged by Catherine Belsey (1980), retreats for the benefit of "the aim […] to produce the impression of faithfulness to ordinary experience" (Attebery 3; cf. Pearson and Reynolds).

[19] For a history of English South African literature and its phases, see, for instance, Herlitzius (72f.), Michael Chapman (1996), Mbulelo Vizikhungo Mzamane (1997), Ursula Edmans (1982), or Kenneth Parker (1978). For a problematization of the different phases, see Herlitzius (72–138).

[20] The term 'cultural worker' was frequently used during the Black Consciousness Movement, underlining its populist approach and intention to write for 'ordinary people' (Zander 193).

[21] For further information on the Soweto Uprising and its further causes, see, for instance, Sifiso Mxolisi Ndlovu's contribution "Part 1: Soweto" in *The Road to Democracy in South Africa – Volume 2 (1970–1980)* (Ndlovu 317–350).

This day triggered major socio-political changes in the years to come and those changes were mirrored in the stories for children as well. Hence, in spite of a political regime which regulated every area of living, including what kinds of books were published, South African authors of the 1970s and 80s started to discuss new and controversial topics in youth literature (cf. Jenkins 1993, 2006, 2012). Judith Inggs, moreover, informs us that "[p]olitical and social themes dominated the genre of young adult fiction in South Africa during the 1980s and early 1990s, as writers grappled with issues of race and identity politics" (2016, 9).

Scholars in the field of children's and young adult literature agree that while initially "children's literature was slow to incorporate the harsher aspects of realism, preferring to reproduce the everyday lives of happy middle-class children" (Pearson and Reynolds 63; cf. Pinsent 2005a, 192), newer texts have moved away from representing an idealized world. The "new hybrid realism", as Pearson and Reynolds have called the latest offspring of the realist genre, has become "varied, bold and amorphous", now "reach[ing] deeper into the psyche, further into the future and employ[ing] a wider stylistic repertoire" (73). Regarding didactic and ideological implications, "little" has changed since the beginnings of children's literature. According to Pearson and Reynolds, "realistic writing […] continues to be an essentially didactic mode in that it remains concerned with encouraging young readers to observe and think about the world around them; increasingly, however, it is also doing this in ways that are less obviously one-sided and seductive" (72). At this point it has to be noted that the inclusion of local contents has always been a distinctive feature of South African fiction written in the realist mode (cf. Jenkins 1993; Davies). Scholars have found that stories that matter to people are those set in a local area they preferably know (cf. Kahora quoted in Said-Moorhouse). When it comes to writing for young people, South African writer Joanne Hichens further adds to this notion by saying that authors "have a responsibility, and an opportunity, to explore local stories and settings and create fiction that is rooted in the kind of experience unique to South African children and young people" (quoted in Partridge). Both Kahora's and Hichens's assertions are pleas for the significance of the place and the time of production (cf. Trites). However, the time of production cannot be thought of without the place of production as it is the uniqueness of local issues happening at a certain time and place that make the difference between a Russian youth novel and a South African one, for instance. More generally, Trites argues that "protagonists must learn about the social forces that have made them what they are – and [learn] to negotiate the levels of power that exist in the myriad social institutions within which they must function, including family, school, the church, government" (quoted in McCallum, 218).

When taking the actual number of realist fictions produced for a younger audience over the past years into account, the question whether the concept of a South African realist fiction has become obsolete can only be answered with 'no'.

A statistical evaluation found that 70% of all English teenage fiction published between 2000 and 2013 are novels written in the realist mode (cf. Stadler 2015, 50). Worldwide, most literature for young adults has been and still is being written in the realist mode (cf. McCallum 216). Yet, nowadays, realist fiction is not as prominent in the public eye as, for instance, the fantasy genre due to the latter's successes beyond the book page (cf. Stephenie Meyer's *Twilight* Series, J. K. Rowling's *Harry Potter* Series, Rick Riordan's *Percy Jackson* Series, and Suzanne Collins's *The Hunger Games* trilogy). Regarding the actual number of publications in South Africa, but also abroad, fantasy writing is the second most frequently published type of fiction (cf. McCallum 215; Stadler 2015). However, despite its popularity with the young, the number of fantastical texts produced by local writers is still small at present.[22] Given the dominance of literary texts written in the realist mode in this early twenty-first century, the subsequent chapters on representations of South African space, gender, and social economics will demonstrate whether or to what extent this "less obviously one-sided and seductive" new hybrid realism can also be found in twenty-first century South African teenage fiction (Pearson and Reynolds 72).

[22] Between the years 2000 and 2013 only 14% of all texts for teenagers were written in the fantastical mode (cf. Stadler 2015, 50). I will return to the discussion of the rise of a distinctly South African fantasy/science fiction genre in the conclusion of this thesis.

1 The Spatial Distinctiveness of South Africa[23]

> "Stories [...] traverse and organize places; they select and link them together; they make sentences and itineraries out of them. They are spatial trajectories. In this respect, narrative structures have the status of spatial syntaxes."
>
> (de Certeau 1988, 115)

In this introductory quote, de Certeau points to a specific capacity of the literary text which is fundamental to the study of the representation of South African space in the narratives for young adults: Stories "are spatial trajectories" (*ibid.*). Fictional accounts transport the reader from the real world to an imagined location, namely the place of action represented in the text. The setting of the novel is, however, not only the place where the story happens, but as one of the three classic entities that constitute narrative structures, it is indeed invested with a narrative function itself (cf. Webb 10). It is the latter capacity which is of special interest in this chapter. The contemporary trend of incorporating spatial topics into South African texts aimed at a young audience coincides with broader public and political debates in South Africa and beyond. Presently, the worldwide dispute about the representation of contemporary culture, identity, and the struggle to belong is deeply intertwined with broader theoretical reconceptualizations of the surrounding space. Since the end of apartheid, South Africa has been struggling to come to terms with its past. The redress of spatial interventions in people's lives as well as a redevelopment of the countryside is one of the major objectives of the new government (cf. "National Spatial Development"). In search of a new cultural identity and narrative, people have rediscovered the semantics of physical spaces as a means to write their personal – and fictional – narratives (cf. Webb; Neumann). These stories are as unique and diverse as the space they are setting their narratives in. Thematically, the following paragraphs focus on three spatial clusters which have been found to be most prominent in English-language young

[23] Subsequently, I understand "space" in the geographical sense of the term as referring to "a dimension within which matter is located or a grid within which substantive items are contained" (Agnew 316), i.e. similar to Lefebvre's *physical* space, and "place" as a "specific" location within that wider, more "general" space (cf. Agnew 318). Simultaneously, one has to be aware that spaces are seldom perceived as exclusively geographical entities but are always also understood as being shaped by social concepts. The discussion of Henri Lefebvre's *The Production of Space* (1994) will give more insight into the construction of social spaces (cf. chapter 1.1). More recently, Pierre Bourdieu defines "social spaces" as being "constructed in such a way that agents or groups are distributed in it according to their position in statistical distributions based on the two principles of differentiation [...]: economic capital and cultural capital" (Bourdieu 6).

adult literature since 2000: cityscapes, rural areas, and school settings (cf. Stadler 2015).

Methodologically, this chapter draws on sociological findings (cf. Lefebvre 1994; de Certeau 1988; Benjamin 1997, 2002), literary criticism (cf. Foucault 1986, 2002), and cultural readings (cf. Robinson 2006; Nuttall 2009) and puts them in relation to studies relating to the stages of the development of spatial perception of children (cf. Piaget et al.; Lohaus and Vierhaus). The objective is to gain insight into how the interconnectedness of the individual and its surrounding space is represented. Space is described in literary texts, yet with political and socio-economic changes in South Africa its representation has altered. This chapter will first examine South Africa's spatial distinctiveness from a theoretical point of view. The subsequent subchapters will provide an analysis of different adolescent narrators, investigating how they perceive their urban, rural, or school environments and how these environments shape their development as individuals to a surprisingly great extent. The more general question underlying the investigation of the urban, the rural, and the school setting is whether spatial segregation is represented as a continuing problem in the new South Africa. Are young people able to cross visible and invisible man-made borders between people of different ethnic descents or social classes so that the wish for a redefined social space is satisfied? Or do measures taken to spatially restructure and separate people during apartheid times still affect the everyday lives of young South Africans in the twenty-first century, thus hindering the people from creating a new cultural narrative and national identity?

1.1 Approaching South African Space Theoretically

To write a theory of 'the' South African space is a mission impossible, simply because there is not one South African space but a multitude of co-existing and overlaying subspaces. "Our [, the South African people's,] histories are inescapable", Beverley Naidoo elucidates, "[t]hey run through us like underground streams. Our past, so scarred with struggles over physical boundaries, created deep boundaries in the mind" (267). Hence, the spatial diversity of the country is comparable to a patchwork quilt which is perceived differently by every person who takes a closer look. The nature of South African space forces critics to choose a wide-angle lens in order to establish a first common ground before they can scrutinize a specific place in greater detail. Hence this chapter is interdisciplinary in its approach and international in its selection of spatial theories, valuing both the insider and the outsider position relative to the object of observation, the space of South Africa. Such an approach has become necessary as the political division of our world into 'three worlds' and their classification as developed, developing, or underdeveloped has led to a chasm between 'Western' and 'Third World' academia (cf. Robinson 2006; Comaroff and Comaroff 2012). In their attempts to find new ways of accessing space and to develop a new perception of South Africa, contemporary scholars, such as Jennifer Robinson (1998, 2006) and Sarah Nuttall (2004, 2009; cf. Mbembe and Nuttall), or Achille Mbembe (2012) and Jean and John Comaroff (2012), as we will see in chapter 3, have now begun to bridge this gap between the worlds by including social and spatial theories of different contexts in their reconceptualizations of South African space and its relation to other global spaces. This thesis aligns with the authors' wish to shelve the orientalism debate which has overshadowed academia for so long and hopes to contribute to this process by evaluating the depiction of South African space(s) in the country's youth fiction.

A factor which is imperative when approaching space theoretically is perspective. From which and even more importantly from whose point of view does one analyse a specific place? As this is a study of the literature written for adolescents, it is vital to consider how this peer group perceives space in contrast to adults. In this respect, developmental-psychological studies will help to clarify the idiosyncrasy of the relationship between teenagers and their surrounding social space.

Developmental-Psychological Perspective

Notions of place permeate the construction of cultural narratives. Whilst adults participate in this process quite naturally, young people have to learn the basic principles of spatial perception before they can operate actively in a certain space. Indeed, the development of a full-fledged spatial and geometric thinking takes up the first eighteen years of a child's life. Piaget's findings on the four developmental stages of the child's conception of space – the sensory-motor period (0–24 months), the pre-operational period (2–6 years), the period of concrete operations (7–12 years), and the period of formal operations (12–18) – are still a pillar of this academic field even forty years after their publication (quoted in Lohaus and Vierhaus 25).[24] Seen from a developmental-psychological perspective, the development of a spatial conception happens on two parallel levels: the body, the space of oneself, and the space outside of and surrounding

[24] Piaget et al.'s findings and influence on developmental studies have been heavily debated and re-evaluated amongst psychologists (see, for instance, Dawson-Tunik, Fischer, and Stein). Lohaus and Vierhaus inform us that scholars have meanwhile been able to show that some deviations in the age determination can occur and that Piaget's age statements should only be understood as points of reference, as children pass through the different stages according to their own development speed (cf. 24–25). More specifically, Piaget appears to have rather underestimated children's competences and his age statements have been found to be set rather too high (cf. Lohaus and Vierhaus 30). Nevertheless, Piaget's four developmental stages continue to influence studies in developmental psychology (cf. Case; Miller 2011) and are thus also taken as reference points in this chapter.

oneself (cf. Eggert and Bertrand 191). In the period of concrete operations, children learn how to recognize spatial dimensions (vertical and horizontal); the so called Euclidean space is established, meaning that children are capable of abstraction (cf. Eggert and Bertrand 85 and Piaget et al. 485). With regard to the site of the body, this implies that young people have learned to imagine their own body, they can locate the position of their body and they can imagine being at a different location while developing spatial concepts of both places (cf. Eggert and Bertrand 138). Thus, the point of reference is no longer solely egocentric, but can be transferred to another object or person. The competence to change the point of reference is ultimately a precondition for the ability to change one's perspective, which in turn is a precondition for reading and conceiving real places as well as fictionalized spaces in (young adult) literature.

In the subsequent young adult phase, also called the period of formal operations, the child's conceptions of outside space become ever more complex, drawing on the knowledge of topological, projective, and Euclidean relations which he/she has obtained during the earlier developmental stages (cf. Piaget et al. 15). Seen from a cognitive perspective, children who are in this phase no longer merely rely on their immediate and concrete reality for problem solving but can also muse over hypotheses and abstract propositions and test their quality (cf. Inhelder and Piaget 251; Lohaus and Vierhaus). Moreover, this coming–of–age phase is the first phase in which teenagers become aware of and are confronted with the social production of space, and it is the first time they can actively interact with and react to the conditions of their living space. As young adults, children process their surrounding space in its entirety for the first time and create their identity within and through that space. 'What do I want?' and 'Where is my place in this world?' are two pressing questions during the coming–of–age period. Born with a natural curiosity, young people experience their surrounding space, looking for answers to their questions while simultaneously opening up new social spaces and in this way contributing to the greater process of the formation of a cultural narrative. Thus, youth literature operates in a most crucial phase of human development, a phase where teenagers detect the world for the first time consciously, consequently developing a more complex understanding of their surrounding space.

Space as a 'Third Educator'

Significantly, the relationship between people and space is reciprocal. A place affects people emotionally via its form, features, and atmosphere. It gives them a sense of orientation. We feel protected, safe, and motivated in some settings and endangered in others (cf. Rätzel 95). The youth learns (from) the established spatial practices and either acknowledges or defies them. Hence, the surrounding space obtains the position of an educator. Reggio-Pedagogy,[25] a concept based in educational sciences, establishes space as the so-called 'third educator'. In traditional Reggio-Pedagogy, which describes the situation in a daycare facility, the other two educators are the peers and the pedagogue (cf. Vogel 136). Parents are another important entity in child-rearing, whose area of responsibility is, however, predominantly outside of the daycare centre context and thus not named in Malaguzzi's original concept.[26] The Reggio concept sees space as a pillar in child development, understanding a place as a learning concept in itself that accompanies the coming–of–age phase of young people (cf. von der Beek 197). The concept needs some adaption if applied to the South African context, i.e. the roles of the three educators, the pedagogue (and parents), the peers, and the surrounding space, need to be revaluated according to the country's social structure.

South Africa is a young country not only by the date of its constitution, but also in terms of demography. "The age cohort 15–34 (youth) comprises 38% of the total population (Statistics South Africa, 2010) and this cohort has been growing faster than the population as a whole due to declining fertility levels" ("Social Profile of South Africa" 1). A substantial number of South African children are abandoned:

> Less than a third (32%) of South African children live with both their biological parents and a quarter of children do not live with either of their biological parents. The disruption of the conventional family structure is most evident amongst African children, as only 27% live with both their biological parents, compared to 48% of coloured children and approximately 80% of children belonging to the other two population groups [i.e. Indian and White]. ("Social Profile of South Africa" 3)

In nearly 10% of the cases, it is a teenager who is the head of a household (cf. "Social Profile of South Africa" 3) and not an adult person of reference that the young person could model him-/herself after. Furthermore, "[m]any have little or no access to education, employment and livelihoods, healthcare and basic nutrition" (De Boeck and Honwana 1) and are thus forced to grow up under very harsh conditions. These numbers prove that a simple adaption of the Reggio-model

[25] The term is a translation from the German 'Reggio-Pädagogik'. The didactic concept was originally developed for daycare centres by Loris Malaguzzi in Reggio Emilia, a town in the North of Italy, in the 1960s. The child is at the centre of this approach and understood as the "constructor of his/her own reality" (freely transl. from "Konstrukteur seiner Wirklichkeit", Göhlich 177) (cf. Knauf 2001, 175; Knauf n.d.). The concept was also adopted for the school system. Since then, many scholars have argued that the learning environment such as the classroom is a decisive factor in the progress of learners (cf. Dreier 2008, 2011; Rätzel; von der Beek).

[26] For more information on the role of parents and their involvement in Reggio-Pedagogy, see Knauf (2001, 176).

is insufficient for the South African context. Instead, an extended definition of the first and the second educator is suggested.

As, according to official statistics, parents are often absent in the lives of South African children (cf. "Social Profile of South Africa"), other figures of authority or guidance become important. These may be for instance other adult persons such as an aunt or uncle, the grandmother or -father, but it might also be a gang leader in the case of street children or the caretaker in a children's home. It is also possible that there is no adult educator figure at all present in the lives of the children. The role of the pedagogue is also ambivalent in the South African context as poor teaching quality remains a major problem in South Africa (cf. Bauer; Naidoo; van der Berg et al.). While "there is near-universal enrolment in schools [...], poor retention rates, high drop-out rates and weak pupil performance" speak of the "quality challenges" which the country has faced in the years after 1994 (Metcalfe 93). For many children, peers become the only points of reference in their coming–of–age phase. In the special case of street children, the peer-educators can disappear as well, since these children seldom attend school and often do not trust anybody but themselves due to their constrained situation in life (cf. close reading of *Thirteen Cents*). Ultimately, the 'third educator' position, space, is the only stable category of the three. The surrounding (social) space is an entity that every child is exposed to, underlining all the more its significance in the period of development of every young South African person. The upcoming chapters on urban, rural, and educational spaces will discuss the educator position of space in a child's life and will show that the accessibility of space(s) is a pillar of character self-development.

Establishing Spatial Theory

However, we still cannot just move on to the analysis of fictional texts. Beforehand a theoretical framework needs to be established that correlates the so-called '*spatial turn*' with contemporary attempts to conceptualize the new South Africa. Regarding the field of spatial theorization, the '*spatial turn*' – a term coined by Edward Soja in his *Postmodern Geographies* (1989) – introduced a new era of reflection on our surrounding space and geography. In the late 1980s, Soja called for a re-evaluation of the spatial category in the field of social theory. According to Soja, the dominance of the temporal perspective over the spatial perspective since the mid-nineteenth century had led to an "ontologische Verzerrung" (2008, 244), a distortion of our viewpoint on the social as a whole. Subsequently, "space was treated as the dead, the fixed, the undialectical, and the immobile. Time, on the contrary, was richness, fecundity, life, dialectic" (Foucault 1980, 70). The latter statement by Foucault became a maxim of the spatial turn after Soja had propagated it in his *Postmodern Geographies* (cf. 1989, 4, 10). In order to overcome the disequilibrium between the temporal and the spatial perspective, the social critic was now asked to re-evaluate the notions that equated history and time with development, progress, and dynamics, i.e. with positive expressions of movement, while space was imagined as a fixed and inflexible entity that merely existed to provide a background or stage for action (cf. Soja 1989, 4; Günzel 91). Subsequently, many scholars of the humanities answered Soja's call and integrated space as a field of study into their disciplines. However, it is to be noted that critics need to be careful as there is no master plan for spatial analyses; after all, each space is unique and each "theory is always a particular theory of the world" (Mbembe 2012, 25).

With regard to the South African context, the early stages of the *spatial turn* are of special interest. This is due to the fact that in contemporary South Africa the temporal and the spatial perspectives on social development are out of balance.[27] Since the implementation of black majority rule in 1994, the spatial development of South Africa cannot keep pace with the vast political and social developments happening in the country. Consequently, as I have indicated already at the beginning of this chapter, an analysis of the South African (social) space is, to say the least, difficult. It starts with the very fact that arguably there is no single South African space, but many different (social) spaces which co-exist next to and within each other, resulting in a multidimensional and multifaceted map of sites – a patchwork quilt. Some critics of South African space have continuously emphasized the difference between these spaces, thus repeating and reinforcing the idea of otherness of the many (social) spaces that exist in parallel (cf. Bremner 1998, 2008). This is not the aim of the present study. Instead, this chapter aims to reveal the entanglements of South Africa's (social) spaces – to borrow Nuttall's term (2009). The chapter stands in the tradition of Soja's demand to investigate social issues through a spatial lens. It moreover draws on Henri Lefebvre's concept of how space is produced as a means to structure and forge society and its members (cf. 1994).

Henri Lefebvre, *The Production of Space* (1994)

With his monograph *The Production of Space*, Henri Lefebvre launched a theory of social space that brings together three fields: "first, the *physical* – nature, the Cosmos; secondly, the *mental*, including logical and formal abstractions; and thirdly, the *social*. [The combination of these fields makes up] [...] the space of social practice" (1994, 11). According to Lefebvre, space is shaped by and shapes society and its individual subjects. Moreover, every space created is unique, as each society produces a space for its own members (cf. 1994, 31).

[27] Reasons for this imbalance can be traced back to colonial times, referring here predominantly to the after-effects of colonial legislations, such as the Natives Land Act (1913) or the Native (Urban Areas) Act (1923).

> [This] already produced space can be decoded, can be *read*. [...] Interested [...] members of a particular society would have acceded [...] to *their* space and to their status as 'subjects' acting within that space and (in the broadest sense of the word) comprehending it. (Lefebvre 1994, 17)

While due to their age and associated experience adults generally know how to act and behave in (their) social space, young people still have to learn the codes of conduct. Frequently, the younger generation questions and chafes at restrictions and old established rules during this particular period of self-discovery. This generation's demand for action stimulates conflict in society and bears within it the possibility of change. When talking about Western societies, the second and the third Lefebvrian category – the *mental* and the *social* – are most frequently chosen for observation.[28] The structure of societies of postcolonial countries as well as the perception of these spatial surroundings is an entirely different one and the critic needs to adjust his/her criteria for investigation. Therefore and for historical reasons, the *physical*, Lefebvre's first category, must take up a pronounced part in the assessment of postcolonial spaces. Only by including the spatial component and looking at the South African country as a whole – its countryside and cityscapes – can the critic understand how the *mental* and the *social* categories influence the constitution of this multifaceted social space. Lefebvre elucidates the basic connection between the three categories as follows:

> Every space [i.e. the *physical*] is already in place before the appearance in it of actors; these actors [...] [seek] to appropriate the space in question. This pre-existence of space conditions the subject's presence, action and discourse, his competence and performance; yet the subject's presence, action and discourse, at the same time as they presuppose this space, also negate it. The subject experiences space as an obstacle, as a resistant 'objectality' at times as implacably hard as a concrete wall, being not only extremely difficult to modify in any way but also hedged about by Draconian rules prohibiting any attempt of modification. (Lefebvre 1994, 57)

It is the never-ending attempt to modify and bend the physical outline of a space according to individual or collective taste that characterizes people's interaction with their surrounding space. More often than not, they encounter "obstacles" (*ibid.*) in the modification process, especially when there is no consensus on the means of spatial appropriations.

[28] This is understandable when considering the fact that the bulk of Lefebvre's work is concerned with Western societies, whose national borders and issues of land have been considered as solved since World War II. [The author is aware that this statement is a simplification which can only serve the purpose of this specific monograph. Labelling a society 'Western' is also problematic, as the term is often related to concepts of imperialism. In this book the term is used only to indicate the different geographic location.]

One example of the many concerning spatial issues in South Africa is the repercussions of the forced relocation of communities in the 1980s; another is the after-effects of apartheid legislation, which still affect the everyday lives of a large number of South Africans (cf. van der Merwe and Saunders 1f.). After the end of apartheid it was clear that the spatial structure of South Africa could not stay the same. Since then the South African government has worked on spatial development plans which reverse spatial segregation and give all people access to service facilities and "[a]reas with demonstrated economic potential" ("National Spatial Development" iv). A contemporary example of spatial appropriation is the reconceptualization of township space as tourist attractions in the Gauteng province pointed out by Lindsay Bremner in her essay on the Kliptown Project (2008, 337–347). The topographical outline of the township was supposed to be redesigned so that the new spatial order would reflect an "urban democracy", and although intentions were good and the "architects were asked to mediate between [...] the 'near order' (Lefebvre 1996, 101), that is, direct relations between people and groups interacting in a space [...] [and] the 'far order' – society's significant ensembles and institutions of power" (Bremner 2008, 340), reality lagged behind the high expectations. Bremner ultimately concludes: "Kliptown's motley, creolized community of outsiders and their meandering narratives have, yet again, been displaced" (Bremner 2008, 345). The attempt to represent all residents in the new architecture failed; the undesired inhabitants were excluded from sight whereas "[m]annequins – beautiful, happy, young, and black – [...] instantaneously populated the newly formed spaces" (*ibid.*). Whether the new architecture can attain the aspired "urban democracy" is severely challenged by the essay's author (Bremner 2008, 340).

In her homage to "the beloved country", Helen Moffett provides an accurate, yet more general outline of what the landscape of twenty-first century South Africa looks like:

> Many [...] places are no longer wild; they have suffered the ravages of drought and dispossession, their inhabitants having drifted to cities or been more brutally displaced [...]; or the land has been bought up by investors who fancy owning a hunting lodge or private game reserve. Above all, a certain innocence has gone for good. [...] Now violent crime can and does occur in all but the most isolated beauty spots [...]. (2006a, viii–ix)

A consequence of all the bending and working on places is that today's map of South Africa looks like – evoking the image once again – a patchwork quilt made up of different overlapping (social) spaces, while, simultaneously, every (social) group has its own conception of the (social) space it inhabits. More specifically, the South African country is not only divided into urban, rural, and small-town areas, but these locations are again layered with a variety of social groups living in them (cf. Murray 2008; Nuttall and Mbembe; Putter). Hence without exaggeration, it can be said that conceptions of both South Africa's urban *and* rural spaces are conflicted and the study of only one of those spaces involves the danger of one-dimensionality. Last but not least, the study of school settings, particularly the boarding school experience, will provide further insight into the spatial and social mapping processes of adolescents. Generally, the adolescent protagonists attempt to establish a sense of place and belonging before they begin to mould their identities in relation to their spatial surroundings.

1.2 Spatial Segregation Continued?

> "Every story is a travel story – a spatial practice."
> (de Certeau 1988, 115)

Since the end of apartheid, the country of South Africa has been establishing new order on (at least) three levels: the economic, the social, and the spatial. Naturally, this has consequences for structures in both the public and the private sectors. The entity that is, however, most affected is the South African people, especially the younger generation. In this time of change, they have to reconsider their conceptions of their surrounding space and re-evaluate their individual position "in a country which has to negotiate ancient cultures and the influence of contemporary Western urbanised society" (Webb 9f.). Whilst historical moments such as the implementation of a democratic form of government by the vote of the people in the mid-1990s or the launching of the "Growth, Employment, and Redistribution" and the "Black Economic Empowerment" initiatives have led to rapid political and social developments in the new South Africa, the reshaping of the country's space, i.e. the repeal of the spatial segregation of people, takes much longer and bears the potential for conflict (cf. Bremner 1998).

Since 1996, Spatial Development Initiatives (SDI) have been launched and understood as an important component for restructuring the post-apartheid rural space economy (cf. Rogerson). Investments from the public and the private sectors in undeveloped rural areas with potential for growth are meant to help to better connect the regions to the vibrant city spaces, simultaneously making the former more interesting for new businesses, which in turn will create jobs in those areas ("Spatial Development Initiative" n.d.; cf. Rogerson). In 2007, *The Presidency* published an official "National Spatial Development Perspective" followed by "A National Overview of Spatial Trends and Settlement Characteristics" in 2008. The results of these two documents show that despite the measures taken, spatial development in rural areas continues to lag behind the development in urban areas. This is due to historical processes which still affect the present space economy of South Africa:

> Apartheid spatial planning [had] ensured that the majority of the people were located far from social and economic opportunities. This has created a disjuncture between where people live and where economic opportunities exist, denying the vast majority of the poor access to opportunities for employment, wealth creation and social progress. ("National Spatial Development" 8f.)

As a consequence, migration towards the urban centres of South Africa has become the most striking phenomenon of the past decade. The 2008 analysis of spatial trends comes to the significant conclusion:

> Viewing the data and trends [...], strong evidence seem[s] to be emerging that the future of South Africa and its citizens, and the crucible for government in delivering on its objectives in many ways hinge on the future of the following key areas/settlements*: The Gauteng city region and coastal city regions of Cape Town, eThekwini and Nelson Mandela Bay* [...]. *The cities and towns that fulfil significant economic and public services functions* [...]. *The densely settled clusters and dispersed settlements in the former Bantustans* [...]. The *range of smaller towns, service* centres and nodes scattered through-out the country [...]. (van Huyssteen and Botha 2; emphasis in the original)

The analysts reason that the future of South Africa lies in its urban centres. Not only are these places nodes of migration, but they are highly attractive for a specific group of society, the youth. In high numbers young people migrate to the cities from regions scarred by unemployment, poverty, and a lack of social services in search of a better life (cf. van Huyssteen and Botha). The urban areas have also become the home of "the biggest and most highly skilled portion of the formal and informal labour market, as well as the biggest number of those that are unskilled [and] economically inactive" (*ibid.*). This conglomeration of highly skilled and unskilled (young) people puts the city environment under great pressure with regard to "natural growth", "increasing dependency ratios", the creation of employment opportunities, and service delivery ("National Spatial Development" 44). Despite these constraints and via this shift in the demographic profile, city regions have become multicultural hubs in which "new tools of analysis, new archives and new ethnographies" (Nuttall 2004, 732) have started to emerge, consequently triggering the transformation of the South African space per se.

These spatial trends in South Africa substantiate the theoretical concepts on urban and rural space made by Edward Soja and Henri Lefebvre. Lefebvre asserted that social development happens in the urban context, not the rural (cf. 1994, 234f., 386). However, he admits that urban space "has a symbiotic relationship with that rural space over which (if often with much difficulty) it holds sway" (Lefebvre 1994, 234f.). Also for Soja, urban space has the greater potential for social and economic change, which he calls "urban spatial causality" (Soja 2009a, 31). Urban spatial causality is defined by those advantages and stimuli which emerge from the condition of density and heterogeneity of urban milieus (cf. Soja 2009a, 31; Soja 2008, 241). According to Soja, urban spatial causality cannot be imagined without spatial justice, which "involves the fair and equitable distribution in space of socially valued resources and the opportunities to use them" (2009b, 2). Characteristically, urban spaces generate not only "technological innovation, artistic creativity, economic development, [and] social change", but are also responsible for "environmental degradation, social polarization, widening income gaps, international politics, and, more specifically, the production of justice and injustice" (cf. Soja 2009b, 2). Participants of the social system of the city need to be aware of these mechanisms in order to produce an equal and just space (cf. Soja 2008, 242). Understanding fiction as ethnography (cf. Hemer 53ff.), this thesis is interested in whether the spatial developments of the new South Africa are reflected in its literature for the young, or more precisely, whether the implementation of the democratic system of government after 1994 also had effects on the spatial conceptions of (social) spaces of South Africa and/or the conceptualization of space in fiction. In her study of young adult literature from the 1990s, Judith Inggs points to the "division of [South African] space" and highlights the existence of a "contrast between the physical and the mental space experienced by the characters, between rural and urban space and between an alienation from and a sense of belonging to a particular space" (2004, 26, 25). Is spatial segregation still a topic in the novels published after the year 2000? Most importantly, what is the role of the youth in the transformation of spatial processes and where are their limitations? These are questions to be asked of contemporary literary texts and their representations of urban, rural, and school settings.

1.2.1 Demystification of the Urban

A statistical analysis of youth literature written in English and published between the years 2000 and 2013, which was conducted at the National English Literary Museum in Grahamstown in June and July 2013, has shown that almost 60% of all books featured an urban setting (cf. Stadler 2015, 51). By contrast, in the year 1990, 30% of "English juvenile books published in South African" "had an urban setting" (*ibid.*; cf. Heale 19; cf. Tötemeier 168). As in the last decade of the twentieth century (cf. Jenkins 2006, 182), Johannesburg and Cape Town are also most frequently found at the centre of attention in contemporary youth novels, while small towns, like Welkom or Grahamstown, or other bigger cities such as Pretoria, Port Elizabeth, or East London, are less frequently chosen as settings in South African youth novels (cf. Stadler 2015, 51). The preference for metropolitan areas such as Cape Town and Johannesburg coincides with the country's demographics, according to which the majority of people are living in these two cities (cf. Ndebele 2013). In the past decade, novels with a township setting as well as stories with a setting in more affluent urban areas have been published more frequently than books with a rural or school setting.[29] The dominance of the post-apartheid urban setting in post-millennial adolescent literature from South Africa does not come as a surprise. The city has been the preferred choice for South African authors ever since the 1950s:

> If they were politically or socially aware, rural areas offered them no potential for exploratory fiction, because in the country social relations were slow to change and opportunities for young people of different races to interact other than in master-servant relationships remained limited. (Jenkins 2006, 18)

Since then, the city has gradually replaced the Karoo and the bushveld as the new "spiritual homeland of white English speakers", and "youth literature followed it there" (Jenkins 2006, 171).

Significantly, not only authors of fictional texts explore the dynamics of the city and its transformative processes in their texts. In this early twenty-first century, ordinary citizens and theorists alike have aligned in the belief that the city is 'the' place to be in the present. For the former, it is the place to turn to when in search of employment, social services, or commodities, for instance. For the latter, it is the space where societal change and progress happen due to its heterogeneity. With their focus on urban studies, South African academics responded to the global phenomenon of rural exodus by using the universal trend to argue for a new, a "cosmopolitan" (Robinson 2006, 3) perspective of the city. This call had become necessary as "theories of urban modernity, just like South African urbanism, have often reserved experiences of dynamism and innovation for a privileged few, and especially for those wealthy cities and their citizens who have laid claim to originating modernity" (Robinson 2006, x). As a result, a divide had emerged between the analysis of Western and of other cities. Jennifer Robinson (2006) and Sarah Nuttall (2009), as we will see later, are two scholars who deliberately point to this gulf between "Euro-American" and African cities, to borrow from the title of the Comaroffs' *Theory from the South* (2012), and who have started to develop approaches which can help to bridge the divide. Both Nuttall and Robinson are experts in theorizing the 'now' in South Africa and their works signify a move away from established patterns of thought. In their studies, which were published under the titles *Ordinary Cities* (2006) and *Entanglement* (2009), they achieve a look beyond South Africa's contested spatial history, even though the country's past undeniably continues to shape its present, thereby opening their local observations to a global audience. More generally, the aim of urban theorists of the post-independence era is to (re)conceptualize and (re)define the urban

[29] This confirms Jay Heale's conclusions after his examination of 71 young adult novels published after the year 2000 according to the parameter "geography", which he kindly shared with me in March 2013 (e-mail conversation with J. Heale in March/April 2013).

geographies of the 'new' South Africa and to achieve an open and unprejudiced discourse about the trend of urbanization. The analysis of the (social) structures of the country's urban centres is topical: "South Africa has an uneven population distribution, with the majority living in small unorganized urban settlements. In 2008, 61% of the population was classified as living in an urban environment. However, the majority of the urban population lives in small towns" ("Country Profile South Africa" 58). Consequently, an urban theory of South Africa cannot be written only from a Johannesburg or Cape Town perspective, rather it has to include the smaller towns and their citizens in their accounts of city life.

Jennifer Robinson's point of access for the study of cities is the argument that "all cities are best understood as 'ordinary' [...] [as this] opens up new opportunities for creatively imagining the distinctive futures of all cities" (Robinson 2006, 1). With her call for the rediscovery of the ordinary, Robinson reinvokes Njabulo Ndebele's influential text *South African Literature and Culture: Rediscovery of the Ordinary* (1994). Robinson rebels against old labels like "Western, Third World, developed, developing, world or global" (2006, 1) and outlines how it is our propensity to categorize that preconditions our analyses. Theorists of the urban usually have a specific city in mind when they develop their theories – Walter Benjamin and Henri Lefebvre thought of Paris, for instance, while Michel de Certeau included Paris and New York in his considerations. So it is predominantly that special city that is theorized. Significantly, not one of these authors has ever claimed to have written a theory which can be applied to any 'ordinary' city and yet their findings have often been taken as universally valid. In a postcolonial, postmodern, post-apartheid world, the claim of 'simple' categories in city analyses can no longer be upheld. Instead, critics need to include "a more extensive range of urban contexts" (Robinson 2006, 6) and acknowledge the individual citizen as a dynamic and innovative player in the urban context, so as to arrive at a creative postcolonial urban studies which implies the ability to imagine new forms of urban development (cf. Robinson 2006, 12). In this respect it can be argued that theory lags behind reality, as processes of multiculturalism and diversity are well underway in the cities of South Africa. How difficult it is to theorize the dynamics of just one city can be seen in Nuttall's work on Johannesburg (2009; see also Nuttall and Mbembe).

Nuttall examined Johannesburg, one of the most complex cities of South Africa, in her book with the telling title *Entanglement* (2009). In it, she verbalizes the various discourses flowing through this city and specifies the very essence of their nature. She looks at the various cultural processes which are at work in the city and concludes by calling them 'entangled'. It seems a plain word for a city as eclectic as Johannesburg and yet it is highly appealing:

> Entanglement is a condition of being twisted together or entwined, involved with; it speaks of an intimacy gained, even if it was resisted, or ignored or uninvited. It [...] gesture[s] towards a [...] set of social relations that is complicated, ensnaring, in a tangle, but which also implies a human foldedness. (Nuttall 2009, 1)

Nuttall is convinced that the story of post-apartheid South Africa is not one of "difference", but one of "overlap[pings]" (*ibid.*), a notion that we can also trace in Robinson's 'ordinary' city. With regard to Johannesburg, this means that it is "the intertwining of surface and depth – in its historical and psychic senses – that defines the life of the city" (Nuttall 2009, 83). The present physical outline of Johannesburg is marked by its mining past, in which the city's soil was literally turned upside down. The riches extracted from underneath the city formed the cityscape visibly for every onlooker. The labourers in the mines, however, were seldom seen. Nuttall highlights that although beyond the range of vision, these people are not to be neglected as they are part of the city image and contribute to the identity of that urban space (cf. 2009, 83–86). It is in the stories of the people inhabiting a certain space that the truth about a place is hidden. We cannot analyse a space solely by its physical structure; we need to include its history, its social contexts, and mental conceptions of the individual.

There has always been a tension "between the language of theory, which can seem a language of fixing and prescription, and a sensibility which sought a mode of writing which was experimental, exploratory, closer, perhaps, to literature itself" (Nuttall 2009, 152). The bias between literary theory and literary texts is nothing new and definitely not restricted to the South African context. Following up on Nuttall's call to "find a way of traversing imaginative and theoretical routes which felt to [her] to have been, if not forgotten, then neglected for quite a while" (2009, 152), this thesis works with literary theories on space and brings them into dialogue with contemporary novels written for a young audience. After all, literature is one such space where people of any background can meet (cf. Nuttall 2009, 152). Literary texts deconstruct and translate the structures of a specific living space for the reader. They deliver points of reference and serve as connectors between different and formerly distinct environments. Foucault argued already in the 1970s that "to imagine another system is to expand our participation in the present system" (1977, 230). Nuttall takes up this cue and applies it to the present spatial system in South Africa. In *Entanglement*, she shows ways in which the various ethnic groups can grow together, namely by making them aware that they have always been living next to each other (cf. 2009). Thus, the different (sub)spaces have always been and continue to be intertwined and they have always subliminally affected and influenced each other due to their proximity. In their efforts to theorize contemporary South African (social) space Robinson and Nuttall have successfully begun to untangle the web of supposedly disconnected spaces by outlining their very connectedness. Moreover, they envision this connectedness on both a local and a global level.

Nuttall's and Robinson's theories reveal South Africa's urban areas to be highly complex entities not only with regard to their topography. The city is never just the sum of its topographical features but a space filled with mental constructs, hopes, expectations, and hypotheses. When scrutinizing the city the individual sees not only its physicality but the chances – and often only later, the dangers – which such a space holds. The cityscape is thus initially mystified as a version of the Promised Land. In those cases in which the individual is successful and content with his/her life (style) in the urban area, this myth is upheld. However, if he/she is not, the myth turns sour and the place becomes one's personal hell. It is this double-sidedness of the cityscape which characterizes its nature and which is quasi omnipresent in South Africa's contemporary literature for young adults. In youth literature of the 1990s "[v]ery often, but not exclusively so, [...] the urban environment represents alienation, division, and deprivation of ownership" (Inggs 2016, 41). In my statistical assessment of young adult fiction written between 2000 and 2013, I pointed out that "[r]ather than fostering city myths, twenty-first century output demystifies the city, strips the urban space of its glamour and discloses it as raw, dangerous and unsympathetic" (Stadler 2015, 50). The subsequent case studies of three selected novels will illustrate the double nature of the city in greater detail. It was argued earlier that the city is made up of many different subspaces such as cafes, the university, the suburb, the township, or the centre, each with a code of conduct of its own. In the following, we take a closer look at three of those subspaces, the city centre of Cape Town in K. Sello Duiker's *Thirteen Cents* (2000), a township of Cape Town in Margie Orford's *Dancing Queen* (2004), and a suburb in Johannesburg in Jayne Bauling's *E Eights* (2009).

K. Sello Duiker, *Thirteen Cents* (2000)

Thirteen Cents[30] gives a remarkable and merciless account of a street child's coming of age in the city of Cape Town. The lesson to be learned from the novel is that

> [e]very city has an unspoken side [and] Cape Town, between the postcard mountain and sea, has its own shadow-side lurking in its lap: [It is] a place of dislocation and uncertainty, dependence and desperation, destruction and survival, gangsters, pimps, pedophiles, hunger, hope and moments of happiness. (*TC*, blurb)

Admittedly, this novel is a tough read for a young person. However, the protagonist's fate is symptomatic and should come to be known by the country's youth, as it is also a pressing social issue of twenty-first century urban South Africa that despite its urgency is often neglected by authorities.

A sociological study by L. M. Richter from 1991 found the average age of street children in Pretoria, South Africa, to be between 13 and 14 years. A more recent UN study detected that "[t]here are an estimated 10 – 12,000 homeless children in South Africa" and "[c]hildren find their way to the streets because of

[30] Hereafter cited as *TC*.

poverty, overcrowding, abuse, neglect, family disintegration and HIV/AIDS" (Heiberg 43). We have encountered these reasons already in the previous chapter in the context of the "Social Profile of South Africa" (cf. 4) of the country's youth. Recent reliable figures and statistics concerning South African street children, however, hardly exist. In 2009, *The Presidency* published a "Situation Analysis of Children in South Africa". In it, the report refers to data from the 2001 census, according to which "2,189 homeless children" were identified, however, this figure "ignores children who work on the streets but live in family households" ("Situation Analysis" 85). Moreover, it points to a study of street children in the greater Cape Town metropolitan area conducted in 2000 by the Cape Metropolitan Council, which "estimated some 782 children living, working or begging on the streets" (*ibid.*). The "Situation Analysis", however, indicates that it "is likely" that "the total number of street children substantially exceeds the number of homeless children recorded in the 2001 census" (85). Apart from this material, no further reliable sources are available. For the purpose of this chapter, these sociological findings provide a sufficient first impression. In the following, the fictional living environment in Duiker's novel and the influence of the fictional surroundings on the protagonist, Azure, are of interest. This is to say that the story told in the literary text is not to be equated with reality but rather to be seen as a cultural product.

At the beginning of the text, Azure introduces himself and gives some background information before the reader starts to accompany him in his daily life. Since the death of his parents three years ago, the child has been living on the streets and he knows that they are "not safe. They are roads to hell, made of tar" (*TC* 66). Since the streets of Cape Town are ruled by gangsters, the city is divided up into separate areas. As he is aware of the danger of the cityscape, Azure intends to "Grow up. Fast" and "[u]nderstand quickly" (*TC* 66) in order to be able to survive. He plans a future away from the streets and saves money to leave this hell behind (cf. *TC* 66f.). Unsuccessfully, the orphan tries to stay out of the way of the gangsters and has "to go through [Gerald, the gangster boss] first" (*TC* 33) whenever he needs something, for instance new shoes.

The reader learns that in terms of residency, Azure has already retreated to the outskirts of the city because, as he reasons, "[t]own's too rough for [him]" (TC 33). For now, the street kid has chosen Sea Point to be his temporary home and hiding place. He reflects:

> The way in Cape Town, it's a long road, winding. I'm always lost, that's why I hide out in Sea Point. Get it? "See Point." That's where my eyes are. That's where I can see the best. I miss Sea Point. And I know that I can never go back there. (*TC* 65f.)

After he calls the leading gangster by the wrong name by mistake, the gangster tortures Azure for three days in the most demeaning ways, gives him a new name, Blue, and claims to own the street kid now (cf. *TC* 56f.). This act of claiming his name and person, which is deeply shocking for the youth, triggers a psychosis and, step by step, Azure loses his sense of identity, his grip on reality, and the contact to other people.[31]

Duiker's novel is told by a homodiegetic narrator. Yet *Thirteen Cents* does not merely provide a chronicle of the narrator's fate but portrays a specific subspace of the city, one which even the authorities hesitate to enter. No social workers and only indifferent policemen occur in the novel (cf. *TC* 59). Thus street children appear to be the victims of the demarcation of spaces, left alone in their daily struggle for survival. When Azure can no longer cope with the city's mechanisms – the raping and selling of his body, the betrayal and loss of his trusted persons and prospect of any future away from the streets – he flees to a secluded mountain cave on the top of Table Mountain, where he tries to calm his senses by envisioning ancestors and nature's force, the elements of water and fire, and the annihilation of urban Cape Town (cf. *TC* 109, 119–123, 126–130, 153–164). As he does not have the physical power or influence to fight back, he uses his imagination to take revenge on his oppressors for molesting his body and soul. These dreams and the conversations carried out in them help him to clear his head, at least temporarily. Still, at the novel's end, the reader does not know whether Azure will recover from his traumatic experiences, yet it seems an impossible task for an orphan without any contact person. The novel outlines the city's anonymity, its arrogance, and its corrupt and egocentric adults. This environment is responsible for Azure's deeply traumatized state and his emotional and mental overload (cf. *TC* 142–145). There is no safety net for street children and Azure's instincts lead him to leave the cityscape and to retreat to the most natural place in Cape Town, Table Mountain, in order to find peace.

The image of walking is a distinctive feature of *Thirteen Cents* which cannot go without mention. In fact, in only the first thirty-eight pages, twenty-nine phrases start with "I walk…" or "I go…".[32] Seven times other forms of walking, namely stumbling, staggering, or limping are described (cf. *TC* 2x 26, 2x 39, 40 44, 45). Walking is not only a mantra that literally keeps the protagonist going, but a motif in the novel as such. Given the overrepresentation of "walking", the critic is instantly reminded of the literary concept of the *voyeur* or *walker* (cf. de Certeau 1988, 92) and that of the *flâneur* (Benjamin 1997, 35). Although written within a Western context, both Benjamin's and de Certeau's observations of social space are groundbreaking studies and thus basic to observations of any social space at whatever location. Both concepts appear very similar at first sight, as both *voyeur* and *flâneur* translate into 'walking' the city. However, there are nuanced

[31] See *TC* 127f.: "Now tell me [i.e. Saartjie, a fatherly figure Azure envisions in his dreams] who you are!" "I'm not sure," I [Azure] tell him, "but they call me Blue."

[32] See *TC* 2, 7, 8, 12, 15, 2x 16, 2x 19, 20, 21, 22, 3x 23, 24, 26, 27, 2x 29, 31, 2x 32, 3x 33, 3x 38.

differences which are relevant for the analysis of young adult fiction, such as *Thirteen Cents* by K. Sello Duiker.

While we find de Certeau's *voyeur* on top of the city, at the summit of a skyscraper, for instance, i.e. at a specific location to which this walker has made his way on purpose (cf. de Certeau 1988, 92), Benjamin's *flâneur* is found amongst the masses, strolling in the streets amongst common walkers (cf. Benjamin 1997, 37). At his exalted position, the *voyeur* is "put at a distance" from the crowd (de Certeau 1988, 92), observing the city from above. According to de Certeau, this view "transforms the bewitching world by which one was 'possessed' into a text that lies before one's eyes. It allows one to read it, to be a solar Eye, looking down like a god" (*ibid.*). The *voyeur* stands in marked contrast to the "ordinary practitioners of the city[, who] live 'down below,' below the thresholds at which visibility begins" (de Certeau 1988, 93). For de Certeau, the common walker holds a disadvantaged position, as he is unable to see the full picture: Those "*Wandersmänner* [...] follow the thicks and thins of an urban 'text' they write without being able to read it" (*ibid.*). One of these *Wandersmänner* or walkers is Benjamin's *flâneur*. Whilst the general walker is blind to the spatial practices of a city, yet follows them instinctively (cf. *ibid.*), the *flâneur* is aware of the structure of the social space. Hence, although he does not have the exalted position of the *voyeur*, the *flâneur*, too, when sauntering through the city's streets, is distanced from the surrounding space. He is, however, different from the *voyeur*, emphatically connected to the cityscape.

> Empathy is the nature of the intoxication to which the *flâneur* abandons himself in the crowd. [He]... enjoys the incomparable privilege of being himself and someone else as he sees fit. Like a roving soul in search of a body, he enters another person whenever he wishes. (Benjamin 1997, 55)

Apart from the point of view and their different ways of walking the city, it is above all the emotional component which distinguishes the *flâneur* from the *voyeur*. The *flâneur* is at the same time part of the social space and outside of it. He is to be understood as a subject delivering a multidimensional mater key of the city and not as an individual composed of clichés.

Despite the dominance of the motif of walking the city, Benjamin's concept of the *flâneur* will not entirely fit the type of walking that Azure conducts during the first part of the novel. In the first eight chapters of the novel, the reader follows Azure as he walks amongst the masses from one place to another; he meets friends, business partners, gangsters, and suitors, seemingly progressing spatially and achieving his targets for the day. In reminiscence of the *flâneur*, Azure walks the city actively. As is characteristic of this walker, Azure understands the structure of his spatial surroundings very well and is able to "read" them (cf. de Certeau 1988, 93). He knows which place is ruled by which gangster and where he can go unwatched. The main character, moreover, is emphatically connected to the cityscape, another feature of the *flâneur*, as he comprehends the dark motifs behind the actions of the different grown-ups represented in the novel, the suitor, the whore, the gangster, and is able to draw conclusions on the social space which is shaped by adults: "You must always act like a grown-up" (*TC* 3) as "[t]here's nothing for *mahala* with grown-ups. You always have to do something in return" (*TC* 6). Through Azure, the reader thus gets a master key to Cape Town's adult underbelly. Yet, due to his vulnerable position as a street child, Azure's style of walking is not comparable to the sauntering or to the strolling around typical of a *flâneur*. Furthermore, both de Certeau and Benjamin most likely had an adult walker in mind. Arguably, when choosing a young adult and not an adult *flâneur* or *voyeur*, the perception of the city must be a different one, as the processes of walking and simultaneous space comprehension happen differently. Adults walk amongst the masses of other adults equally, implying that there is no explicit imbalance of power between the respective walkers. In comparison, a younger person is not granted the same rights of access as an adult, but in fact needs an adult to open up certain spaces. Both parties, the youths and adults, know about this disparity in social 'power' which shapes their respective way of flâneurie or voyeurism.

In *Thirteen Cents*, it is not primarily the young adult perception which hinders the protagonist from walking the city in the manner of Benjamin's *flâneur*, but rather Azure's status as a street child which complicates his development into a *flâneur*. In the novel, the protagonist wants to make his readers believe that he knows the cityscape like the back of his hand. However, he is soon shown to falter. After having been brutally tortured by Gerald and several members of the gangster's gang, Azure is no longer able to pretend to understand the space of the city (cf. *TC* chapter 9). This experience has left deepest marks on Azure's body and mind: "My feet are sore, they have walked too much. My eyes hurt. They have seen too much. And it never ends. It just keeps going" (*TC* 65). After the incident Azure "walk[s] around town like a lost dog all day. Everyone seems to know where they are going except [him]" (*TC* 67). The street child has lost the previously portrayed self-confidence about his accurate perception of his surrounding space and has become even less than a common walker. His wandering through town leaves an impression of repetition, redundancy, and walking in circles. Thus, the notion that walking means progress is turned upside down in this part of the novel.

It was mentioned before that Azure climbs Table Mountain at two different points in the novel. "Going to the mountain" is a cultural reference to rites of initiation, which are traditionally performed by several South African ethnic groups.[33] The result of traditional rites of passage is that after the initiates have returned from the mountain they have formally come of age and are thereafter accepted as full members of society. Azure's trips to the mountain are not conducted in the manner of ritualized rites of passage. Rather, Azure makes these

[33] Such rites of passage will be discussed in more detail in the chapter on machoism and masculinities (cf. 2.1).

trips in order to escape from the crowded city and to regain his ability to understand the social space beneath the mountain. His first walk to the mountain happens shortly after he is forcefully initiated into Gerald's gang (cf. *TC* 104–131). Azure himself has gained nothing from the initiation. His status as a street child remains unchanged. However, his latest, traumatizing experiences trigger something else in the protagonist, an urge to leave the cityscape behind. Although de Certeau has of course neither read *Thirteen Cents* nor written on it, his words are most fitting in this context: Making his way to the mountain, Azure takes on the position of de Certeau's *voyeur* as a means to escape his torturers and the very "bewitching" mass of people "by which [he felt] 'possessed'" (de Certeau 1988, 92). In an effort to see more clearly again and to get a better sense of the space that surrounds him, Azure "move[s] up into the light" (*TC* 106), represented by the mountain of Cape Town. Observing the city from above, Azure finds: "I have never been on my own this long in Cape Town. It feels good. I don't feel rushed" (*TC* 110). The exalted and somewhat distanced position of the *voyeur* has given back some power to the traumatized child. After four days he walks back down to Cape Town and "[e]ven though [he] look[s] thinner, [he] feel[s] stronger and protected by an invisible silence" (*TC* 132). Yet, when reality catches up with him soon after his return to the city, Azure loses this new-found strength again.

Having nowhere else to go, as all of his former points of reference have vanished, Azure makes a second trip to the mountain (cf. *TC* 154–164). In the final pages of the novel, Azure once again looks down at the city, to use de Certeau's words once more, "like a god" (1988, 92), yet this time, he envisages an apocalypse and thus the destruction of his former area of living, the urban space. This is both an image of empowerment but also one of surrender because at the moment of his vision, Azure is lying exhausted and feverish at the top of Table Mountain, leaving his ultimate recovery open for debate. Outlining the brutal effects which a traumatizing event can have on a person's sense of orientation and location, the novel thus indicates that Azure's special life situation makes a reconciliation with his surrounding space impossible. As Duiker's protagonist's means of walking change with his experiences, his young protagonist is to be understood as a decidedly alternative interpretation of the classic adult walker.

Margie Orford, *Dancing Queen* (2004)

Dancing Queen[34] is a youth novel written by Margie Orford, a prizewinning journalist and film-maker, who is most famous for her crime fiction for adults. The novel appeared as part of the Junior African Writers Series (JAWS), which deals with health, life skills, HIV, and AIDS. In terms of focalization there are three different homodiegetic young adult narrators, who take turns in narrating the story.

[34] The title is herafter cited as *DQ*.

One of these is speaking as a ghost, namely Nolitha, or Princess as she is otherwise known, telling her story through letters which she wrote before her death. Bongani, Nolitha's first boyfriend in Cape Town, and Shireen, Princess's female best friend in the city, are the narrators of the second and third chapters. It is this mix of narrative voices which considerably adds to the value of this novel, which retraces the story of the death of the protagonist, Nolitha, in consequence of her infection with the HI virus. The strength of the novel lies not only in its emphatic depiction of the silence surrounding the topic HIV/AIDS in South Africa and its cry for gender equality, but also in its apt visualization of the contrastive perception of rural and urban South African spaces.

Telling their stories, the teenage characters simultaneously narrate their sense of a certain place. In *Dancing Queen*, space holds an educator position in the sense of the Reggio concept. The topography of the city plays a decisive part in the main character's fate: The *physical* space becomes an insurmountable "obstacle" for the main character, to put it in Lefebvrian terms (Lefebvre 1994, 57). In this novel also the two other educator positions – the peers and adult authority figures, such as the pedagogue and parents – are represented. After winning a scholarship for the Cape Town Performing Arts Academy, Nolitha moves from her rural village, Tshatshawe, to Cape Town. The book thus invokes the famous 'Jim Comes To Joburg' pattern, which has already been discussed in the introduction. After her arrival in the city, Nolitha quickly makes friends with a teenage boy and girl from the city, Bongani and Shireen, who "taught [her] everything she needed to know about the city" (*DQ* 5). Lastly, as Nolitha is attending school regularly and her teacher is shown to have an eye on Nolitha's whereabouts, it can be said that the pedagogue, here Miss Njobe (cf. *DQ* 8), contributes to her upbringing as much as her parents and her aunt and uncle do.

The following analysis will continue where the previous theoretical argumentation left off and apply Soja's notions of urban spatial causality and *social justice* to the literary text (cf. 2009a, 31; 2009b, 2): Country girl and dancing talent Nolitha is allowed to move to the city after winning a scholarship for Cape Town's Performance Arts Academy. Unfortunately, and contrary to her initial beliefs, living in the city does not lead to fame and fortune, but misery and death. Had it not been for the "expensive" (*DQ* 18) life in the city, the long distance between school and place of residence, and the necessity of transport between the two places, the protagonist might still be alive. However, on her arrival in the city, the main character's "heart was exploding with joy" (*DQ* 4), still hardly believing her luck in being able to live in the big city where she is sure to become the next big dance star. Her aspirations and expectations of what can be achieved in the city have been fueled by the people of her home village, who even express hopes that her success "will put [the village] on the map", too (*DQ* 13). Princess's mother is convinced that in order for her daughter to "make something of her life" (*DQ* 12), she needs to go to the city. The initially positive attitude of the village people and the mother towards the young girl's move to the city shows that the myth of the city – a place where you can supposedly rise from rags to riches and have better chances to live a good life than in the countryside – still persists in the rural mind. These opinions and attitudes towards the city make up what Lefebvre termed *mental* space (cf. Lefebvre 1994, 11). Furthermore, the mindset of the people is congruent to Soja's theoretical conception of the spatial capital of the city, which is ranked higher than that of the village, as the city provides a better platform to thrive (cf. 2008, 241), a notion which the village people support. However, when Nolitha has to return to the village because no one in the city is taking care of her after she has contracted "that disease" (*DQ* 2; cf. *DQ* 8), the village people respond contemptuously. They spread rumours of her having been "loose" in the city and make her relocation to the city responsible for the illness (cf. *ibid.*). Hence, the mentally constructed space of the city has both positive, mystifying and negative, demystifying connotations in the rural areas. The attitude shifts from positive to negative when the city experience turns out to be lethal for the youth. Moreover, a deliberate act of silencing is carried out as the villagers are not willing to delve into the real reasons behind the contraction of the HI virus, but rather put the blame on the bigger entity, namely the space of the city, which is conveniently far away from their own area of living. As the accused (*mental*) space is not directly accessible, the allegation cannot immediately be confirmed or proved wrong, which is the desired effect of the silencing method. What people fail to include in their considerations about Nolitha's situation is that the real, the physical outline of the cityscape does not correspond to their *mental* construct of it. As they imagine the city as a holistic and not as a layered space, they fail to understand that it is the topographical layout of the cityscape and the spatial difference between, for instance, the centre of the city (place of work and education) and the townships (place of living) on the outskirts of the city that foster Nolitha's disempowered position in the urban environment.

Generally, both the rural and the urban space appear to have codes of conduct of their own. These have to be disentangled by the young characters. As a result of their place of origin, Bongani and Shireen are well versed in urban codes of conduct, while Nolitha is shaped by her rural upbringing. Whenever a character moves away from his/her place of origin, he or she enters a new negotiation process. When her friends from the city, Bongani and Shireen, attend Princess's funeral in the village, "both look out of place in this rural area" (*DQ* 5). They appear "cool and urban" (*ibid.*) and are easily distinguishable from the rest, also due to Shireen constantly typing into her cellphone; she is afraid that the city might "vanish" (*DQ* 27) during her stay in the Eastern Cape. Living in a rural area is not an option for the city girl as it consists only of "chickens and dust" (*DQ* 29, cf. also *DQ* 5, 27). But Nolitha is also instantly branded as a rural person when she first comes to the city due to her appearance and her conservative mindset. Her "wiry legs" (9) are characteristic of "kids that have to walk for miles to school every day" (*ibid.*) and whereas Shireen likes to party and have a drink and a smoke from time to time, Princess is "straight" (*DQ* 31), proud to be a virgin (cf. *DQ* 29), and allows the city to change her only in little respects, for instance, with regard to her clothes (cf. *DQ* 31).

On her arrival, the teenage girl is clearly overwhelmed by the traffic in Cape Town and afraid of "all those *skollies* at night" (*DQ* 13). Bongani maps out the city for her and gives her valuable tips on how to 'survive' in that space: She is not to walk alone at night (cf. *DQ* 14), for instance, and she is not to use an unknown taxi as the drivers would strip her of her valuables because they could tell that she is new to the city and comes from a rural background, two features which instantly mark her as an easy victim (cf. *DQ* 13). Princess is not oblivious to the dangers lurking in the city and it is not carelessness that brings about her death, but rather her dependence on her relatives' willingness to let her stay in their house in Khayalitsha and consequently the need for transport to and from the city. Public transport is not an option for Princess as the routes do not run close enough to her aunt's house in Site B of "the huge township that sprawls out across the Cape Flats" (*ibid.*). Thus, Nolitha depends on taxi lifts by Jabulani, a friend of her uncle's. All is well while her aunt is riding with her in the car. However, when her aunt loses her job and money is scarce in the third year of Nolitha's stay, Jabulani takes advantage of the situation, offering to Nolitha's uncle that the teenager could have free lifts to school and furthermore come to clean his house to earn some extra money for the family on Saturday afternoons. In the following, Nolitha's uncle makes it a prerequisite for her staying in the house that Nolitha be nice to Jabulani (cf. *DQ* 32f.). It does not take long for Jabulani to trick the girl into a dependent relationship where he demands sexual intercourse as payment for the taxi rides from the township to her school in the city and back, as well as for the money he has given to her relatives for food. As the protagonist's dream is to be trained at the Cape Town Performing Arts Academy, she is dependent on lodging with her relatives and thus sees no other option than to do what Jabulani demands (cf. *DQ* 34). It is the location of the place of residence of the family – a township, which is located far away from the city – and the city's insufficient infrastructure, an inadequately developed public transport system and the consequent high costs of taxi rides, which put the life of the teenage girl in danger. These socio-economic and spatial issues catch the young girl off guard and force her to do things she does not want, ultimately leading to her infection with the HI virus.

Clearly the cityscape in Orford's youth novel is almost devoid of what Soja describes as *social justice*, a principle wedded to his notion of urban spatial causality. As urban areas provide more options for prosperity, it is the citizens' task to distribute these options in a fair and just manner. Only then and through equal eligibility to the process of (re)structuring the city can *social justice* in Soja's sense be achieved (cf. Soja 2009b, 2). The girl in *Dancing Queen* is in an inferior position to the locally established hierarchies, which follow patriarchal structures, and it is she who suffers from the consequent social injustice. Although Princess did not cause her aunt's unemployment, she is singled out as the scapegoat. The authority figures, who are clearly the men in *Dancing Queen*, do not act on her behalf and the majority of the women in the novel succumb to their husbands' wishes.[35] Instead of support she is met with anger and refusal, and made to feel unwelcome and guilty. This negative conduct is a symptom of a social system which is out of balance and socially polarized (cf. Soja 2008, 242). Hence, in the course of the novel, the cityscape is demystified in so far as it is stripped of its formerly attractive mask.

Jayne Bauling, *E Eights* (2009)

Jayne Bauling won the Senior Award in the Macmillan Writer's Prize for Africa for *E Eights*[36] in 2008. According to the "Macmillan Catalogue", the book is part of the approved books for schools and compulsory reading in Grade 9. The novel is set in the suburban flatlands of Johannesburg and is told from the perspective of Chabi Mnisi. She and her friends find it necessary to develop their own spatial codes and spatial practices as the models followed by adult characters, such as Chabi's father, are not suitable for their present situation in life. Since the adult's conceptualization of the surrounding space fails to represent their current circumstances in the suburb, the youths generate a parallel space to the adult world, which is reminiscent of Homi Bhabha's utopian third space. It is only after a near-death experience that the two spatial concepts start to merge into one, leaving the reader with the impression that E Eights has transformed into a culturally hybrid space.

In an interview conducted by Jonathan Rutherford in 1990, the renowned postcolonial critic, Homi Bhabha, talked about a space that allowed for negotiation, the so-called 'third space'. This type of space emerges from Bhabha's considerations on cultural difference and cultural diversity. "This third space displaces the histories that constitute it, and sets up new structures of authority, new political initiatives, which are inadequately understood through received wisdom" (Bhabha quoted in Rutherford 211). Hence, it is a space that "enables other positions to emerge" (*ibid.*). The term 'third space' is equated with hybridity.

> [T]he importance of hybridity is that it bears the traces of those feelings and practices which inform it, just like a translation, so that hybridity puts together the traces of certain other meanings or discourses. It does not give them the authority of being prior in the sense of being original: they are prior only in the sense of being anterior. The process of cultural hybridity gives rise to something different, something new and unrecognisable, a new area of negotiation of meaning and representation. (*ibid.*)

[35] Her teacher, Ms Njobe, and Bongani's mother are an exception to this rule (cf. *DQ* 23f.).
[36] The title is hereafter cited as *EE*.

Considering hybridity as a mere amalgamation of precast elements would miss the point. Instead it is the strategic selection of constituents which characterizes the production of a third space (cf. Wieselberg). Notably, Bhabha's third space is to be understood as a utopia. It represents a wish, a suggestion of reality and not reality itself. The outline of the new, 'third' space is produced by its practitioners. They negotiate and decide on the structure of this free zone while the key components of the third space are openness and pliability. Significantly, the hybrid space is for those whose freedom and equality is endangered, such as migrants or child soldiers, making it an ideal element in narratives of young adult fiction as we will see hereafter. Earlier in this chapter, Inhelder and Piaget's study of the developmental-psychological phases of children helped to outline the developmental stage of teenagers with regard to spatial conceptualization (cf. Inhelder and Piaget 251; Lohaus and Vierhaus 29). The subsequent analysis will use these findings in order to explain the spatial practices of the main character and her friends.

The title, *E Eights*, refers to a run-down apartment block in one of Johannesburg's suburbs, normally called "Elizabeth Heights", but since "the first 'H' in 'Heights' has fallen down the wall" (*EE* 3), the inhabitants call it E Eights. The homodiegetic female narrator, Chabi, which is a short form of Masechabe (cf. *EE* 9), makes the reader picture the building in detail: The garages make up the ground floor, on top of which are two further storeys of flats (cf. *EE* 3). The block is but one of many in the suburb of Windsor, which are all named after British aristocrats, "Dukes, Queens, Earls, Countesses and a whole lot more" (*EE* 3). The protagonist and her friends perceive the names given to their house and the area as odd and inapt, which is why they try to find new ones for them. Instead of E Eights, the main character's brother, Nathi, suggests "Uhuru" (*EE* 19), meaning freedom in Swahili, whereas their father finds "Little Lagos Extension Ninety-Nine or something to that effect" (*EE* 12) much more suitable, referring to the many Nigerian people who have been immigrating to South Africa since the end of apartheid. These two propositions spell out the two contrastive attitudes towards foreigners in South Africa, which are represented by the young adults living in E Eights on the one side and Chabi's father on the other. The two clusters, xenophobia and space, complement each other due to the nature of the topics and are thus dealt with simultaneously in the following paragraphs. The xenophobic attitudes of the parent and his consequent insular conception of *spatial capital* and *spatial justice* ultimately lead to the young people's construction of both a revised *mental* and *social* cityscape (cf. Soja 2008; Lefebvre 1994).

E Eights has been Chabi Mnisi's and her family's home since her mother's promotion. Originally, the Mnisis are from Kabokweni, which lies in the South African province Mpumalanga. Apart from the protagonist's family, Felicity Vilonel, otherwise known as Fliss, and her mother are the only other two South Africans living in the block. The rest of the apartments are rented out to Zambians, Nigerians, and people from Mozambique and the Democratic Republic of Congo (cf. *EE* 4–7), who have come to Johannesburg in hope of a better life. The apartment block appears like a collage containing many of the different nationalities now living in the new South Africa, which has become a node of (im)migration (cf. Pinnock's *Skyline* 2000). Once again, the 'Jim Comes To Joburg' pattern is invoked. The children living in E Eights grow up together as friends and enjoy the cultural diversity, eagerly anticipating every new person moving into the block, whereas it is precisely this multiculturalism which Chabi's father detests (cf. *EE* 13). As the father does not approve of his children meeting friends of foreign descent (cf. *EE* 12f., 27, 47f.), the youths see themselves forced to do so behind his back. Hence, they tell their father that they are going to meet a South African friend at the friend's apartment, but actually relocate to a second place where they then meet further friends of foreign origins (cf. *EE* 35–38). This second place is an adult-free zone, and hence a space where the spatial concepts of the older generation do not apply, a parallel space.

Clearly, from the outset of the novel the father's sense of place is utterly different from that of his children, Chabi, Nathi, and Khensani. Since the youngsters grow up in a multicultural and multinational environment, they do not perceive the other kids as 'foreign' but as belonging to the block as much as they do. They make no distinction between their space and their friends' space. To her father, their foreign neighbours are a "gang of thieves" (*EE* 49) and the deportation centre at the end of the road is the only place where all of them belong, while Chabi imagines it to be literally "the end of everything" (*EE* 18) and speaks of it with a "shiver" (*ibid.*). The novel, thus, illustrates the difference in child and adult perceptions of the exact same place, here the deportation centre. This difference in perception of a place, the father's wish that his children keep their distance from foreigners, and finally the utterance of the father to some men on the street that he wishes the apartment block "cleansed" of at least "some of these people" (*EE* 42) triggers a process in which the teenagers construct their own spatial practices and spatial codes and consequently their own social space.

The creation of a parallel, *mental* space by the teenagers can also be explained from a developmental-psychological perspective (cf. Inhelder and Piaget 1958). As the coming–of–age phase is the first in which young adults can actively engage with and react to the conception of their surrounding space – also because they are now able to form hypotheses and engage critically with a topic – they are likely to do so. This process, however, is not to be understood as a mere act of open rebellion against the parents' will, but is in fact a necessary act of formation in the course of finding their individual identity. In the novel, this is acted out as follows: After the father has told the men on the street whom he believes to be "[p]lainclothes police" (*EE* 41) about the new Somali family in the apartment block, both of Hawa Dahir's parents disappear and are not to be found again. Chabi and her friends decide to help Hawa and hide her from the men who are probably responsible for the disappearance of the parents. Daniel's apartment appears to be the ideal hiding place as his father is seldom at home (cf. *EE* 37). Subsequently, the characters contemplate the problems that will arise for Hawa due to her parents vanishing and they conclude that the adults' method – handing her over to the authorities (cf. *EE* 65) – is not an option. The decision to hide Hawa at Daniel's place supports the previous argument that it is natural for the young adults to share their space with the immigrant girl, an idea Chabi's father would not even consider. While the parent prefers the spatial segregation of different groups of people, the children – and also Chabi's mother and a few other adults in the novel (cf. *EE* 72) – have moved beyond this notion and advocate a shared space. "I don't see why different age groups or religions should stop people being friends", Fliss states (*EE* 39). The youths' questioning of the persisting spatial practices enables them to construct a new social space, a space which goes hand in hand with their notion of the new South Africa as a place "where everyone wants to come" (*EE* 39) due to its transformation. However, despite their best efforts, the teenagers fail to find a solution for Hawa's difficult case. While the group of friends is still busy discussing their options, the Somali girl disappears in the course of a fire accidentally set by Fliss's mother in flat number ten of E Eights (cf. *EE* 75f.). Due to the homodiegetic narrative perspective, the reader does not get any further details about the whereabouts of Hawa's family or Hawa thereafter. Chabi believes she has seen Hawa at an intersection, supposedly well, however she cannot find her when she goes looking for her after that (cf. *EE* 77). Nevertheless, meeting Hawa has changed Chabi's perception of South African space and the country's people.

It was stated earlier that the Mnisis have not always lived in the city of Johannesburg. Their small-town background makes Bauling's novel particularly interesting for this literary analysis of the representations of South African cityscapes with regard to another aspect, namely the adjustment process to the cityscape which the individual family members go through after their move. Since their arrival, the Mnisis have been living in a two-bedroom apartment, which is too small for a family of five. The two sisters and the parents each share a room, while Nathi, the main character's little brother, has to sleep in the living room (cf. *EE* 13). Due to the nature of the flat and the building, privacy is scarce not only within the family but also with regard to the other inhabitants of the block. While this lack of privacy and the proximity to other people makes the mother uncomfortable, the younger characters are not bothered by it (cf. *EE* 12f., 27, 38); again, this is a further indicator for the argument that the novel's young generation is more willing to share space than the older generation. Nevertheless, Chabi is very aware of her family's situation and the effects which the confined space of the apartment have on the other family members. Indeed, she is not particularly fond of their new life in the city, finding it "so…hard. Everything is so different [from life in Mpumalanga], and difficult. People [are, too]" (*EE* 26). As a reaction to her father's xenophobic attitudes and her encounters with xenophobia at school (cf. *EE* 17, 27) Chabi, however, decides to accept the hardships of the city space as a challenge, which she masters by refabricating the existing social space according to her means.

Chabi's mother, too, finds life in Johannesburg exhausting: The topography of the city forces her to fight her way through "ten traffic jams" per day to get to her job "in one of Sandton's smart office blocks" (*EE* 11). She is drained due to both her demanding job and because she is the sole bread winner in the house since her husband has lost his job. Although she is worried about their present living situation and disappointed with her husband, as he has let life in the urban area turn him into an overweight, "hate-filled man" (*EE* 26), Chabi's mother keeps busy to ensure a future for her family in the city. This is indeed harder than she had expected: Being so successful at her former company had "deceived [her] into thinking that [she] was a big fish" (*EE* 26). When her daughter asks her "'What will you do?' She pushes herself upright, claps her hands [...] and laughs. "Grow myself into a very big fish indeed'" (*ibid.*). While Chabi's mother stands her ground, convinced of staying in the city and dead set on claiming her space, the protagonist's father has fallen victim to the commodities of the city.

While living in Mpumalanga and Nelspruit, Chabi's father had been the supportive husband every wife wishes for. However, since he has lost his job in Johannesburg and is unable to find a new one, he has changed, now indulging in every "good[y]" and consumer good available in the Kwickspar near the apartment block, a behaviour he formerly mocked (cf. *EE* 8). His children witness how their father "with all his couch-potatoeing in front of the TV, feeding his face or nursing a beer [...] balloon[s], and yet [...] seems so much smaller than the man he used to be" (*EE* 9). Instead of assessing his situation objectively, he rather looks for a scapegoat, which he finds in the immigrants to South Africa. Consequently, he develops very strong xenophobic attitudes, which he expresses openly on the street with the result of a family being separated (cf. *EE* 10). Eventually, Chabi can no longer hold in her disappointment in and anger with her father's lack of ambition and his narrow views of the social space of the new South Africa (cf. *EE* 49). The young girl's outburst triggers not only tension and discomfort but a change in the family. Moreover, when E Eights is accidently set on fire and Chabi's father is terrified of losing his children in the flames, the adult realizes that he has to change his attitudes. Thus, the novel ends hopefully for Chabi and her family (cf. *EE* 76f.). After the fire, Chabi's father returns to Mpumalanga, where he finds a new job. He furthermore loses the weight he had gained from consuming too much in the city and is working to overcome his xenophobic attitudes (cf. *EE* 77). The rest of the family stay in Johannesburg.

In sum, *E Eights* depicts two different South African spatial practices: one that is still characterized by the markers of spatial segregation acted out by Chabi's father and a second one which advocates a shared space represented by the younger generation. It is this second approach, lived and practiced by the youths of the apartment block, which makes the ending of the novel hopeful beyond its pages. Significantly, the novel's tone and style is not condescending and depicts a wide range of characters, making it a valuable fictional assessment of the new South Africa. Whilst in reality, in many areas the different ethnic groups are still living spatially separated, this divide is not upheld in the novel. The younger generation opens up the possibility for a refined *mental* and *social* space, a Bhabhaian third space, as it were (cf. Rutherford 1990). Ultimately, the novel empowers the younger generation, showing the young readers the potential of their voice.

Résumé

This chapter has critically addressed the claim of the demystification of urban South Africa. The different novels depict the entanglement between rural, suburban, township, and city centre spaces (cf. Nuttall 2009). All the novels chosen for case studies in this chapter debate the image of the city as a place for "innovation and dynamism" (Robinson 2006, 2) and depict those problems that come with rapid urbanization, social injustice being a characteristic feature of many of the depicted places. It should be noted that this is not a situation unique to South African cities. In fact, worldwide, cities have become nodes of migration and hence hotspots of inequality and development alike. Young adult novels "written in the early 1990s reflect[ed] a sharp division of space and place according to race, moving in the latter part of the decade towards the contestation of space and movement between and across spaces" (Inggs 2016, 27). In the 2000s, all the young adult characters continue to perceive the cityscape as an "obstacle" or a challenge (Lefebvre 1994, 57), one which only Chabi of E Eights learns to overcome. The protagonists' living situation and social background plays a decisive part in their ability to access the space of the city.[37] The empowerment of young people and hence their forging of an identity is connected to them being able to access and to influence their surrounding space. In contrast to the image of the monstrous city which lets its innocent citizens starve in plain sight of the aspired freedom and riches – a space which only the juvenile characters of *E Eights* successfully subvert by creating a parallel space, the rural is depicted as more peaceful and as a place of teenage empowerment.

[37] The relevance of the socio-economic background will be further discussed in chapter 3.

1.2.2 Revaluation of Rural Settings

Elwyn Jenkins's monograph on the *National Character in South African English Children's Literature* (2006) opens with a discussion of the literary representation of children in the countryside, pointing out that previous to the 1970s, the Karoo and the bushveld were the "spiritual homeland of English-speaking white South Africa" and the most frequently chosen setting in South African children's and young adult literature (cf. 1–19). Interestingly, "from the 1970s until the end of the 1980s, [...] no physical space as easily identifiable as the Karoo or the bushveld replaced them" (Jenkins 2006, 18). During those years "no local youth literature in English could foster a love of a homeland" and it "is only since the coming of democracy in 1994 that the cities" have replaced the Karoo and the bushveld as "the spiritual homeland of white English speakers" (Jenkins 2006, 19, 171). This trend continues in this early twenty-first century: Between the years 2000 and 2013, only 22 novels, i.e. 14% of all novels written in the realist mode, set their stories in an exclusively rural South African area, whereas nearly 60% of texts were set in urban areas (cf. Stadler 2015, 51). Another 16 novels (10%) are set in both rural and urban contexts. Seven novels depict how characters migrate away from the rural space toward the city; three novels engage with urban to small-town migration, while only one novel deals with urban to rural migration (*ibid.*). Of all the novels that were classified as being written in the realist mode, the great majority of texts are set in the Gauteng and Western Cape region, as Johannesburg and Cape Town are located there. Two novels have their setting in the Northern Cape, 13 in the Eastern Cape, six in the Free State, eight in KwaZulu-Natal, three in Limpopo, and five in Mpumalanga. Thirty-five texts are classified as "unspecified" as the texts did not provide enough information to locate the place of action in the story at a distinct place or region in South Africa (*ibid.*). The statistical assessment leads to the conclusion that South African literature written in the realist mode represents South Africa's regional diversity. The "diversifying of places and communities in which stories are set" is indeed a reason to "celebrate", as "[many] books now exist in which young South Africans can recognize their own world", Beverley Naidoo explains (267, 268).

The dominance of the urban setting in contemporary literature for young people automatically implies the underrepresentation of non-urban settings in fictional texts. Elwyn Jenkins found that after the 1950s, "rural areas offered [...] no potential for exploratory fiction, because in the country social relations were slow to change and opportunities for young people of different races to interact other than in master–servant relationships remained limited" (2006, 18). Today, rural settings are chosen to discuss environmental and conservational issues alongside character development. In light of the socio-economic harshness of the city, characters are seldom portrayed as developing feelings of belonging or a sense of being at home in urban novels. Country children on the other hand are depicted as having a deep relationship with their surroundings. Overall, rural spaces are shown to be more open and accessible and thus more empowering for young adult characters than their urban counterparts. Moreover, rural life is shown to retain a longstanding characteristic: Its space is still shaped by slow development and old customs. Significantly, characters growing up in a rural environment are generally shown to be appreciative of the stability and reliability of non-urban life. In both David Donald's *Call on the Wind* (2007) and Gillian D'Achada's *Sharkey's Son* (2008) the surrounding space appears like an educator figure in the lives of the two male protagonists. In these novels, the natural, non-urban space is depicted like another character amongst the novel's list of (human) characters. Living in harmony with one's natural surroundings is a leitmotif in both novels.

Rural settings as well as the appreciation of nature as an actor amongst human characters have been studied by literary scholars with the help of ecocritical theorizations (cf. Glotfelty and Fromm). Elwyn Jenkins, for instance, has discussed and highlighted the significance of ecology in South African youth literature on various occasions (cf. 1993, chapter 3 and 4; 2002, chapter 4; 2006, chapter 3). Bryan Caminero-Santangelo and Garth Myers clarify that "ecocriticism [is] 'the study of the relationship between literature and the physical environment' when such study moves beyond treating the environment as background (setting) or symbol" (3). When debating the position of humans in the natural world in their stories, environmental children's literature has been found to traditionally follow one of three approaches (cf. Sigler): This type of fiction either embraces the domination model, "assum[ing] the primacy of humans, who either sentimentalize or dominate the environment" (Martin 2004, 217–218), the stewardship model, "which is less so but still anthropocentric, position[ing] humans as caretakers of the earth" (Martin 2004, 218), or the "typically non-Western [...] biocentric model" (*ibid.*), which "decenters humanity's importance in nonhuman nature and nature writing (thus rejecting anthropocentric views) and instead explores the complex interrelationships between the human and the nonhuman (a biocentric view)" (Sigler 148). Elizabeth DeLoughrey, Renee Gosson, and George Handley moreover point to the fact that "ecocriticism overlaps with postcolonialism in assuming that deep explorations of place are vital strategies to recover autonomy" (5). Despite this connection, "post-colonial criticism has given little attention to environmental factors" until the mid-2000s (DeLoughrey, Gosson, and Handley 5). As others have already illustrated the evolution of a postcolonial ecocritical theory elsewhere in elaborate detail (cf. Caminero-Santangelo and Myers), it is not my intention to embark on a discussion of its origins in this chapter. Instead, I will rather focus on the formation of a so-called African ecocriticism.

Since the beginning of the new millennium, critics like Anthony Vital or the already quoted co-editors Caminero-Santangelo and Myers have worked to establish an ecocriticism which is distinctly African, acknowledging, however, that such an African ecocriticism must be part of the more general postcolonial ecocriticism (cf. Caminero-Santangelo and Myers; Vital). An African approach to ecocriticism became necessary because earlier British and American ecocritics had focused rather uncritically on "nature writing" (Martin 1994, 4) and its preference for the need to preserve and conserve African nature. According to Caminero-Santangelo and Myers, "first-wave ecocritics" from British and American contexts had not shifted their attention to the untangling of "the extensive intertwined history of nature and culture in Africa" (7). Julia Martin highlights that for environmental issues to become meaningful in the South African context, "environmental priorities" must not be "in keeping with the […] colonial project", which would be tantamount to the discourse of preservation and conservation, but must be thought of along the lines of "the struggle for social and political justice" (1994, 3, 1). Postcolonial ecocritics start their observations from the premise that "all representations of the material world are situated" and provide "viewpoints of the world that are historically, politically, and culturally positioned" (Caminero-Santangelo and Myers 5). Consequently, both Martin and Vital believe that representations of African environments need to be assessed differently than, for instance, Wordsworth's descriptions of nature (cf. Martin 1994, 4; Vital 88). The upcoming analysis is therefore conducted in light of Huggan and Tiffin's call for critical studies of "how postcolonial writers from a variety of regions have adapted environmental discourses" (Huggan and Tiffin 15).

In the following, the representations of an Eastern Cape cove in David Donald's *Call on the Wind* and of a Western Cape lagoon in Gillian D'Achada's *Sharkey's Son* become the focal point of discussion. The two novels are a response to the unique historical and cultural situation of the respective environments. They underpin the notion that different cultural regions exist within the same country. Both novels depict young male characters who have gained impressive knowledge about the natural peculiarities of the places where they grew up (cf. Huggan and Tiffin 15). Both texts feature protagonists coming from non-affluent backgrounds, where money and material goods are scarce. If there is some extra money, it is spent on practical goods such as a fishing rod in *Call on the Wind*, or a fridge in *Sharkey's Son*. Interestingly, both novels feature young males who are brought up by a caring father figure. In both novels, the mothers of the boys died when they were still very young. In this respect the novels are an exception regarding the corpus of this study. In the majority of cases the absence of father figures is characteristic of the young adult genre. In both of the novels examined here, school plays a minor role in the formative processes of the protagonists. While in *Sharkey's Son* school is described as a nuisance that keeps Grant, the protagonist, from doing what he really wants, which is being in the natural world, *Call on the Wind* does not feature any educational setting at all. In both novels nature is described as a loyal companion and educator figure in the lives of the protagonists.

David Donald, *Call on the Wind* (2007)

Donald's *Call on the Wind*[38] is set in a small Griqua fishing village on the Tsitsikamma coast in the Eastern Cape region of South Africa. The novel contains an extensive "Glossary of Afrikaans and Colloquial Languages" (*CW* 120-124), as well as a "Postscript", which mentions that "[t]his story is based on truth" (*CW* 118). *Call on the Wind* is thus intended to be a realistic depiction of the life of a small fishing community in a remote cove on the Eastern Cape coast and thus differs from, for instance, Leon De Villier's *Shorn* (2009), which "invents a mystical new world" by "creat[ing] an alternative and primitive civilization" comprised of "white characters in a typically black tribal environment" (Vorster 126). An illustrated map preceding the acknowledgements and the table of contents serves as a first introduction to the spatial outline of the cove and its surroundings. The natural beauty of the place and its idyllic location are portrayed in this map. Further black and white illustrations of key scenes follow at different selected sections in the story. An emblem of an osprey is used to signal flashbacks or time leaps within a chapter.

The novel holds a special place in the contemporary corpus because it interweaves a typical coming–of–age tale with the story of the rite of passage of a small fishing community. The book shows how a young person's energy and will to thrive and explore new paths beyond the known inspires an entire community in its darkest hours to believe in a fresh start at a new place. The resettlement of the community becomes necessary after a maritime accident which causes the death of the majority of the men in the community and destroys the community's fishing boat, hence the basis of their self-sustaining lifestyle. The community, which is rich in terms of social cohesion but poor regarding monetary funds, cannot afford to buy a new boat and, due to the deaths of its men, no longer has the manpower to generate enough food and revenues to sustain the entire community at the cove. The life that the protagonist Isaak had previously established for himself outside of the community in the town of Knysna becomes a model for a potential future of the members of the community. The protagonist's success in the urban area facilitates the community's decision to "leave the cove and find new homes and work" in Knysna (*CW* 115). The novel ends with the group, having packed up its few belongings, turning to leave for their new lives in the city. Whether they will succeed in their new lives is left open. Significantly, the novel's ending is not to be misunderstood as a devaluation of life in secluded areas. In fact, the peace and content that the people have experienced while living in the rural area is foregrounded throughout the novel. Had there not been an accident, the people would never have thought about leaving their cove.

Isaak's deep appreciation of the nature around him and his life in the community shape his adolescence and his life as an adult. The novel begins shortly

[38] The novel is hereafter cited as *CW*.

before Isaak's eighteenth birthday (cf. *CW* 33–34). With his birthday, Isaak becomes a full member of the fishermen crew, meaning that he is now allowed to cast his own hand lines and no longer has to take on the more menial chores (cf. *CW* 39). The four seasons, the sea, the weather, wild animals, and a "cluster of huts tucked away in the forest" (*CW* 11) shape the everyday life of the small community. Whenever the fishermen catch more than the community needs the women make their way to Plettenberg Bay, where they sell the fish to buy food and goods which they cannot produce themselves (cf. *CW* 12). Throughout the novel it is emphasized that everybody in the community has a fixed role and tasks which he or she has to fulfil so that the well-being of the community can be ensured. When Frik, a young man in the community, is shown to prefer to flirt with the ladies and lie in the sun instead of collecting firewood or working on the fishing boat, the narrator gives the reader insight into Isaak's uncompromising condemnation of such spoilt behaviour (cf. *CW* 21, 36). As Frik's absence on the fishing boat endangers the lives of the other fishermen, the rest of the community also starts to scorn him: "He was ignored. He was cold-shouldered. He began to realize that he wasn't wanted" (*CW* 37). Frik ultimately leaves the community. Isaak's character is described as the exact opposite of Frik's. He genuinely puts the community before his own wishes, despite being "unsure of whether fishing was what he wanted to do for the rest of his life" (*CW* 43). Unlike the rest of the fishermen crew, who have by now become used to the business of fishing, Isaak is shown to severely struggle with having to kill the fish he catches. As Isaak is portrayed as a likeable character, the reader sympathizes with his dislike of killing the fish. However, the reader is also aware that fishing is the major resource of the community, without which it cannot survive at the cove. *Call on the Wind* asks the reader to weigh the killing of the fish against the community's need to eat. In this respect, David Donald's novel, as well as Gillian D'Achada's *Sharkey's Son*, as we will see later, addresses the controversial topic of hunting in South African children's literature from a different angle. In nineteenth century children's books, hunting was frequently connected to colonial practices and shown to be a means to "[tame] the African wilds" (cf. Jenkins 2006, 44–48). According to Jenkins, "whale hunting and the slaughter of seal cubs to protect fishing resources" last featured as topics in Laurens van der Post's *The Hunter and the Whale* (1967), Dianne Hofmeyr's *When Whales Go Free* (1988), and Dale Kenmuir's *Son of the Surf* (1988) (Jenkins 2006, 44). Hofmeyr's and Kenmuir's books both depict "angst-ridden boys who reject their father's role in these traditional harvestings. This rejection is central to their strained relations with their fathers, while readers are swayed to disapprove of the slaughter because the boys are portrayed sympathetically" (*ibid.*). Neither Donald's nor D'Achada's novel depicts hunting as a pastime or as a sport, but as a means to assure a livelihood for the family. Overall, catching fish in order to sustain a community is not depicted as ethically unsound. Significantly, Isaak's leaving the village to follow a different career in the city only a few months after becoming a full member of the crew does not complicate his relationship to his father or the other crew members. Thus, *Call on the Wind* guides its readers in their development of an ethical standpoint on fishing and the value of natural life as such and is infused with a didacticism that speaks of a general appreciation of the lives of humans, animals, and plants.

In chapter five of *Call on the Wind* a visit from Isaak's cousin Braam leads to Isaak leaving the coastal village for the town of Knysna. Braam convinces Isaak and Isaak's father that the protagonist's talent as a singer will earn him more money in the city than his hands at the cove. With the consent of his father, who sends his child away in the hope that Isaak's move will help the community more than his staying, Isaak starts his new life at Knysna as a worker at a sawmill (cf. *CW* 44–45). The protagonist struggles to adjust to the densely populated and noisy city. He cannot "believe that there [are] so many people living together" in one place (*CW* 49). In the chapters which describe Isaak's life in the city the main character's appreciation of the quiet and slowness of his home village and its related diversity of fauna and flora makes itself felt most significantly. However, his homesickness and longing for more natural surroundings do not keep Isaak from working dutifully at the sawmill and from following his career as a singer. He and his band are soon making good money with their music. Isaak's thoughtful songs about his home village and his work at the sawmill bring about the band's success. The main character's knowledge of trees and the forest also help him to move up the ladder at the sawmill. Having "grown up with a wild forest all around him", Isaak becomes the new "'tree-spotter' to go ahead of the cutting and felling team" (*CW* 62–63). Although he initially enjoys being back in the forest, he soon grows aware of the double-edged character of his promotion: His work in the woods means the death of many trees.

> As [he] approached the part of the forest where trees were being felled, it looked just as though a tornado had ripped through it. Giant kalanders, some as ancient as those he knew at home, lay crashed to the ground, their great branches twisted and shattered like huge broken arms and legs. Othe[r] trees lay across them. And, with their weight and size, all these felled giants had crashed through the forest around them, smashing the younger and smaller trees into twisted spikes, stumps and heaps of broken branches. (*CW* 63)

This extract illustrates that Isaak's perception of trees and the forest differs from that of the foreman and the people in the city. While the latter see them as material goods that ensure their monetary profits or provide building material, Isaak can only focus on their "huge broken arms and legs" (*ibid.*). To him, the trees are like human characters, whose absence leaves a blank (cf. *CW* 65). The main character thereafter decides to save as many trees from cutting as possible. "'You I will not mark,' he murmured quietly to the tree. 'Grow strong, tree. And shed your seeds around. Perhaps you can father a few new yellowwoods around here at least'" (*CW* 65). His experiences as a tree-spotter fuel Isaak's fears that the woodcutters will one day destroy his home forest as well (cf. *CW* 64). Isaak expresses his fears in his songs, through which the protagonist starts to instill notions in the hearts of the people of Knysna that "trees were [not just] trees" which "people used [...] for wood" (*CW* 66).

In *Call on the Wind*, David Donald discusses deforestation alongside the cultural and social specificities of the Eastern Cape. The novel also touches on a city–countryside pattern, whereby Knysna is described as the busy opposite of the rural area, a pattern which we have already encountered in the previous subchapter (cf. chapter 1.2.1). The novel depicts the communal life of people in a secluded cove and gives insight into their austere way of living. The novel's rich documentation of types of animals and information on dendrology introduces the reader to the diversity of the local flora and fauna in the Eastern Cape region. Descriptions of life in the city are provided alongside and not in opposition to the rural lifestyle. Both areas are shown to have their dangers: in the city it is gangs (cf. *CW* 57) who threaten people at night, at the cove the bad weather is responsible for endangering the fishermen's lives. Eventually, due to social circumstances, namely the death of the majority of its fishermen, the community has to change its place of residency from the cove to the city realm. Isaak's earlier success in the city helps the older community members to familiarize themselves with the thought of leaving their natural surroundings for the city. The young adult has become a respected member of the community and it is his life that will serve as a model for the future of the community.

Gillian D'Achada, *Sharkey's Son* (2008)

D'Achada's *Sharkey's Son*[39] was the 2007 winner of the Gold Medal of the Sanlam Prize for Youth Literature and has been included in the Department of Basic Education's National Catalogue for Senior Phase Learners. In 2013, the book appeared in its third impression. A school edition of the book in the form of an ebook, which includes pre- and post-reading activities as well as notes on the genre, appeared in 2014. Moreover, Emma Reid has put together a "Teacher's Guide and Activity Resource for Grades 5–7" (n.d.), which can be accessed on the publisher's website. As this is a book that is read in South African schools, the novel's didacticism or ideology, to borrow John Stephens's terminology, regarding the coastal environment is of particular interest.

Sharkey's Son voices a discourse that denounces the "environmentalism of the affluent" (Caminero-Santangelo and Myers 10; cf. also 4, 7) and can thus be seen as a book that speaks out against a culture of preservation and conservation at indigenous people's cost. *Sharkey's Son* is set in the Western Cape region and although, like in *Call on the Wind*, a lagoon serves as the major place of action, the living situation of D'Achada's protagonist is quite different to Isaak's in *Call*

[39] The novel is hereafter cited as *SS*.

on the Wind. Overall, tourism and 'civilization' have already taken a tight hold of this otherwise unsullied rural area. Many of the original Lagoooners have already sold their estates to rich town people, with the result that great "parts of Langebaan had changed [in the last fifty years] since the people from the town had 'discovered' it and started building huge white mansions that greedily gobbled up the strandveld, the grassy banks adjoining the beach" (*SS* 2). Sharkey and his son, however, cannot imagine living anywhere else but near the lagoon; the selling of their house has not been considered an option so far.

The protagonist, Grant, his father, Sharkey, as well as their friends at the Langebaan lagoon, are described as being a people of their own. They share a deep sense of belonging to the place and understand themselves as a part of their natural surroundings. Moreover, they speak and act differently than those who have recently arrived at the lagoon in the past years, and they make sure to clearly differentiate themselves from the "Capetonians", who come to visit the lagoon on the weekends (cf. *SS* 47). The "Langebaners" are shown to have their own rules of conduct and sense of community. The young protagonist informs us that

> [u]sually Langebaners didn't mind their friends coming into their homes when they weren't there, but normally this was just done to drop something off or to wait around for the owner of the house to return. Even in Langebaan it would be considered unacceptable to enter someone else's house in order to rifle through their things. (*SS* 13)

Over time, the Langebaners have developed a deep knowledge of their place. During his short life the main character has already learned to read the signs of the sea and the wind, its dangers and pleasures: "Like all Langebaners, [Grant] knew that the sea was the best healer" (*SS* 21) or that you have to take a step to the side after every fifth step in order to walk out of a current (cf. *SS* 89). Grant's connection to and knowledge of the place is also apparent to the other characters in the novel. "Grant the seagull" (*SS* 111) is how the protagonist is described at one point in the novel. Having been raised by his father alone, Grant has developed into the same West Coast loner as his father. In fact, Grant is shown to have had no friends of the same age prior to the book's events. His father is his "only real friend" (*SS* 10):

> Grant knew that most of the other Lagooners didn't altogether approve of the way Sharkey was raising him, but it suited him just fine. His father understood his need to walk to school in the morning by himself, to amble home on the hot, windy afternoons by a different route every day, to go swimming on Saturdays in Churchhaven, on the other side of the lagoon, and perhaps come home only on Sunday. (*SS* 3)

Grant has lived in accordance with his natural surroundings for as long as he can remember. Simultaneously he has developed a feeling of deep connection to his place of origin. He treasures the brownness and emptiness of the lagoon, while the beauty of the place is, for instance, lost on Ally, a girl who has lived in cities for the majority of her life (cf. *SS* 53). In fact, Grant "feel[s] richer in his little stone house in Langebaan, with only a rough wooden shelf and a small bar fridge in the kitchen, than he d[oes] in Uncle Roy's house in Cape Town that had private bathrooms off each bedroom" (cf. *SS* 75). Consequently, "[r]ich and poor all depends on where you are – and who you are" (*SS* 75), Grant concludes after a conversation with Ally.

Throughout the novel, Grant describes Cape Town as the antithesis of his life at the lagoon and communicates his dislike of the big city at various instances throughout the novel. The topic emerges in chapter 2, shortly after the protagonist's father has supposedly left Grant behind to take a job in Lüderitz, leaving Oom Daan, a friend of the family, with "instructions for the house to be sold and for Grant to be taken to Cape Town" (*SS* 9). Grant is outraged and cannot and will not believe what Oom Daan is telling him. Both he and his father "hate[d]" Cape Town (*SS* 9). "How many times had Sharkey said those words: 'This house belongs to me and my boy. It's not for sale.' Now why would he sell it? It just didn't make sense" (*SS* 9). Subsequently, the novel invites the reader to join thirteen-year-old Grant on his adventurous journey to find out why his father would leave him for a job in Lüderitz, especially when he had R50 000 resting in a "FLASH account" (*SS* 12). When Oom Daan informs Sharkey's son that he will pick him up and drive him to his uncle in Cape Town and that he will sell the house in Sharkey's name, Grant follows his instincts and runs off to find out the truth about the whereabouts of his father by himself. The protagonist decides to follow Sharkey to Lüderitz and makes his way to the dune track. At first his "West Coast instincts guid[e] him, sure as a sonar, through the thick white mist" (*SS* 18). But then, tricked by "a snorting, rolling-eyed monster", which was "really only a dune buck", Grant "accidently stumble[s]", getting "quantities of thorns in his feet" as a result (*SS* 19). Thereafter, Grant is in need of two new found friends, Smiler and Amy, to help him recover. Like in *Call on the Wind*, nature and its phenomena feature like characters in *Sharkey's Son*. The flora and fauna of the place influence the happenings throughout the story and the actions of the characters in the novel to a great extent. The tone used to describe the natural phenomena, like the tide, the mist, the strandveld, and so on, is respectfully gentle. Grant and the other inhabitants of the area know that they have to subjugate their needs to the place's peculiarities and not the other way round. Otherwise they will get hurt rather sooner than later. Direct speech acts and personifications underline the understanding of nature as a character: "Who are you? the mist mocked, unmistakably the master of this night and this place and this time. Grant pulled his woollen cap further down over his ears and eyes so that he wouldn't have to hear its taunts and see its hostile rushing, rushing" (*SS* 20). Throughout the book, nature is shown to shape the Langebaners' lives. The local people can only make a meagre living at the lagoon and mostly rely on tourists and the sea to provide enough for them. Despite the socio-economic constraints connected to life at the lagoon, the locals perceive themselves as rich and Sharkey is shown to go to great lengths so that he and his son can keep living at the lagoon (cf. *SS* 75).

The reader learns that Grant's father has previously had trouble with the police because of smuggling. Apparently, Sharkey was denied a fishing license by the government after the banning of shark nets in South Africa (cf. *SS* 6). However, "fishing was his life" and unlike others who "joined the army or [...] left" the area, Sharkey "refused to go" (*SS* 6–7) and so had no other option but to fish "on the sly" (*SS* 7). The novel comments on the non-transparent decision-making process of ministers (cf. *SS* 7) and the life-changing effects such political decisions have on an individual. Sharkey was never able to find out why he was denied the license and the reader is left to speculate about the reasons as well. Toward the end of the novel, it becomes clear that it had in fact been against the country's constitution to deny a man "the right to make an honest living" (*SS* 112). This "clause" may help Sharkey's lawyer to "overrun the court's decision" (*SS* 112). Hence, the novel discusses the power imbalance between authorities and locals and their right to their place via Sharkey's story. Sharkey, who is involved in "smokkeling" (*SS* 105) in order to sustain his family, has been caught "lots of time[s], and given warnings. But he's a stiffnecked Sandvelder, you know, just like [Grant]" and so "decided to do just one last smokkel, a big one, a thousand kreef. And got caught" (*SS* 105). Two corrupt Special Forces cops "tried to cut in on it, and when that didn't work they decided to steal" Sharkey's other profits instead (*SS* 105–106). Grant is shown to need all his knowledge about the environment in the process of solving the riddle of Sharkey's disappearance. The story ends with mixed feelings for Grant. His father is sent to prison for smuggling, thus leaving him to live with somebody else. However, he is not sent to Cape Town as initially planned, but is now allowed to stay with Oom Daan and his wife at the Lagoon until his father's return (cf. *SS* 106). Grant's stubbornness, which makes him a true Sandvelder (cf. *SS* 106), has paid off and he can continue living at the lagoon.

Résumé

The ecocritical lens lends itself to discussions of South Africa's natural environments and their fictional representations. Both *Call on the Wind* and *Sharkey's Son* display a deep appreciation of the country's flora and fauna without leaving pressing social and political injustices out of sight, thus presenting their stories according to the biocentric model (cf. Sigler 148). If African ecocriticism is about the disclosure of realities of lives in the natural environment, then South African writers such as David Donald and Gillian D'Achada make the critic's work easy. South African authors who write about rural South African spaces discuss environmental conditions alongside cultural and socio-political issues. DeLoughrey, Gosson, and Handley argue that "deep explorations of place are vital strategies to recover autonomy" (5). Through their fictional works writers of the new South Africa manifest their autonomy in such regional discussions. Their characters, too, achieve this personal autonomy over their lives, even if that means leaving a certain environment for another. Significantly, the character's autonomy is not tied to their age. The young characters are shown to shape their environment and both Isaak and Grant are perceived as empowered, also by the other characters in the novel. Their knowledge about their environment leads to their empowerment and makes their tales convincing. By contrast, we have seen that knowledge about the spatial structure of cities does not automatically lead to the empowerment of a protagonist. In fact, in both *Thirteen Cents* and *Dancing Queen* the cityscape renders the child protagonist inferior.

Interestingly, stereotypes characterize the characters' perception of urban and rural spaces alike. Therefore, it is difficult to speak of a re-evaluation of rural settings in general terms, as both rural and urban settings are shown to have problems of their own. The discussion of the coastal settings has provided insights into the cultural diversity of these spaces as well as the socio-economic restrictions that come with such locations. Game reserves are another rural setting that still features in youth literature. Fanie Viljoen's *Scarred Lion* (2011) is an example of such a novel. The farm, which has long been the archetypical setting for South African fiction (cf. Jenkins 2006, 5–13), appears to have lost its significance in this early twenty-first century. No book in the corpus examines farm life in present-day South Africa.

1.2.3 The Appeal of School Settings

School stories have a long, yet interrupted history in South African publishing, as Elwyn Jenkins illustrates in *National Character in South African English Children's Literature* (2006). Initially the genre was picked up by Afrikaans writers of children's literature, and they are "the only colonial writers who really made school stories their own" in the South African context (Jenkins 2006: 14). May Baldwin was the first to write a South African school story in English, titled *Corah's School Chums* (1912). The novel considers the "English/Afrikaans rivalry" of that time, including other typical features of the school story such as "rivalries, cattishness, petty crime, pranks and bullying" (Jenkins 2006, 14). Later examples of school stories written in English, such as George and Lorrie Raath's *Chums of Meredrift School* which was published in the 1960s, "made no impact" on the national canon and although they "follow the events of the school year with perhaps a theft or some serious rivalry to liven them up", they cannot easily be compared to original English school stories, as they lack the "tension between formal school rules and the informal behavioural norms of the children" (Jenkins

2006, 15). Moreover, "the schools were coeducational, the activities are very South African (such as preparing for a military cadet parade), and they are not infused with notions of public school spirit or class distinction" (Jenkins 2006, 15).[40] P. W. Musgrave found the genre to be "almost dead before the Second World War" (1). According to Isabel Quigly, they no longer met the *zeitgeist* (cf. Quigly 1).

In recent years, this type of fiction has gained new prominence. Yet this prominence does not necessarily result from a high number of school story publications. In fact, only 14 out of 158 novels written in the realist mode in the period between 2000 and 2013 made schools the prime setting of their novels, thus comprising only 9% of the corpus (cf. Stadler 2015, 51). However, amongst these 14 books is the "biggest-selling [juvenile] novel in South African history" (Gray), namely John van de Ruit's *Spud* (2005). This *Spud*–phenomenon can be compared to the *Harry Potter*–phenomenon, except that *Spud* does not contain any magic and, admittedly, has not had the worldwide reception that J. K. Rowling's books have had, with the latter ranking amongst the most frequently bought books in world history (cf. Stadler 2014; Stadler forthcoming). In her essay "Inscribing Whiteness and Staging Belonging in Contemporary Autobiographies and Life-Writing Forms", Wamuwi Mbao names *Spud*'s effectiveness in bridging the gap between "highbrow and lowbrow audiences" (63) as its formula for success. Apparently, the novel caters to a number of needs of the reader, most importantly to a feeling of nostalgia, which, according to Mbao, "arises out of a perceived lack, or from perceptions of dislocation and uncertainty" which are widespread in and hence characteristic of post-apartheid South Africa (64). Although I do see Mbao's point, I will follow a different line of argumentation in the following, namely that it is firstly due to elements of comic relief (cf. Stadler 2014) and secondly due to the boarding school setting that *Spud* – and to a lesser extent also Fiona Snyckers's *Trinity Luhabe* Series (2009–2013) – has been so successful in South Africa.

In this chapter, I will focus on the boarding school and the campus experience of young people not only because it is a boarding school novel that is the most frequently sold young adult novel in the history of South African book publishing, but also because attending boarding school is a formative experience that a great number of South African children still go through. Education remains a heavily debated subject in present-day South Africa, as the following two examples illustrate: Firstly, in 2012 and 2013 the so-called Limpopo textbook crisis could be followed all over the media. In these years the government failed to order and provide the relevant textbooks for teaching in the Limpopo area (cf. Veriava ii–v).

[40] Contrary to the "South African Schools Act, 1996" which defines "public schools" as funded by the government (cf. chapter 3, section 12.(1)) and "private schools" as privately funded "independent school[s]" (cf. chapter 6, section 53), Jenkins uses the British distinction between public and private schools in the above quote (cf. Jenkins 2006, 15). Following Jenkins's lead, "public schools" are hereafter understood as fee-paying independent secondary schools and "private schools" as state-controlled institutions.

It goes without saying that a lack of teaching material correlates negatively with the learning process of children. Secondly, the quality of both public and private schools is regularly put up for discussion, although generally the reputation of South African public schools exceeds that of the country's private schools. A recent article in the *City Press* by David Harrison informs us that "[t]hree-quarters of children in South Africa never experience quality learning before they go to school and public spending on preschool education is only 1% of the basic education budget" (2014). Discussions about the quality of education are altogether fuelled by the high costs connected with schooling in South Africa. Kentse Radebe explains that "[s]ome of these costs are higher than the costs of university study" (2013). As a result people from a given social milieu usually all attend a public school or all attend a private school. Exceptions are pupils like John 'Spud' Milton who receive scholarships which allow them to transcend the borders of their usual social space. Ultimately, in such a school culture the quality of schooling is related to the amount of money that parents are willing or able to spend. Thus, inequality remains an issue in South Africa's educational system.

Michel Foucault, "Of Other Spaces" (1986)

Foucault's theory "Of Other Spaces" (1986) will serve in the following as a basis for discussing the boarding school and later the university campus context and their representation in John van de Ruit's *Spud* (2005), Anoeshka von Meck's *My Name Is Vaselinetjie* (2011), and Fiona Snyckers's *Trinity Rising* (2009). Foucault originally delivered the text as a lecture in 1967. He did not authorize it for publication during his lifetime. Although this implies that the essay is not part of his official oeuvre and is hence often excluded by critics, Edward Soja argues that "Of Other Spaces" "significantly [adds] to a practical and theoretical understanding of [...] the geohistory of otherness" (1996, 154). The text introduces a significant spatial concept, the heterotopia, which I believe substantially helps to understand the boarding school and campus context. Foucault comprehends our contemporary space as consisting of sites[41] which stand in relation to each other. Comparing Foucault's and Lefebvre's lines of argumentation, Soja concludes that "although less infused with allusions to the production process, the sites and situations of Foucault take on insights that reflect Lefebvre's critique of everyday life in the modern world and his trialectic of the perceived, the conceived, and the lived" (1996, 156). Foucault – like Lefebvre (1994) and Soja (1996) – looked for a third dimension in order to explain contemporary spatiality, as the two-tier model of the perceived/physical and the conceived/mental space appeared to be outdated

[41] "The site is defined by relations of proximity between points or elements, formally [...] describe[d] as series, trees, or grids [...] or more concrete [...] in terms of demography [...] [,] the human site or living space" (Foucault 1986, 23).

(cf. Lefebvre 1994, 11, 38, 40). He started to look for "other spaces", those "that have the curious property of being in relation with all the other sites, but in such a way as to suspect, neutralize, or invert the set of relations that they happen to designate, mirror, or reflect" (Foucault 1986, 24). The heterotopia is one of these sites. Heterotopias are "singular spaces to be found in some given social space whose functions are different or even the opposite of others" (Rabinow 20). Unlike Bhabha's utopian third space (cf. Rutherford), Foucault's heterotopias are real places,

> places that do exist and that are formed in the very founding of society [...], a kind of effectively enacted utopia in which the real sites, all the other real sites that can be found in the culture, are simultaneously represented, contested, and inverted. Places of this kind are outside of all places, even though it may be possible to indicate their location in reality. (Foucault 1986, 24)

A heterotopia is a purposeful site that exists within and yet outside of society, a place which is different from but nevertheless part of our reality. Ultimately, Foucault's concept of the heterotopia is a means to structure the surrounding space. The heterotopian site can be understood as an island in that surrounding space. However, like spaces outside of the heterotopias, it too is made up of numerous subspaces, which are hierarchically ordered in public and private spheres. Thus, heterotopian spaces follow similar rules of space construction to spaces outside of the site. Most importantly, however, they fulfil "different or even [...] opposite" functions to other social spaces. Foucault differentiates between two forms of heterotopia, the crisis heterotopia and the heterotopia of deviation (Foucault 1986, 24). "Crisis heterotopias" are "privileged or sacred or forbidden places, reserved for individuals who are, in relation to society and the human environment in which they live, in a state of crisis" (*ibid.*). According to Foucault, these are "adolescents, menstruating women, pregnant women, and the elderly" (*ibid.*). Adolescence was first described as a period of crisis by the psychologist Erik Erikson in 1968. More recently, South Africa's "Social Profile" (2012) has established children and young people as vulnerable groups, who are 'at risk' in the current society. 'At risk' and 'in crisis' are thus terms recurrently used in relation to the period of identity formation of young people. Foucault names the "boarding school" as one of the few last "remnants" of these crisis heterotopias in contemporary society (*ibid.*); also children's homes can be added to this category. Otherwise, crisis heterotopias have by now been almost entirely replaced by "heterotopias of deviation" (Foucault 1986, 24–25). The latter are spaces reserved for those "individuals whose behaviour is deviant in relation to the required mean or norm" (*ibid.*). Clinics, prisons, sanatoriums, and retirement homes are examples of heterotopias of deviation (cf. *ibid.*). The purpose of these institutions is to remind the deviant individual of prevailing social norms in the space outside of the heterotopias of deviation. Close readings of John van de Ruit's *Spud* (2005) and Anoeschka von Meck's *My Name Is Vaselinetjie* (2011) will illustrate how heterotopian sites function not only as places of order but also as instruments of power.

Initially, the order of a space is expressed via its geographical outline. However, it is the architecture of a space that turns it into an instrument of power which establishes relationships between people (cf. Foucault 2002). The heterotopia is an empowered place as it includes some people, but excludes others. Boarding schools open their doors to only a privileged few. Children's homes fulfil their function at the other end of the social ladder. They, too, are only open to a selected set of people. The difference between the children inhabiting these heterotopias is that those attending boarding schools usually come from privileged backgrounds to which they regularly return, while those children living in children's homes seldom have a social environment outside of the home. The social perception and reputation of the two institutions can moreover be described as oppositional. Both the boarding school and the children's home are heterotopian sites, as they are part of and yet outside of society. They are places where either "privileged" children or those who are "at risk" mingle (Foucault 1986, 24). Each of these spaces is made up of different spatial and social hierarchies, to which the inhabitants have to adjust. How the established spatial and social structure of the heterotopian site superimposes itself on its inhabitants can best be observed through the perception of new arrivals. Interestingly, in John van de Ruit's *Spud* (2005) and Anoeschka von Meck's *My Name Is Vaselinetjie* (2011), the main characters' descriptions of their first encounter with the new space and their corresponding mapping processes are similar and independent of external perceptions or prejudices of these spaces. As mapping processes are implicit processes, the protagonists remain predominantly passive in these inaugural situations, meaning that they seldom speak but mainly observe and take note of pre-existing structures. The respective narrators translate these processes to the reader; actual verbal and behavioural responses only follow significantly later.

John van de Ruit, *Spud* (2005)

Van de Ruit's novel is part of the four-volume *Spud* Series, which was published between 2005 and 2012. Given the success of the printed books, volumes one and two have been turned into movies (Marsh 2010, 2013), thus following a more general trend in this early twenty-first century, in which bestselling teenage fictions, such as J. K. Rowling's *Harry Potter* Series (1997–2007), Suzanne Collins's *Hunger Games* Series (2009–2011), Veronica Roth's *Divergent* Trilogy (2011–2013), Stephanie Meyer's *Twilight* Series (2005–2008), etc. have been adapted for movie theatres. Written in the diary format, the novel has been called both a *Bildungsroman* (cf. Robertson 36, footnote 5) and an autobiography (cf.

Mbao 63). Van de Ruit's first novel, *Spud*,[42] follows John Milton's coming of age in a prestigious boys-only boarding school in rural KwaZulu-Natal. Spud is the new nickname John Milton receives after his arrival at the school. Apparently, every new student is "re-christened" (*S* 9) after their arrival, underlining the start of their new lives within the boarding school site. The nickname, Spud, refers to his still childlike body, which has not entered puberty yet (cf. *S* 13). Keith Gray confirms in his review what readers might have guessed because of that nickname:

> There's plenty of crude humour. [The novel is] unflinching in portraying the uproarious and puerile wit of teenage boys, therefore realistic about the way adolescent males interact with each other – so much so that the author can appear more interested in chasing the joke than digging a little deeper into the issues he raises. But the overall feeling is one of warmth and affirmation. Friends are made, problems solved and bullies overcome. (2008)

The book opens like a dramatic work, providing a list of "dramatis personae" of those people who will feature in the subsequent diary entries. We enter the boarding school setting together with Spud on Monday, 17th January 1990.

> An African guard salutes us and then opens the huge white school gates. We pass through and drive along a beautiful avenue of trees called Pilgrim's Walk towards the school's gigantic red brick buildings which are all covered in green moss and ivy. My father is so busy pointing out a pair of mating dogs to my mother that he doesn't spot the speed bump that savages the underbelly of the car. Our station wagon limps up to the school and slides in between a Rolls Royce and a Mercedes–Benz. (*S* 4)

We are instinctively aware that we have left the outside world, entering into the boarding school via its gates. The first impression is somewhat intimidating for Spud as the architecture is so "gigantic" (*S* 4). The protagonist's reaction is immediately ridiculed by his father's perception of the scene. He appears to be unimpressed by the towering buildings. Rather, it is the "mating dogs" (*S* 4) which catch his attention and with whose help van de Ruit humorously underlines the difference between the adult and the child perception of this situation. Spud's mapping process nevertheless continues in the subsequent scene:

> The main quadrangle is surrounded by buildings, which remind me of those medieval castles in our old history books at primary school. We head towards a building that looks older than the rest. Its red brick has faded to peach brick and the moss and ivy are as thick as a hedge. The prefects lead us up a dark narrow staircase, through a long dormitory containing about fifteen empty beds and into another dormitory, this one dark and creepy with long hanging wooden rafters and dark brick walls. It is small and cramped with just about space for eight beds. It feels

[42] The novel is hereafter cited as *S*.

> spooky and smells like old socks and floor varnish. One of these eight beds is mine. The dormitory is divided into cubicles by five foot wooden partitions which separate one cubicle from the next. Each cubicle has two wooden beds, two cupboards, two footlockers, a blanket, pillow and mattress. Under each bed there are two drawers with golden doorknocker handles. (*S* 5–6)

With the help of the previous lines, Spud establishes the spatial hierarchy of the place for the reader and for himself. Firstly, we perceive the exteriors of the buildings of the boarding school. Inside, the layering continues. There are different dormitories and in these dormitories a further hierarchy is established via the interior decoration. The opening speech of the headmaster further underlines what Spud has already begun to grasp, namely that with his passing of the entrance gates he has entered a space that differs from the spaces he has encountered so far: The headmaster, Mr. "Glockenspheel keeps referring to the school as an 'institution' and the boys as 'subjects'. He also keeps repeating himself about discipline and stern punishment for wayward subjects" (*S* 6). The heterotopian site is clearly established in these few sentences. The boarding school is understood as a society that exists within the society of the outside world. The setting of the novel is thus a place that follows its own rules. Later in the evening the establishment of hierarchies continues, this time on a social level. Spud writes in his diary that Robert Black "appoints himself as the king of the dormitory. He includes enough swearing in every sentence to satisfy the group that he means business and is to be heartily respected and hero-worshipped" (*S* 8).

The next morning, daily rituals including their detailed protocols are introduced. During "Roll-Call", those whose names are read out loud are supposed to respond with "Sharks" even though "nobody can explain why" (*S* 9). Such rituals fill the social hierarchy prevalent at the boarding school. It is also common practice that older school boys play tricks on the new arrivals, taking advantage of their ignorance, as Spud soon finds out:

> I nearly missed roll-call because an older boy told me it took place in the common room and that I should report there immediately. When I arrived in the common room I found it completely deserted. Stupidly, I sat on one of the old red chairs thinking I was the first to arrive when actually it turned out that roll-call was taking place outside in the quad. (*S* 9)

The older prefects are responsible for showing the new arrivals "around the school and tel[ling them] what everything meant" (*S* 10). It turns out that "every room has a code name and every quadrangle is identical, no doubt designed to completely confuse new boys. Our lesson timetable was like reading a page of hieroglyphics" (*S* 10). After these first days' experiences, Spud confides in his diary about his fears and considerations about leaving the school:

> Can't sleep, I lie in bed, homesick. (I even miss Mom's cooking!) [...] My new home is like a war zone and while I take heart in the fact that there are two easier

> victims than me in our dorm (Gecko and Vern), I have the uneasy feeling that my time is coming. [...] I never seem to be sure what happens next. [...] I wonder what my parents would say if I gave up my scholarship and came home. (*S* 11–12)

Although there are initial processes of adjustment, the overall first impressions of the boarding school have had an intimidating effect on the protagonist. Spud realizes that the boarding school site has its own rules and feels crushed and disempowered because of the gigantic architecture of the building as a result. In addition to the spatial hierarchy, Spud witnesses the quick emergence of a social hierarchy amongst the new arrivals, which he fears falling victim to.

In the subsequent chapters, the reader follows Spud's attempts to further adjust to the spatial and social hierarchies of the heterotopian site. He becomes part of the 'Crazy Eight', a group of young boys which forms itself out of the schoolboys that share Spud's dormitory. The more he feels accepted by the other school boys, the more his earlier feelings of anxiety and disempowerment are replaced by feelings of unity and belonging to the place (cf. *S* 86). Gray has noted that the overall tone of the novel is "one of warmth and affirmation" (2008). This is mostly due to the humorous and partially satirical depiction of events in the novel. Overall, this style of writing is underrepresented in contemporary South African literature for young adults. Not many authors have adopted this method to approach the troubled history of the country. Yet, van de Ruit, who is also a successful comedian, points out that

> South Africans want to laugh, they want to watch, they want to see themselves on the screen. We want all these things, we are no different to anybody else. There is no short cut, and there is no silver spoon. You just got to fight for your piece of land and you got to work hard on it. I say, never cut off your dreams, you never know when they are going to come true. (van de Ruit 2012)

According to van de Ruit, humour is an unprejudiced tool to bring people of supposedly different places and with different social or ethnic backgrounds together. Also Fiona Snyckers has employed this element in her chick-lit-like fictions on the trials and tribulations of Trinity Luhabe, the daughter of an ex-Robben Island inmate, now mining magnate, and an ex-apartheid activist mother (cf. *Trinity Luhabe* Series 2009–2013), as we will see after a short analysis of Anoeschka van Meck's *My Name Is Vaselinetjie* (2011).

Anoeshka von Meck, *My Name Is Vaselinetjie* (2011)

Vaselinetjie originally appeared in Afrikaans in 2004. The first English translation followed in 2009. In 2005 the novel received the Rapport/Jan Rabie Prize for fresh, new literary voices in Afrikaans, the MER Prize for Youth Literature, and the M–Net Prize for an Afrikaans text in short format. In 2010 it was moreover transformed into a play staged at the Suidoosterfees in Cape Town and the Klein Karoo Nasionale Kunstefees. A teacher's guide for the Afrikaans version is available from the publisher's website.

My Name Is Vaselinetjie[43] is the tale of an abandoned white baby girl who is found by an elderly coloured man. He and his wife raise the baby as their own daughter. Due to her skin colour, however, the local school kids start to make fun of her and her adoptive parents eventually see no other option than to send her away to a children's home near Johannesburg. This novel touches on many uneasy topics, such as the effect of poverty on a child's life, language issues, issues of multiculturalism, and belonging. Rather than focusing on the thematic composition of the novel, in the following I will examine how the setting of the children's home impacts the coming of age of the young female protagonist. Although the novel also includes a public school setting, which is characterized by a social hierarchy of its own (cf. *V* 23–26), I will limit the analysis to the heterotopian site of the children's home, as the latter is foregrounded throughout the novel.

Vaselinetjie experiences as a new arrival at the children's home are similar to Spud's emotional roller-coaster ride when he arrives at the boarding school. When she enters the children's home via a safety gate, the spatial order and architectural outline of the space have an intimidating effect on the young person (cf. *V* 13–14). In *Vaselinetjie* it is the matron who explains to Vaselinetjie that "[t]here are several units in the building, but they all look alike. We call them houses and they all have different names. Each house has its own matron who looks after the children in their houses. All the front doors open into a long passage at the centre of the building" (*V* 15). Coming from the unurbanized lands of the Northern Cape, the new spatial situation is almost unbearable for Vaselinetjie. She "wanted to shut her eyes tightly and scream and scream until she woke from the nightmare. Each bed stood a metre away from the next and had a locker and a tall, narrow clothes cupboard. Some of the cupboards had no doors" (*V* 15). Her emotional response to the spatial design of the places shows that the protagonist is at first unable to cope with the idea of life in such close quarters and the related intimacy. Moreover, Vaselinetjie struggles with the unfamiliar sounds and noises that come with her new chaotic living situation: "The next morning Vaselinetjie was startled awake by the noise of fifteen girls living together in cramped quarters. A crazy hullabaloo of voices talking and laughing and shouting from room to room" (*V* 16). As in *Spud*, names and personal belongings that constituted the young person's identity outside the walls of the children's home no longer count when entering the heterotopian site. "Here you get only a number", her roommates explain, while "rifling through the contents" of Vaselinetjie's open suitcase (*V* 16). Her "stuff" is no longer hers. All her belongings "have to go to the laundry first and then you

[43] The novel is hereafter cited as *V*.

can label" them, i.e. reclaim them and call them yours again, Vaselinetjie learns (*ibid.*).

As in *Spud*, Vaselinetjie finds out about the social hierarchy in the children's room as soon as she has grasped the spatial hierarchy of the place. In this case it is a "senior" who introduces the new arrival to the rules in the dormitory, and as in the boarding school setting it is the older girls who make sure that the younger ones follow the rules: "Kitcat stepped forward and Vaselinetjie ducked instinctively" (*V* 17). As she has previously experienced violent bullying in her home town, Vaselinetjie is also afraid that "the white children [in this new setting will] beat her up" (*ibid.*). Vaselintjie's previous experiences influence her mapping process of the spatial and social hierarchy. Vaselinetjie is not aware that her looks and the way she expresses herself are antagonistic; although the protagonist is white, she talks as if she were of coloured descent. As a result, Vaselinetjie's looks and language confuse her fellow roommates, which is why mutual distrust characterizes the first encounter between the girls (cf. *ibid.*). Hence, on her arrival, the protagonist is intimidated by the architecture of the space, where "[t]here was nowhere to be alone" (*V* 20), and feels out of place and excluded from the unfamiliar social hierarchy. Soon, however, the other girls start to integrate her into their group by introducing her to the daily routines and the tasks which every girl has to fulfil in the home (cf. *V* 18–20). Ultimately it is time, the personal development of the protagonist, and her reconsideration of her self-image that lead to Vaselinetjie's integration into the children's home community. After her first year at the children's home, Vaselinetjie becomes a senior herself, which is tantamount to a step up rise on the social ladder and a step up rise on the spatial ladder of the children's home as well. As a senior she no longer has to sleep in the crowded dormitory but can now move into a double bedroom at the corner of the building. In *My Name Is Vaselinetjie*, the children's home is "gradually transformed into a place to which meaning is attached" (van Zyl abstract). Ultimately, the heterotopian site is perceived as "a landscape of belonging" as expressed by the protagonist's "solidarity with the [...] children in the home" (*ibid.*).

We have previously looked at boarding schools and children's homes as heterotopian sites and have accompanied Spud and Vaselinetjie during their first moments in these settings. Both protagonists experience similar mapping processes: The spatial outline of a place and its integrated hierarchies are described as impressive experiences for the protagonists in the novel. Both analyses underline the significance of the process of getting accustomed to the new place and that these processes received primary attention. As soon as they have become acquainted with and accustomed to the new settings, they are able to understand the social hierarchies which are superimposed on the physical outline of the place. The decryption of these social hierarchies takes considerably longer and is described as being more complex than the decoding of spatial hierarchies. In the two novels, the setting "functions both as a microcosm of the world and as an alternative to it; as a place of socialization and of subversion, and as an educational establishment in which the lessons learned generally take place outside the classroom" (Pinsent 2005b, 8). In the course of the novels, both protagonists attach increasingly more value to deciphering the codes of conduct of their surrounding social space, realizing that this type of knowledge decides about their integration into or exclusion from social groups. In the case of *Spud* and *Vaselinetjie*, both main characters are shown to be successful in finding their place in the respective boarding school/children's home community.

Fiona Snyckers, *Trinity Rising* (2009)

Fiona Snyckers's novel *Trinity Rising* (2009) is part of the three-volume *Trinity Luhabe* Series (2009–2013). In the trilogy's first installment, the reader accompanies eighteen-year-old Trinity during her first year at Rhodes University in Grahamstown. *Trinity on Air* (2010) goes on to narrate the protagonist's path of trials and tribulations when entering the job market at the age of 23. The content of the most recently published novel, *Team Trinity* (2013),[44] actually predates that of the two earlier published novels, as it deals with Trinity's teenage experiences at a boarding school. The non-sequential publication indicates that the publishers had not initially intended to publish sequels of *Trinity Rising* (2009).[45] The question is whether author and publishers decided to break with chronology and to set the third novel of the volume in Trinity's teenage years at a boarding school setting because of van de Ruit's earlier success with the boarding school setting in the *Spud* Series. A reference to *Spud* in *Team Trinity* certainly supports this notion (cf. *TT* 9). Both series follow a young protagonist in his/her phase of identity formation. Both series employ humour as a means to discuss socio-critical content. Otherwise, their approaches to portraying their protagonists' coming of age differ. Van de Ruit's novels chronicle Spud's entire development between the ages of thirteen and eighteen. Snyckers's series follows Trinity's development at different phases in her years of identity formation, namely during her early teenage years in *Team Trinity*, her nineteenth year of life in *Trinity Rising*, and her twenty-fourth year of life in *Trinity on Air*. All of Snyckers's stories are narrated in the first person.

Interestingly, while Trinity's first encounters with the boarding school setting in *Team Trinity* are designed similarly to those in *Spud* and *Vaselinetjie*, Trinity's mapping processes of the university campus in *Trinity Rising* are not as systematically narrated. Like Spud and Vaselinetjie, Trinity's first act when entering the boarding school grounds in *Team Trinity* is to physically discover and mentally map her new spatial surroundings as a means to adjust to the new place:

[44] The novel is hereafter cited as *TT*.

[45] The novel is hereafter cited as *TR*.

> I turn around and look up at Sisulu House, which is going to be my new home for the next three months. Okay, it's pretty, I'll give you that. Built in a gracious mock-Tudor style with half-timbering and authentic turn-of-the-century period features, Sisulu House boasts some of the finest blah blah blah. I got all of that out of the brochure Mom has been boring me with all holiday. [...] I trudge up the stairs and hesitate for a moment, not sure which way to turn. Oh yes, right. Then I stand at the entrance to the Grade 10 dormitory and take a proper look at it. This could be worse, I'll admit. This could be a lot worse. It's a big, sunny room, with six beds in separate little cubicles. We each have our own bedside cabinet and built-in cupboard. (*TT* 14)

Unlike Spud or Vaselinetjie, Trinity arrives prepared at the boarding school site and is already aware that these sites are organized differently than public or private school environments. The confined spaces in the form of dormitories, dining halls, and common rooms characterize the everyday lives of the boarders in *Team Trinity* as do a number of rules that they are expected to observe (cf. *TT* 4, 8, 10–12, 14–15). Hence, in this novel the boarding school is once again described as a heterotopia in the Foucauldian sense. After her walk through Sisulu House, Trinity's next project is to prepare herself for meeting the other girls in the house. Aware of the difficulties and prejudices that new arrivals face in a boarding school, Trinity intends to look her best in order to be quickly accepted in the house's community (cf. *TT* 24–25). Fitting in (cf. *TT* 18, 27) is one of Trinity's highest priorities; this is a wish which we have also encountered in the previous narratives by van de Ruit and von Meck. Again, the deciphering of the social hierarchies, rules of conduct, or seating orders prevalent in the school setting follows after Trinity has decoded the spatial surroundings (cf. *TT* 19).

In contrast to this systematic introduction of spatial and social hierarchies in the opening pages of *Team Trinity*, the protagonist does not provide such detailed insights into her mapping processes of the campus setting in *Trinity Rising*. The reasons for this are her opposing emotional attitudes towards the two places and the age at which she enters the two institutions. Her becoming a boarder at Sisulu House in her early teens was a decision made by her parents. However, it was she herself who decided to enroll in a university which was "a thousand kilometers away from home" (*TR* 15). Her earlier experiences at the boarding school help the eighteen-year-old protagonist to adjust to the spatial outlines of the campus almost immediately and Trinity is shown to move on to decoding the prevalent social hierarchies sooner than in *Team Trinity*. "I've come here to have fun, and that's exactly what I'm going to do", Trinity clarifies (*TR* 15). The campus qualifies as a heterotopian site as there, too, Trinity has to succumb to the specific rules of the space, realizing that she has to adjust to the spatial confinements that come with moving into a student's house. In the manner of the chick-lit genre, Snyckers subsequently displays Trinity as a confident, articulate, and light-hearted young woman who is so busy organizing her social and business life that she cannot quite focus on what she is actually supposed to do, namely to study. Despite its rules, regulations, and standards of penalization, which students receive via their e-mail account (cf. *TR* 10, 47, 86, 106–107), Trinity encounters the university as a more open and at first glance less rigid institution than the boarding school site. Trinity is depicted as using every last bit of this freedom and almost overdoes it. Having asked for extensions for assignments once too often or failing to hand in the assignments at all, Trinity is soon in danger of failing her first year at university. Despite all her private 'dramas' – related to dieting, fashion, falling in love with her tutor, and a feud with her former schoolmate Sophie that leads to a disciplinary hearing at the university – Trinity eventually passes her final exams and gets the boyfriend she has been looking for since the beginning of the story.

The novel ends with an e-mail from Trinity to the warden of her residence, asking whether it is possible that "the person with the most stuff [gets] the biggest room" (*TR* 370). This is a wish that Trinity has recurrently voiced and fought for in both *Team Trinity* and *Trinity Rising* since the day of her arrival at the boarding institutions. Snyckers repeatedly invokes this spatial image to make the reader laugh and simultaneously question Trinity's obsession with material goods and her compulsion to follow the latest fashion trends. When a second-year student decides to quit her studies in *Trinity Rising*, Trinity is the first to stand in line for her "bigger, warmer and lighter" (*TR* 65) room. Contrary to Spud or Vaselinetjie, Trinity and her fellow girls[46] consider the student residence's premises a negotiable commodity. Some of the girls, including Trinity, even try to bribe the warden (cf. *TR* 65). Eventually, all their attempts to undermine spatial and social hierarchies remain unsuccessful. Much to the benefit of the social climate in the residency, the room is given to a new girl. As one of Trinity's housemates puts it: "I can handle not getting [the room] myself – just as long as they didn't give it to one of you guys" (*TR* 66). While at the end of her first year at university, Trinity finds that she "really *ha[s]* changed" (*TR* 349), as she now only buys two pairs of trousers instead of four or five and reads books like *Pride and Prejudice* instead of fashion magazines (cf. *TR* 350), she still does not want to cut back on space. As already indicated, in the final pages of the novel, Trinity is already making preparations for her second year at Rhodes University by sending out an e-mail in which she requests "the biggest room" in the residency for the following year for – obviously spurious – reasons of "fair[ness]" and "academic success" (cf. *TR* 370). Ultimately, Trinity's notions of space are markedly different from Spud's and Vaselinetjie's, namely more emancipated. Due to her outgoing and self-confident personality, and because she comes from a family whose "surname opens doors for [her]" (*TR* 70), Trinity is not afraid to explicitly voice her wish for

[46] The reader does not get to know much about the socio-economic background of Trinity's friends, though it can be said that while none of them is as well off as Trinity, the other girls do not come from impoverished backgrounds either. Having grown up in upper middle class families, it is safe to assume that they, too, are used to having a certain amount of space just for themselves.

more space in the boarding facilities. She even feels a sort of entitlement to call a certain amount of space her own. By contrast, neither Spud nor Vaselinetjie question the pre-established spatial hierarchies, as they both enter the respective boarding school and children's home site as outsiders, a position which they are both aware of and which influences their confidence in claiming a space for themselves.

Résumé

Team Trinity, *Trinity Rising*, and *Spud* show that the model of structuring school stories according to the school year has persisted since the genre's invention (cf. Jenkins 2006). Both John van de Ruit and Fiona Snyckers follow this pattern, yet with distinct styles. While van de Ruit draws on the diary format to structure *Spud* (2005), Snycker uses chapters but also includes e-mails, formal letters from the university, and text messages as structuring devices in *Trinity Rising* (2009) and *Team Trinity* (2013). All of these stories are set in smart educational environments, a boys-only boarding school in rural Kwazulu-Natal, Sisulu House, and the prestigious Rhodes University in Grahamstown, not in small-town or township establishments. Jenkins has observed that affluent settings have also been a favoured choice of twentieth century school stories written in English (cf. Jenkins 2006, 15). However, since 2011, less affluent school environments have also become more and more represented in youth novels for South African teenagers. A most prominent example is the so-called *Harmony High* Series, which is published by Cover2Cover and comprises stories written by different authors, but dealing with the same set of characters (cf. Haden's *Broken Promises* 2010; Dyer and Haden's *Jealous in Jozi* 2011; Dyer's *Two–Faced Friends* 2012; Mazantsi and Roth's *Too Young to Die* 2012; Gamedze and Dyer's *From Boys to Men* 2013). Clearly, the appeal of including a school setting in youth novels lies in their closeness to the adolescent experience of life. After all, children spend a considerable amount of time in educational settings. The majority of texts published between 2000 and 2013 feature a school environment alongside a number of other settings, such as the home or places where youths spend their leisure time, and thus mirror the everyday lives of young South Africans. Hence, *Spud*, *My Name Is Vaselinetjie*, *Team Trinity*, and *Trinity Rising* remain exceptions in making the school, the children's home, and the university campus the sole setting of their novels. In all these cases, the school is treated like a multicultural hub and a space where new forms of society and notions of belonging can be tested. On their entrance into a new (social) space, all the children are shown to have the will to actively shape their surroundings and to agree to compromises in negotiating those social spaces.

Conclusion

The aim of this chapter on South Africa's spatial distinctiveness has been to highlight the influence that spatial and social hierarchies have on the development of those coming of age in the literary texts of contemporary South Africa. In more general terms I aimed at reintroducing theories of social space in the literary analysis of twenty-first century South African texts. Clearly, academic studies should not stop at investigating the representations of the new metropolis in the novel, but should extend their interest to areas and places which appear to have faded into obscurity in this new millennium – the space of the rural and the small town. Generally, notions of space have been and still are a matter of heated discussion in South Africa and beyond and are thus also deeply embedded in the country's literary texts. This chapter's close reading sections show that the more the juvenile protagonists know about spatial and social hierarchies, the more they want to participate in shaping these (social) spaces. In the course of this chapter it has become apparent that conceptualizations of rural and urban places are inherently intertwined; their perception is defined by their geographical other. Analyses of a novel's *physical* setting have helped to examine the *mental* and *social* conceptions which shape and transform a site. Close readings of *Thirteen Cents*, *Dancing Queen*, and *E Eights* showed that the borders between the city and the country are fluid, with people constantly being on the move in order to find a place where they can feel at home and which gives them a sense of belonging – a place of safety and peace. In these novels city life is shown to be uncomfortable and depressing for adults and potentially perilous for children.

Obviously, the new South Africa is a highly amorphous space. It provides an ideal testing ground for both 'older' spatial theories – Lefebvre's trialectics, de Certeau's *voyeur* and Benjamin's *flâneur*, etc. – as well as 'new' concepts by Robinson and Nuttall. The variety of settings in South African youth fiction corresponds to the range of theoretical approaches necessary to decipher the various cityscapes, countrysides, and educational environments. Simultaneously, all spaces are shown to be 'entangled' (cf. Nuttall 2009) and going through 'ordinary' (Robinson 2006) processes of spatial appropriation in relation to the neoliberal political climate. Of the selected set of texts, the responses of *Thirteen Cents* and *E Eights* to Soja's call for "alternative [ways] of envisioning spatiality" (Soja 1996, 163) could not be more different; while the former envisages the end of urban space as such, the latter points to utopian subspaces emerging within the cityscape. In contemporary South Africa, considerable steps towards the achievement of the aspired 'rainbow nation' have been undertaken, yet it is the persistence of certain spatial divisions – together with persisting gender and socio-economic inequalities – that slow down spatial development. The young adult characters in the novels are shown to be aware of the spatial segregations that continue to trouble the new South Africa. The analyses have helped to underline the understanding that accessibility to (social) spaces is fundamental for the development of young people. Many times they are shown to feel exiled and excluded from a particular (social) space. Many main characters are portrayed as carving out spaces for themselves and as influencing their surroundings actively. Others are shown to fall prey to the social and spatial circumstances presented to them. In light of this social reality, this chapter can only be a first step in the analysis of spatial and textual issues related to the youth of contemporary South Africa. Future studies will need to extend their insights into the obstacles that the younger generation encounters when looking for their place in the social space of South Africa in the years to come.

Till today, the critique of the binary opposition male and female, popularized particularly by second-wave feminists in the 1970s, and the social constructedness of masculinity and femininity concepts have characterized the language of gender discussions (cf. Irigaray 1985 a, b, c; Cixous 1991, 1981a, 1981b; Wilkie-Stibbs). In his 1996 article "Gender, Genre and Children's Literature", John Stephens presented a table with clusters of adjectives traditionally ascribed to masculinity and femininity:

> The ideal masculine schema includes such characteristics as being strong, tough, independent, active, aggressive, violent, unemotional, competitive, powerful, commanding, and rational. The feminine schema includes such characteristics as being beautiful, soft and yielding, passive, self-effacing and caring, vulnerable, powerless, and intuitive. (18f.)

Nine years later, David Russell produced a similar catalogue of schemata, ascribing "competition, self-assertiveness, individual rights, and social rules" to the male and "human relationships, responsibilities to others, cooperation, community values, tolerance for opposing viewpoints" to the female (2005, 28). The danger that our linguistic restriction to the two word clusters, male and female, delimits our discussions of gender exists and is particularly evident in our attempts to define sexual identities, whether these are homo-, hetero-, bi-, or transsexual.

With the emergence of Queer Studies, also called Sexual Diversity Studies or Lesbian, Gay, Bisexual, and Transgender (LGBT) Studies, in the 1970s and the subsequent development of queer theory in the 1990s, the gender debate headed into a new era. Deeply influenced amongst others by Judith Butler's notions on the social constructedness of gender identities and gender performance (cf. 2011), LGBT Studies has expanded what previously had mostly been a two-fold discussion of heterosexuality and homosexuality to include so-called 'deviant' forms of sexual identity, thereby creating a new space for debate about norms and the elusiveness of labels such as 'gay' or 'lesbian'. Internationally, the inaccuracy of labels such as 'LGBT', 'MSM' (men who have sex with men), or 'WSW' (women who have sex with women) is by now widely acknowledged (cf. Asthana and Oostvogels; Boyce; Cáceres and Rosasco; Muños-Laboy; Parker and Cáceres; Sandfort and Dodge). Regarding the South African context, however, scholars have to be aware that they "cannot simply transport [their] research assumptions about MSM from societies in the global North, where 'MSM' and 'gay' have largely been conflated and used synonymously, to describe a single target population" (Lane 71). Pierre Brouard from the Centre for the Study of AIDS

(CSA) at the University of Pretoria explains that "[i]n our attempts to understand same-sex practice, we [in the South] have avoided complex identity politics, understanding that identity labels such as 'gay' and 'lesbian' may be Western constructs, of little value and use in an African context" (59). For instance, the label 'lesbian' has been found to take on many forms in South Africa: "'tommy boys', 'Galla man', 'dyke', '*manvrou*', 'butch and femme'" (Matebeni 100). Lorway's research into "HIV risk and male–male sexual practices in the Windhoek urban area" (2007) made evident that sexuality "cannot be viewed as a fixed set of predictable roles or behaviours that can be readily mapped onto the parameters of Western sexual identity categories of lesbian, gay, bisexual, transsexual and heterosexual" (Lorway 278). And yet, when trying to describe same-sex relationships and to explain how people feel and act (cf. Bloch and Martin), scholars, writers, and laymen alike repeatedly return to the dichotomy because "[m]asculinity and femininity are inherently relational concepts, which have meaning in relation to each other, as a social demarcation and a cultural opposition [and t]his holds regardless of the changing content of the demarcation in different societies and periods of history" (Connell 44). Brouard even states that despite the shortcomings of conventional gendered terminology, it can at times be "useful" because "the words people use to identify themselves are a window into how they view their practice" (59; cf. Block and Martin).

The limited range of vocabulary employed and the apparent incapability to find other means of describing gender are also evident in both fiction and non-fiction. By continually drawing on gender-stereotypical language to describe a character's development or by setting a novel in a specific place due to a protagonist's gender, a text reproduces the social discourse. Are literary works thus also responsible for a perpetual repetition and continued institutionalization of gender stereotypes? It should go without saying that the use of gendered language does not imply that there is no critical display of gendered behaviour in the literature for young people. Internationally, efforts have been undertaken to alter those styles of writing that reinforce traditional gender binarism. However, "[t]he degendering of literary texts has proved to be a multifaceted problem to which writers have needed a continuing commitment" (Pennell 55). Also in South Africa the "degendering" of youth novels has been a major challenge since the late 1980s (cf. Inggs 2009, 103). More recently, Inggs came to the conclusion that "[a]lthough South Africa is a multicultural society, and is therefore not homogenous, nor primarily western, the novels tend to reflect stereotypical gender roles [...] with the exception of the few novels that explore less heteronormative identities" (2016, 67). Hence, at present, a general liberation of gender norms appears to be unrealistic. My corpus analysis of twenty-first century South African youth novels supports this notion from a statistical point of view, showing that "generally, more males (46%) feature as protagonists than females (36%)" (Stadler 2015, 47). Sixteen percent of the 158 realist novels examined in the analysis had protagonists of both sexes (cf. Stadler 2015, 51). When adding the factor 'ethnicity' to the assessment, black males comprise 25% of all main characters; both black females and white males each comprise 18% of the protagonists, while 13% of the texts had white female protagonists. Coloured males only made up 1% of all texts while coloured females were represented in 3% of all texts (cf. Stadler 2015, 52).

Thematically, the corpus analysis showed that young adult novels published between 2000 and 2013 discuss teenage sexuality and gender identity across the whole spectrum, namely with regard to machoism and masculinity (chapter 2.1), homo- and transsexuality (chapter 2.2), and to young females and their lives (chapter 2.3). These will be the focal point of discussion in the upcoming chapters. It will be particularly interesting to see what kind of stories female or male narrators tell and whether they can be classified in terms of Stephens's or Russell's abovementioned catalogues. The results will be used to comment on conventional gender attributes and contemporary gender issues as well as on closely related South African trouble spots, namely sexually transmitted diseases, violence against (adolescent) women and children, as well as prejudices against adolescents with a different sexual orientation than the heterosexual norm. This chapter also draws on the results of chapter one when it reassesses the spatial topic via a gendered perspective. Here, the thesis contrasts the perception of space of male and female narrators, arguing that contemporary young adult literature portrays the South African 'macho state' while simultaneously communicating a more explicit stance on gender issues. Pennell is sure that "[c]hildren's literature can make a significant contribution to whether or not child readers understand the patriarchal social order and oppositional gendered social relations to be immutable" (55). Thus, young adult literature plays a most significant part in the development of a new gender culture in South Africa.

2.1 Machoism and Masculinities

> "In Alex[andra Township, in the North of Johannesburg], the highest compliment is to be called an ingagara. The hegemonic construct of the *ingagara* refers to a male who is well respected and who is considered macho. [He] is associated with having many girlfriends, an expensive car and fashionable clothes."
>
> (Selikow, Zulu and Cedras 27)

The new Constitution of South Africa and consequently the new unlawfulness of discrimination "against anyone on one or more grounds, including race, gender, sex, pregnancy, marital status, ethnic or social origin, colour, sexual orientation, age, disability, religion, conscience, belief, culture, language and birth" ("Constitution", Section 9.3) have led to a "transition in gender/power relations" and hence to a "crisis of masculinity" in the post-apartheid years (Walker 225). Changes in legislation have altered the position of women in the new state, giving them more rights in both the public sphere (e.g. equal payment in the workspace) and the domestic sphere (e.g. the enforcement of stricter sentences in cases of domestic violence and a quite liberal abortion legislation) (cf. Walker 227). Celebrated by women's rights activists, the new rights of women and their advancement "in education [and] economically" has had a countering effect on many South African males, indeed making this particular group "feel threatened" and "weaker" because of the changed rights of their female contemporaries, Vusi, a young black male from Alexandra Township explains (Walker 229). In fact, in the years after the implementation of the 1996 Constitution scholars witnessed that the progressive legislation and concomitant sexual liberalization resulted in an initial "increase in gender violence" with South Africa having "the highest per capita rate of reported rape in the world – 115.6 cases per year for every 100,000 of the population" in 1998 (Walker 228). For further information, Walker relies on Smith (2001), who found that during that period child and infant rape was on the increase: "13,540 children under the age of 17 were raped, of whom 7899 were under the age of 11" (Walker 228).

Roughly a decade later, in 2014, the picture has hardly changed. Generally, researchers continue to encounter difficulties when trying to find reliable data concerning gender-based violence. Interestingly, the 2012 official "Gender Statistics" published by *Statistics South Africa* does not contain detailed information about the problem, admitting that "Stats SA does not have reliable data on this issue" (2). The report does, however, mention that serious gender-related challenges persist, including "unacceptable levels of gender-based violence" ("Gender Statistics" vi). M. V. Phyega's "Analysis of the National Crime Statistics 2012/13" provides more information on those 'unacceptable levels of gender-based violence' stating that the "[s]exual offences ratio decreased by 10.9% from 2004/5 to 2012/13" from 142.5 cases in 2004/5 to 127 cases per year for every 100,000 of the population in 2012/13 (2013, 18). More specifically, rape was reduced by 3.3% between 2009/10 and 2012/13 to 94.5 persons among every 100,000 people. Also incidents of sexual assault "ha[ve] reduced by 6.2% […] to an all-time low of 13.7" persons among every 100,000 people (2013, 19). These figures could give rise to the conclusion that gender relations are gradually beginning to change. Although the number of reported cases of gender-based violence is still alarmingly high compared to other countries, their slow decline supports notions that today more South African men are willing to find ways to combine "traditional/conventional male practices and the desire to be a modern, respectable, responsible man" than immediately after the implementation of the new Constitution (Walker 225). The above numbers from 2013 also indicate that "[n]ew notions of manhood", which Walker had already proclaimed in her 2005 article (236), are only now finding wider acceptance and more followers in South Africa.

And yet, one needs to be cautious not to overestimate and misinterpret the abovementioned decline in sexual assault cases. Firstly, also today, the number of unreported cases of assault or rape has to be estimated much higher than the reported cases. In her article Walker highlighted that it is assumed that "only one out of every twenty rapes is reported" (228). Moreover, a culture of silence persists regarding gender violence (cf. Thorpe), which has been frequently represented in contemporary fictions such as Kagiso Lesego Molope's *This Book Betrays My Brother* (2012) or Kgebetli Moele's *Untitled* (2013). Secondly, the decline in gender-based violence has to be seen in relation to developments in the public sector – the sphere which has traditionally been ascribed to men. With the new Constitution, the male 'right' to the workspace was rendered inoperative and the new body of constitutional principles was thenceforth seen by some men as a threat to their position as the provider of the family. "Some men felt redundant" because women were able to earn their own living now, Walker's interviewees confess (229). Since the last decade, however, it has become evident that despite the right to equal payment and job opportunities, the "[u]nemployment rate remains higher among women. While education is an enabler, disappointingly women are not as enabled by their education status as their men counterpart. [...] Furthermore, women with tertiary education earn around 82% of what their male counterparts earn" ("Gender Statistics" vi). Such findings show that legislation and daily practice still differ to a large extent and men continue to hold the "dominant, privileged position" they previously feared to lose (Walker 229). However, it would be shortsighted to assume that the momentary affirmation of their societal position marks the end of the crisis of masculinity in South Africa. Walker's interviews display the insecurity and anxieties that young male South Africans have felt concerning their position and role in the newly formed country at the turn of the century (cf. Walker 229–236). Such notions have found their way into the literature of the country and particularly in the last decade fictional texts were used to debate new and old conceptions of (hegemonic) masculinity. As the 'crisis of masculinity' has become a heavily debated topic in recent South African texts such as Niq Mhlongo's *Dog Eat Dog* and *After Tears* or Kgebetli Moele's *Room 207*, the question arises of how young adult literature has responded to or integrated issues of machoism and masculinity in its narratives. Is "to be called an *ingagara*" still the highest compliment, as the introductory quote asserts (Selikow, Zulu and Cedras 27, emphasis in the original)?

While Masculinity and Men's Studies have by now manifested themselves as an academic field, research has so far mostly been undertaken "in cultural studies and the studies of general literature", according to Stephens (2002, x). Reynolds finds that the discipline has previously predominantly focused on "mature expressions of masculinity, offering autobiographical, anthropological, sociological [...] explanations for and apologies/defenses of contemporary manhood", whereas boys and boyhood have not been at the centre of attention (2002, 99). Although a growing number of publications discuss male representations in children's and young adult literature (cf. Stephens 2002, x), there is no such analysis for the contemporary South African context. In his preface to *Ways of Being Male* (2002), editor John Stephens quotes Richard Fletcher (1995), who says: "Feminist thinking – that girls deserve the same opportunities as boys – has become recognized as common sense. But we are still confused about directions for boys" (quoted in Stephens 2002, ix). Subsequently, this chapter is thus interested in the "directions" South African young adult literature gives to boys and young men.

In 2002, Perry Nodelman explained the difference in conventional conceptions of femininity and masculinity as follows: "Traditionally femininity manifests itself as a form of dress, a costume or role one puts on, therefore something that is understood as repressing individuality [...]. Masculinity is often understood as not being a form of dress – as resistance to the act of putting on costumes or being repressed by conventional roles" (1). This binary cannot be transferred to the South African context, as also the introductory quote from Selikow, Zulu and Cedras reflects: "[A]n expensive car and fashionable clothes" are essentials for 'real' South African men (cf. 27). The assessment of more than 250 teenage novels further supports notions that in and outside of South African literature masculinity concepts are as much constructed as conceptions of femininity. Like female characters, male protagonists are shown to draw on specific 'dress codes' to establish their maleness.

In the following, violence and materialism have been selected as the two prime "patterns of conduct" (Bhana 207) to be examined in relation to South African masculinities as these reoccur in the majority of fictions containing a male main character. Other "patterns of conduct associated with hegemonic masculinity are usually authoritative, aggressive, heterosexual, physically brave, sporty, and competitive" (Bhana 207). The sociologist Jacklyn Cock states that "for many South Africans, 'violence is proper and appropriate to manliness,' because in much of the country, violence 'involves weapons that are understood as legitimate symbols of masculinity'" (quoted in Romero 166). Such views of South African masculinity can be found across the colour bar. "For some Africans, traditional weapons, for others knives, AK–47s, and handguns. For white South Africans violence is acted out by way of shotguns, rifles, and handguns"; throughout South Africa, a "culture of violence" persists due to "a culture dependent on weapons" (Romero 166). Moreover, Morrell's studies show that school and other educational settings play a major role in the instigation of violent masculinities (2001a, 2001b). This connection is particularly significant in the context of black working-class townships (cf. Bhana 205), but also in the context of boarding schools for boys. Both the township and the boarding school have been taken up as settings in novels for boys, as we have already seen in the case of John van de Ruit's *Spud* (2005) in the previous chapter. *Young Blood* (2010) by Sifiso Mzobe will be examined as a case in point regarding the township setting in the following.

The desire to consume and possess a certain set of material goods which have become representative of social affluence is the second pattern of conduct under scrutiny. In accordance with a more global trend, South Africa's young males follow a specific materialist convention in order to signal their belonging to a certain social group. With the acquisition of material objects, clothes, electronic devices, jewellery, or cars, which are connected to a certain societal status, young males buy a form of dress which in turn ensures their acceptance as 'real men'. In doing so they subject themselves to the prevalent "hegemonic masculinity", which has been defined by Connell as "the configuration of gender practice which embodies the currently accepted answer to the problem of the legitimacy of patriarchy, which guarantees (or is taken to guarantee) the dominant position of men and the subordination of women" (Connell 77). This shows that instead of being "somehow natural and free – the state [a young man] achieves by resisting societal norms and being one's true self" (Nodelman 2002, 2) – males, too, become victims of societal expectations and cultural norms precisely because they are expected to lash out against codes and conventions. Novels, such as *Young Blood* by Sifiso Mzobe or *A Man Who Is Not a Man*[47] (2010) by Thando Mgqolozana, show that the very expectation to resist societal norms and to be one's true self can confuse the coming–of–age process of young males to a surprisingly large extent.

Besides violence and materialism, the expectation to follow cultural norms is the third most pervasive element in young men's lives and is thus worth taking a closer look at. Particularly in South Africa's indigenous contexts, rites of passage into adulthood still define conceptions of masculinity and femininity and are understood as a prerequisite for maintaining one's place in the community. In the case of young Xhosa initiates, for instance, the rite of initiation includes the retreat of the young males to a mountain or a secluded hut after they have been circumcised, according to Mgqolozana's protagonist (cf. Meissner and Buso). Within this particular context, abiding by the laws of the tribe is tantamount to acceptance and a future life in the community as Mgqolozana's main character informs us. Those who do not undergo the procedure of circumcision cannot come of age and cannot become a member of the adult male group that shapes the communal life. Instead, they face social ostracism and "resign themselves to a lifetime of shame and ridicule [... and] traditional penalties demanded by other men whenever they are found out", Mgqolozana's first-person protagonist confides (*MWNM* 2).

Before analysing Sifiso Mzobe's gangster novel *Young Blood*, two novels will be placed at the centre of attention to illustrate the pressure that cultural norms can put on young males in South Africa, namely Russell Kaschula's *Take Me to the River* (2006) and Thando Mgqolozana's *A Man Who Is Not a Man*. Both choose a direct approach to the controversial topic of male circumcision. Kaschula's shorter novel explicitly advocates a safer method for the ritual after the death of one

[47] The novel is herafter cited as *MWNM*.

initiate in the beginning of the novel. Mgqolozana addresses in detail the social ostracism following a failed initiation to manhood. Apart from *Take Me to the River* and *A Man Who Is Not a Man*, a short biographical novel by Mbu Maloni titled *Becoming Indoba – A Real Man* published by the FunDza Literary Trust in English in 2013 in their mobile library is the only other novel for adolescents in the corpus that explains the rite of passage of young Xhosa males. The reader's responses to Maloni's text, which is freely accessible online and allows readers to comment on the text, illustrate the delicate status that the topic still occupies in public discourse. The user comments are displayed beneath the text and can be read by everyone accessing the site. The following are examples of online responses to *Becoming Indoba – A Real Man* (2013):

> Its so gud 2 hear wats happening in da entabeni. tanx 4 sharing mbu! dnt mind al doz craze s***t talkers. if dy dnt wana share, askies 4 dm. .bt u felt free to share wth ur readers. dnt feel bad, dats wat writers n journalists do. u r a real man mbu.
> *alfatima* 7 Nov 2013 at 16:13
>
> [Response:]
>
> > Congratulate mbu! bt knw tht real man dsnt talk abt wht happning at the mountain bcoz u wil mde adas 2 be afraid 2 go 2 the mountain
> > **0000COMRS+LEBEBS** 24 Nov 2013 at 13:29
>
> dont be to hard on him hes telling us abwt his experience,y r ull tripping?
> *(x)Jezzy(x)* 7 Nov 2013 at 01:02
>
> Yo yo yo i dnt bliv u rote dose thngs I THOT THEY WER SUPOSED 2 B A SECRET arent they???? #confused#
> *DAZZLING+DIVA* 3 Nov 2013 at 23:17
>
> ("Responses to Becoming Indoba")

These few examples already show how controversial the topic of a male's rite of passage still is amongst South African teenagers today. While *alfatima* appreciates the insights given by the story, DAZZLING+DIVA is "#confused#" as the user "THOT THEY [the information about how initiation rites are conducted] WER SUPPOSED 2 B A SECRET" (*ibid.*). The user *0000C0MRS+LEBERS* explains the silence surrounding traditional rites with the fear that future initiates might no longer undergo circumcision if they knew the details. This user also believes that 'real men' would not talk about the experience and thereby indirectly denounces the 'masculinity' of the author, Mbu Maloni. These reactions show not only the topicality of the issue, but also the emotionality of the debate and the continued significance of tradition and cultural distinctiveness for young South Africans.

Russell H. Kaschula, *Take Me to the River* (2006)

Kaschula's *Take Me to the River*[48] was published in 2006. That same year, the novel was also published in isiXhosa, titled *Emthonjeni*. Thus it is one of the few texts for youths that are available in the mother tongue of 16% of the population (Lehohla 2012a, 24). N. S. Zulu reads *Emthonjeni* "as a creolization[49] of South Africa's past essentialized cultural identities" aiming "to reduce their dominance and power in creating national harmonization" (abstract). The fact that the novel is considerably shorter than Mgqolozana's *A Man Who Is Not a Man* as well as the choice of a generous typeface hint that Kaschula's *Take Me to The River* is aimed at a predominantly male audience that has not yet reached the age of circumcision. Both novels are constructed within a cultural framework in which young Xhosa males are traditionally circumcised after they have completed their final year of high school. The rite signals the end of their youth and the beginning of their lives as 'real men'. Kaschula chooses a different point of view than Mgqolozana to look at the controversies and common assumptions around the circumcision process, making Zama Gobodo, the younger brother of Xolilizwe, the main character of this coming–of–age story. In chapter two the reader learns that three years before the time the story is set Xolilizwe died as the result of an unprofessionally performed circumcision. The reader finds out that for Xolilizwe's and Zama's parents, as well as for Lumkile's, following the tradition had been more important than the initiate's well-being. Not until more than two weeks after the eldest son had still not emerged from his hut did the parents bring Xolilizwe to a hospital. However, by then it was too late and both antibiotics and the removal of his entire penis could not stop the infection in his body, leading to his death (cf. *TMR* 25–26). In *A Man Who Is Not a Man*, Lumkile has learned early in his life that "[i]t is better to die than to go to hospital. It would be the end of you anyway. [...] There is no living space for failed men in our society. Either you become a man the expected way, or you are none at all" (*MWNM* 65). Thus in both novels, death is presented as the better option in case your circumcision fails than going to a hospital. With his death, Xolilizwe escapes the social ostracism which Mgqolozana's protagonist will have to endure for the rest of his life.

As we will see, Mgqolozana's autodiegetic narrator also has a younger brother who is the only person attending to him in the hut after his circumcision. Toward the end of *A Man Who Is Not a Man*, the reader learns that it will now soon be time for the younger brother's circumcision (cf. *MWNM* 179). However, the reader

[48] The novel is hereafter cited as *TMR*.

[49] In order to define creolization, Zulu draws, among others, on Ashcroft, Griffiths, and Tiffin, who define it as "the process of intermixing and cultural change that produces a creole society" (58), and "Brathwaite [...] stresses that 'creolization is not a product but a process of both acculturation and interculturation the former referring to the process of absorption of one culture by another; the latter to a more reciprocal activity, a process of intermixture and enrichment to each other'" (Zulu 1).

does not learn whether this rite of passage will differ from his older brother Lumkile's failed rite of passage, as Lumkile's traumatizing experience is hushed up even in his family. By contrast, in Kaschula's novel the experience, which is traumatic for both parents and younger brother, leads to the parents' reconsideration of how the circumcision was executed, not to a questioning of the tradition as such. Zama himself wants to be circumcised in honour of his brother (cf. *TMR* 104). When his time of initiation has come, his father and mother want him to go to the doctor and take antibiotics beforehand. "[T]hings have changed now. No one minds if you take antibiotics beforehand", Zama's father proclaims (*TMR* 101). In order not to lose another son, the father also makes sure this time that the *ingcibi*, i.e. the traditional healer, is qualified to perform the operation (cf. *TMR* 101–102). Kaschula's novel not only portrays parents who adapt their conception of tradition to present circumstances, but crosses yet another invisible border. In the course of the novel, Zama becomes best friends with Pieter, his classmate and neighbour of coloured descent. At the end of the novel, Pieter also decides to get circumcised as a sign of friendship and understanding. With this step, *Take Me to the River* breaks with long-established cultural boundaries between social groups and shows that traditions that once belonged to a distinct group can be adapted, transformed, and become meaningful for other milieus as well. With their decision, Zama and Pieter mix their cultures, hence creating their own tradition, which signals understanding across the colour bar. Regarding its presentation of a reformed rite of passage that draws "from the good of Xhosa tradition and Western medical practices" (Zulu 3), Kaschula's novel is amongst the most progressive in the corpus. The author invokes a space in which "race and culture, as concepts that emphasized racial differences in the past", are "de-essentializ[ed]" and give way to a process of "national harmonization, reconciliation and healing" (Zulu 5). Significantly, the author gets this message across without making the story sound condescending and without denigrating "South African hybridization and therefore multiculturalism as 'something artificial, [socio-politically] engineered'", as scholars like Nuttall and Michael (2000) or Martin (2005) have tended to describe the "fragile situation that emerged after a negotiated political settlement" in 1994 (Zulu 5). This aim is also achieved by maintaining traditional conceptions of masculinity throughout the novel. Zama is portrayed as a typical young boy, who skips school, cycles, fishes, and is adventurous and bold. "Zama couldn't wait to become a man. He knew that he wouldn't cry, not a single tear!" (*TMR* 20). As in *A Man Who Is Not a Man*, Zama is aware of a concept of masculinity that does not allow men "to show any emotions, otherwise [you] would remain a boy, and never become a man" (*TMR* 20). Likewise, the traditional roles that men and women have in the initiation process of a young boy are invoked in the novel (cf. *TMR* chapter 2). In this roughly one-hundred-page novel, Kaschula does not present notions that would lead to a questioning of traditional masculinity concepts per se. Instead, his focus is on the establishment of a creolized space in which friendships and relationships across the colour bar can become a given.

Thando Mgqolozana, *A Man Who Is Not a Man* (2010)

A Man Who Is Not a Man is the rebellious testimony of a young Xhosa male against the cultural norms of his community and against the culture of silence that surrounds failed circumcisions. Lumkile decides to tell his story a few years after the failure of his rite of passage. In the prologue and the epilogue of the novel, both of which are set in the present and are meant to serve as a frame to the story of Lumkile's circumcision a few years earlier, the reader is frequently directly addressed. This creates an intimate atmosphere between reader and narrator. The protagonist's intention to lay bare the details of his rite of passage to a potentially uninformed, multiracial, and multinational audience containing both males and females is in itself an act of rebellion against his culture's customs. "[W]hat happens at the mountain stays at the mountain" (*MWMN* 180) is the rule that must be obeyed not only in real social contexts (cf. "Responses to Becoming Indoba"), but also within the fictional frame. The procedures and rituals connected to a young male's initiation process are to be kept a secret from those who have not yet or will not undergo the procedures themselves: women, children, and people who do not belong to the social group. By disclosing the rite–of–passage ritual as well as its flaws, Lumkile breaks with his culture's tradition and risks social ostracism. Furthermore, the title and cover of the novel may well be considered an affront: Displaying a young Xhosa initiate covered in ritual clay and labelling the image "*A Man Who Is Not a Man*" must appear absurd to those in the know because the image of Xhosa initiates is culturally linked to the concept of becoming a 'real man'.

Lumkile's identity formation as a young Xhosa male is at the centre of the novel. Narratives of hegemonic masculinity permeate the text from the start: "Me, I was a real boy from the word go, with both my balls fully descended and the promising look that I would one day own a formidable lion" (*MWNM* 1). The animal metaphor underlines the young boy's natural right to one day become the sovereign of his own 'kingdom', where he as man/lion can do as he pleases. Growing up in a Cape Town township, Lumkile has learned early to take and do what he likes. Drugs, crime, and violence shaped his early years in the city to such an extent that he considered them normal (cf. *MWNM* 15–24). In his early phase of identity formation, Lumkile forms himself according to the images of the hegemonic masculinity prevalent in his surrounding space. In this case the images Lumkile draws on can be compared to Bhana's findings, who analysed the behavioural patterns of "young black, Zulu-speaking boys between the ages of six and ten who attend a working class, township school in Durban" (206). *Tsotsi* images of a "flashily dressed black male street thug [who is] frequently a member of a gang and armed with a knife or weapon" defined the hegemonic masculinity in that township school (Bhana 206). In *A Man Who Is Not a Man*, Lumkile paints his younger self in the colours of this *tsotsi* image in chapter two of the novel: He and his boys "were the role models of [their] kasi [i.e. township]. When they saw us, young boys got inspired. Oongwana – chicks – were flattered by our attention, while the grown-ups were extraordinarily polite" (*MWNM* 16). Material objects are also relevant in Lumkile's early processes of identity formation. In fact, growing up without any caretaker and just enough money to buy himself the next zol, "[a] marijuana joint or hand-rolled cigarette" (*MWNM* 188), Lumkile falls prey to the belief that expensive clothes would differentiate him from his peers and earn him respect. However, as soon as he owns the material objects he desired, "Levis jeans", "All Star takkies", "a Starter t-shirt and Pierre Cardin cap", he realizes that in fact, these things are not what he "wanted and needed the most" in life after all (*MWNM* 32, 33).

In the novel, Lumkile's change of heart regarding the value of material objects as well as the use of violence and drugs is connected to his relocation to his mother's home in the rural Eastern Cape. Having found out that his former partners in crime in Cape Town had been locked up in prison and a psychiatric hospital, Lumkile realizes that "right here in Ngojini was the life [he] could claim as [his] own" not in the kasi, where "[i]t was always about overcoming the next obstacle" (*MWNM* 36–37). Consequently, Lumkile decides to no longer model his identity according to the *tsotsi* image. With this turn in the story, Mgqolozana also reinvokes and underlines an urban myth that has already been addressed in the previous chapter, namely that rural areas are morally superior to urban spaces with the latter leading to a person's ruin. In this vein, Lumkile embraces rural life and culture after his return to the land of his ancestors and his ritual initiation into manhood turns out to be as important to him as receiving a university pass after his final year of school:

> [He'd] become what [his] city friends would have called "softies". [His] joy lay in simple things: the greenness of sowing fields, the thorniness of bush, the shape of mountains, the gayness of dogs, the pureness of the atmosphere and freedom from toxins, speed and noise. [He] couldn't imagine breaking into another person's house [...]. [He] no longer had in [him] the readiness to kill if it came to the crunch. And [he] wasn't constantly looking at cars to check if they had mgqala–gqala [i.e. an alarm system]. (*MWNM* 66–67)

Lumkile's transformation appears to be substantial. Significantly, Mgqolozana's protagonist's character development happens before his failed circumcision; Lumkile himself calls it his "conversion" (*MWNM* 40). He has turned soft or, to put it in Bhana's words, become a "*yimvu* (Zulu for sheep, used metaphorically to describe passive, quiet, harmless boys)" (207). Despite his change and contrary to how his social surroundings think of *yimvu*, Lumkile still perceives himself as a full man, an even better man than his new classmates, whom he describes as "clumsy", "unwashed", and "stupid" (*MWNM* 40–41). Circumcision and good grades become his main objectives as these will allow him to live a good life as a 'real man' away from his kasi origins. Lumkile's character development illustrates the fluidity of masculinity concepts and their dependence on specific contexts (cf. Bhana 207). It also unmasks conventional conceptions of masculinity, showing Lumkile to be able to choose between *tsotsi* and *yimvu* masculinity freely.

Novels such as *A Man Who Is Not a Man*, which interrogate hegemonic masculinity concepts, appear to find themselves in good company internationally, as Nodelman's research shows. In "Making Boys Appear: The Masculinity of Children's Fiction", he found that presently

> [a] lot of books about boys that purport to transcend the formulas of popular fiction are about boys seeing through the conventional constructions of masculinity, learning to be more sensitive or more loving or more openly imaginative or literate, or less caught up in the pleasures of aggressive bullying. (Nodelman 2002, 11)

Within the South African context, such explicit dissection of particularly black masculine identities has only recently become more visible in texts aimed at and about young South Africans. This has to do with the fact that it is only in the last decade that discussion has shifted "from a focus on men to a focus on masculinity", which, in the South African context, "allows the importance of race and class to be recognized" (Morrell 2005, 285). On a broader scale it then becomes clear that the transformation of gender roles can only be examined "in tandem with racial liberation" (Messner quoted in Morrell 2005, 276). Since the colonial period race has been "a marker of inferiority", also having "a specific gender impact on black men: it emasculated them" (Morrell 2005, 282, 283). Their attempt to regain their status as 'real men' often resulted in "efforts to reestablish or perpetuate power over women" as an end to the greater constraint, oppression due to class and race, could not be achieved (Morrell 2005, 283). The integration of such notions as "race as historically received, materially located identity" as opposed to "race as a lived identity" in the contemporary masculinity discourse is essential as it "permits new forms of organization" for men to emerge (Morrell 2005, 283, 285).

A Man Who Is Not a Man is not only the coming–of–age story of Lumkile, it is also the story of his rite of passage as a young Xhosa initiate. When the narrator is admitted to hospital in the aftermath of his circumcision, he has to decide whether to become "a man who is not entirely a man" or "a dead man" (*MWNM* 3). In Xhosa culture, being a real man implies undergoing the rite of initiation alone and enduring the pain after circumcision only with the help of a personally assigned attendant who helps and advises the initiate through the different stages of recovery. When the narrator leaves his initiation hut on the mountain and turns to the help of official doctors at a hospital outside of the community due to an infection after the circumcision, he becomes a so-called "failed man" in the eyes of his social group. However, Lumkile's case is not as straightforward. While he has followed the protocol in detail, "gone for the required blood test", "got his circumcision licence", got circumcised by a "licensed traditional surgeon", and "followed all the right procedures at the mountain", his attendants, his grandfather and uncle, fail their relative at this most important stage in life by being absent (*MWNM* 138). Only his much younger and inexperienced brother attends to him in his hut, while his grandfather is getting drunk and his uncle chooses to earn money instead. The reader learns that it is not due to conventionally assumed reasons such as the protagonist's fragility or failure to bear the pain that he is a failed man, but because his attendants were not there to show him how to properly nurse himself back to health. These latter crucial details will however never be known by anyone outside the male community – "what happens at the mountain stays at the mountain" (*MWMN* 180). Hence, although it is not his own fault, he will forever be branded a failed man. Lumkile's story culminates in an epilogue in which he calls to the elders and caretakers of children to ensure the safety of the young initiate: "So long as our parents faltered, so long as the supposed custodians of our customs did not care for our well-being the way they were supposed to, and kept getting away with it, the government could try what it liked but the problem would only get worse" (*MWNM* 138).

The main character's story is told backwards, inviting the reader to absorb the narrator's story with the hopeful ending in mind that he presents in the first chapter. Already in the prologue Lumkile announces that in the aftermath of the initiation process he was forced to "gain a new understanding of [him]self" and the world around him (*MWNM* 3). In the seven years since his failed initiation, he has been able to develop a new concept of self-independence from the world's perceptions; the reader learns: "I no longer look at my world in the same way, through the world's eyes; a recipe for discrimination, that! I have had to learn to look through my eyes, and then adjust the world's view of the way it looks at me" (*MWMN* 3). For him, writing down the story is his "way of bringing finality to that process" of reconsidering learned perception (*MWMN* 3). Mgqolozana's novel, which publicizes a topic which community members do not want to become public, can hence be understood as a South African answer to the Western tales of rebellion which Nodelman mentioned in his study (cf. 2002). The novel rebels against conceptions about what a real man is and seeks sympathy for alternative versions of maleness. Ultimately, the narrator concludes that "[s]trangely enough, my supposedly 'failed' circumcision has made me feel more like a real man, not less. If manhood is about enduring pain in its figurative and literal sense, then I dare say I have more than earned it" (*MWMN* 182). These words demonstrate that there is no unitary concept of masculinity, but that it is "both in motion and rigid" (cf. Fink 127), as the protagonist draws on hegemonic conceptions of masculinity but simultaneously deconstructs them, showing that he has been able to develop a new masculine identity because of his experiences.

Sifiso Mzobe, *Young Blood* (2010)

Mzobe's *Young Blood*[50] is the last novel to be discussed in greater detail in this subchapter on contemporary masculinities in South Africa. In 2013, the novel appeared in its fourth impression. By then it had already won the 2011 Herman Charles Bosman Prize for English Literature, the 2011 Sunday Times Fiction Prize, and the 2012 Wole Soyinka Prize for African Literature. Telling the coming–of–age story of Sipho Khumalo, *Young Blood* (2010) has been called a representative of the South African version of the contemporary *Bildungsroman* (cf. Jones 2013). It has been illustrated already in the introduction that *Bildungsroman* remains a contested term in the South African context. Rita Barnard considered the South African 'Jim Comes To Joburg' stories the closest equivalent to the European form of *Bildungsroman* in the country, even though closure was not achieved in those South African texts (cf. 547). Jones notes that

> [u]nder apartheid, the 'Jim Comes to Joburg' narratives chronicling the arrival and settlement of rural black migrants to the city were unable to convey social legitimation because black South Africans were not considered citizens. Consequently, there could be no harmony between the black individual and the state. (211)

Today, however, Jones notes, "there exists a compensatory desire to align individual change with romanticized discourses of the "new" South Africa" (Jones 211), leading to a reconsideration of the *Bildungsroman* genre in the country. In his novel *Young Blood*, Sifiso Mzobe plays with this desire for unity between the state and the individual which could not be achieved under apartheid, thus presenting to the reader his version of the contemporary South African *Entwicklungsroman*, which can be considered the young adult version of the *Bildungsroman* (cf. Inggs 2007, 47). For the purpose of achieving unity between state and individual, Mzobe follows the *Bildungsroman* convention by including an element of closure in the novel; the protagonist is eventually integrated in "society via the reconciliation of interiority and exteriority" (Jones 211). Mzobe himself admits to the didacticism he infused the novel with in an interview, saying that he "wanted his novel to be a cautionary tale for the young people" (quoted in Jones 211–212). This 'cautionary' element, or the element of closure, is precisely what leads Megan Jones to a less enthusiastic verdict than the many literary prizes the novel received would suggest. Although she can see elements of "societal critique" in the novel (211), Jones has a problem with *Young Blood*'s "overriding aims" to assimilate "the individual within some form of meta-narrative" (Jones 211). The lesson that the protagonist learns at the end of the novel, namely that "'crime doesn't pay' or at least, the physical and psychological costs of crime are not worth paying" (*ibid.*), leads to his voluntary reintegration into his initial social

[50] The book is hereafter cited as *YB*.

environment. Such is also a narrative typically invoked in the *Bildungsroman* genre and one which raises Jones's concerns. Unlike "Niq Mhlongo's novel *After Tears*, Ralph Ziman's 2008 film *Jerusalema* and the musician Spoek Mathambo's video for the single 'She's Lost Control'", whose texts "interrogate the possibility of social coherence" and "figure the township as abandoned, distorted or dystopian", Mzobe's *Young Blood* remains a 'normative' fiction to the last page (Jones 211, footnote 14). To her, a closure that is founded on the "conspicuous destruction" of Sipho's previous attempts to ascend the social ladder, to "elevate the body and mark public spaces", resists her understanding of an achieved unity of state and individual (Jones 223). With her insightful essay, Jones shows that, as "processes of unequal enrichment persis[t] in post-apartheid South Africa", the *Entwicklungsroman* remains an incomplete and contested genre in the country (*ibid.*).

Young Blood depicts a prototypical type of violent and materialist masculinity stereotypically associated with the 'new' South Africa. The desire to develop his individual identity according to the socially accepted form, i.e. the hegemonic form of masculinity of Umlazi Township in Durban, characterizes the protagonist's coming–of–age throughout the novel. Like in *A Man Who Is Not a Man*, violence and materialist aspirations serve as markers that the young male follows on the expected path to manhood. Wearing the 'right' clothes, by the brand Hugo Boss in this case, is as important to the main character, Sipho, as it is to Lumkile in *A Man Who Is Not a Man*, as owning expensive clothes is tantamount to receiving more prestige, higher respect, and greater awe (cf. *YB* 172–173). In the novel, such emotional reactions to material possessions and the resulting behavioural patterns have led to the establishment of a social hierarchy based on the individual's purchasing power. In this respect, the novel mirrors contemporary patterns of social hierarchy construction. Anthropologists such as Douglas and Isherwood (1996) or Fine and Leopold (1993) found that "the *social* meanings of commodities, essentially inanimate goods, are far more significant to the ways in which our society works than the *utilitarian* meanings of these goods" (Maxwell 203; emphasis in the original). Sipho is not content with the simple and modest lifestyle his parents, a nurse and a mechanic, can provide. He decides to leave school and pursue a supposedly faster road to success, one which enables him to make money much faster than by repairing cars with his father. By making car theft his new profession, he knows he has chosen "money over freedom" and that with this step he "was saying goodbye to [his] childhood, embracing manhood from a different angle" (*YB* 107–108). In his new profession, which also involves the reselling of stolen goods, he indeed is able to make money fast: "I bought a four-component music system for R500. Then we went to the university up in Westville and opened shop […] I sold the music system for R1500. I returned Musa's R500. […] R1000 was in my back pocket – the quickest pocket money I ever made" (*YB* 70). Within the couple of months covered in the novel's content, Sipho is able to save more than R20,000. In order to demonstrate his business success he decides to buy a Hugo Boss outfit to replace his no-name clothes. The utility of goods becomes less significant with the increase in purchasing power, whilst the significance he places on the social meaning of consumer goods has risen (cf. *YB* 121). His efforts to fit in in the new milieu are rewarded: "I can see you are a go-getter", (*YB* 118) Mdala, a higher ranking gangster, praises Sipho, subsequently asking him to join in in his upcoming drug scheme.

In his new line of business, there is a further signifier of masculinity that is ascribed even more power than following the dress code and that is the owning of one's own car. Gartman points out that since their invention, cars have "commonly [been] revered as symbols of the good life aspired to by all, and turned up in Cole Porter songs, Fitzgerald novels and Hollywood movies" (60). Miller, who "examines the car as a vehicle for class, oppression, racism and violence" points to the fact that many contemporary critics have interpreted "the car as a symbol or as the token for modernity", which leads them to "rushed conclusions" (2001, 2, 10–11). According to Miller, scholars not only "ten[d] to assume that contemporary car use is associated with an increased sense of mobility and speed" they also "asser[t] a relationship between the car with masculinity and violence that verges on the essentialist" and do not give credit to "the centrality of the car to the mundane tasks of women" or "caring parents" (2001, 2, 10–12). While such misreadings may be true for other texts, the critical assessment of South African fiction for teenagers has shown that in terms of gender, cars are indeed predominantly constructed as masculine. An exception can be found in *This Book Betrays My Brother* (2012), in which the car is, amongst other things, a sign of parenting in Miller's sense. In the novel, the mother is shown to drive – or "chauffeu[r]", as Miller has called it (2001, 12) – the female main character to her friends or activities in order to protect her from the streets, which are considered dangerous. In *Young Blood* cars clearly belong to the male sphere and are signifiers of the male's social mobility. Driving in fast and prestigious cars is tantamount to progress in both spatial and social terms. With a car you can cross and transcend the invisible borders drawn between social spaces and change your location quickly. Sipho moves unimpeded between townships, cities, and suburban areas (cf. Jones 2013). Cars also signify the individual's progression on the social ladder. The BMWs Sipho is driving earn him respect from both his fellow gangsters and his family, who assume that business must be going well. Except for one instance (cf. *YB* 103), the driving of cars is done by males. Females only feature as sitting next to the driver or in the back seat together with another man. Large sections of the novel are given to Sipho's descriptions of how he masters the driving of cars:

> I released the handbrake and stepped full power on the accelerator. The 325is stalled, and took a few digs on the tarmac. When I released the clutch it was like we were inside a bullet. […] I went full on the gears, double-tapped the accelerator from first to second. Simply to show off, I tapped it three times from second gear to third. (*YB* 21)

> I shoved the M5 as hard as I could. On the freeway to Pinetown the accelerator pedal locked onto the floor. The sound from the tailpipe was like gunfire as the engine clocked again and again. (*YB* 77)

Sipho's hard and uncompromising way of driving as well as his ability to fix cars and override anti-hijack systems earn the protagonist respect and are his entry ticket to a small but effective car stealing gang after he has decided to leave school (cf. *YB* 26, 149). He becomes Musa's "soldier" (*YB* 31). Moreover, not only the fellow gangsters attribute success and mobility to a prestigious car, like the BMW 325is Sipho is driving; women do, too.

Young Blood is the epitome of what Wilkie-Stibbs has called men's "objectivity and outsidedness through which women are turned into objects through the agency of '*The look*,' 'the logic of *The [male] gaze*'" (41, emphasis in the orignial). Throughout the novel, Sipho presents women as accessories that come with a nice car. The great majority of "chicks" (*YB* 25) in the novel are described as nameless, silent, and dull "ghost[s]" (*YB* 103) who vanish after last night's party has ended. At these parties, men pay the girls' expenses for food, drinks, and drugs. The young females repay these expenses with meaningless sexual encounters. Although Sipho has a girlfriend, Nana, he does not miss a chance to score with other women, leading to physical encounters and sexual intercourse with several of his female party acquaintances throughout the novel (cf. *YB* 23, 102). Simultaneously, Sipho tells Nana that he is faithful to her. Such behaviour is accepted and encouraged by his fellow gang members but also by the nameless girls at the parties, and adds to the consolidation of Sipho's position in the gang. *Young Blood* thus becomes a double 'regulatory fiction' in Donna Haraway's sense[51] in that it perpetuates socially accepted gender concepts by following Sipho's striving to incorporate the features of the hegemonic masculine identity of that particular subspace.

Also in its final pages, Mzobe's novel stays a regulatory fiction when the norms of gangsterism are replaced by the norms Sipho initially fled from, namely those that permeate the social milieu of his home township. In the last chapter of the novel with its telling title "Pillars of Sand", Sipho's promising career as car thief and his plans to enter the drug business are stopped dead in their tracks when he is caught by the police while driving in his new stolen car. With a bribe as high as his savings, R20,000, Sipho is able to convince the three cops to not press charges against him. After the incident the protagonist is left with nothing. The same night, his gangster bosses, Musa and Mdala, get involved in a gun fight,

[51] 'Regulatory fiction' is a term introduced by Donna Haraway in the early 1990s to describe the regulatory practices that supported the formation of conventional gender concepts in Western countries after the Renaissance (cf. Navarro 1993). Such narratives contain a "regulatory framework that influences, directs, and delimits possibilities of action" and "prescribe[s] and proscribe[s] restrictive norms of femininity and masculinity" (Mallan 72).

leaving one fatally injured and the other condemned to flee. In the aftermath, Sipho decides to end his career in crime, revoking his earlier choice for money over freedom (cf. *YB* 108). Earlier, Sipho had described "freedom" as being able to play soccer and living the normal life of the township (cf. *YB* 108). Now he starts at a technical college, where he trains to become a motor mechanic (cf. *YB* 222). With this decision Sipho consciously rejects the regulatory framework of the criminal world, simultaneously subjecting himself to the regulatory framework of conventional township life. In the latter life, Sipho once again has no money and has to rely on his parents or his girlfriend, who gets a weekly allowance from her well-off parents, to pay for his food or transportation (cf. *YB* 221). Considering the dangers he has been through and the luck he had in escaping a prison sentence, Sipho accepts this new, old, and slower life with almost no sign of emotion. It should be noted that despite the narrative being told from Sipho's perspective, the reader is seldom given insights into his emotional responses to the surrounding events and has to make do with short remarks in subordinate clauses. In one of the rare moments when Sipho is alone and allows himself to reflect on the events, the protagonist admits to being "[s]haken" (*YB* 226) by last year's experience, yet he still makes sure to maintain his masculine attire in public. Keeping up his appearance and "concentrate[ing] in class" are Sipho's means of dealing with "everything [he] saw in the year that [he] turned seventeen" (*YB* 228). When he is told about the death of his fellow gangster, Musa, he "looked away from Sticks for fear of tears, but [his] eyes were dry" (*YB* 228). Instead of an open emotional response, Sipho "sa[ys] a silent goodbye to [his] friend Musa" (*YB* 228). Thus, traits of "hegemonic masculinity" (Connell 1995, 77) are shown to help the main character to find his way into the new/old life. These traits are not deconstructed thereafter. Pennell argues that in order to break up gender binarism, "the operations of traditional normative masculinity must be made visible" (Pennell 56). At the end of the novel, Sipho is successfully and voluntarily reintegrated into his surrounding social order, indicating the moment of closure that has been so central to the European *Bildungsroman*. Thus, the ending of Mzobe's novel provides the "normative" closure that leaves Jones (2013) uneasy. With Sipho's submission to the norms of the South African state, therewith signalling his unity with a state that is still in turmoil, the novel neglects an element of disintegration that is central to the "new hybrid realism" previously invoked by Pearson and Reynolds (72). Although the novel goes "some way in contesting the reification of townships as sites of violence and suffering", it "reiterate[s] the destruction of poor black bodies as symptomatic of their social exclusion", thus catering to "a mass-mediated view of the townships as breeding grounds of brutality" (Jones 220).

Resumé

The previous analyses have shown that *Young Blood, A Man Who Is Not a Man* and *Take Me to the River* "are examples of YA fiction that are representative of the ways that contemporary writers are attempting to reflect back to readers ways of 'being–in–the–world', highlighting the fluid and multiple geographies and environments young people inhabit" (Mallan 79).[52] The young male protagonists are shown to form and change their masculine identities in response to their spatial and social surroundings. Assessing different novels from the period between 1989 and 2006, Inggs found that while "novels generally confirm the existence of a 'hegemonic masculinity'" and "tend to reflect stereotypical gender roles", there are at least some "leading male characters [that] reflect Romøren and Stephens's sensitive 'new man' schema (225) in that they are gentler, more attentive and more considerate than the typical hegemonic male" (Inggs 2009, 103). Overall, however, "traditional gendered subjectivities" have not really been challenged in youth novels published been 1989 and 2006 (Inggs 2009, 103). In fact, this remains basically unchanged to this day (cf. Inggs 2016, 81). Although contemporary fictions have moved from what Pennell called depictions of "unitary masculine subject[s]" to outlining the complexities underlying masculine identity formation, these novels still depict "intersubjective experiences with women and girls [as being] premised either implicitly or explicitly upon unequal relations of power" (Pennell 56; cf. Inggs 2016, 75). Notably, these power relations are not a one-way street. Mzobe's *Young Blood* is a case in point. The book is a tale ripe with patriarchal normativity and morale also due to the fact that "women are presented as materially rapacious" (Jones 216). In this novel, the female side characters are only attracted to affluent young males, thus driving these men to inconsiderate behaviour and criminal actions in order to satisfy their needs. Inggs detected a similar set of behaviours in her analysis of Phalime's *Second Chances* (cf. Inggs 2016, 74–75). Consequently, as they are "more likely to be[come] perpetrators and victims", young males are shown to pay a higher price than their female contemporaries (Jones 218). In *Young Blood*, only men become gangsters and although women, too, are "involved in street crime" (Jones 218), like consuming drugs or driving in stolen cars, only the males are convicted for these crimes. Moreover, "there is also an underlying text that places blame on the female characters' naivety and poor judgement and lessens the responsibility borne by the male characters" (Inggs 2016, 75). Jones points to Swartz (2009), who "calls the specificities of place associated with varying types of moral action 'a located morality'" (218).[53] Only if such located moralities as well as "the operations of

[52] In her article, Mallan examined "The Regulatory Fictions of Online Communities" (2008), yet her conclusion also holds true for offline communities.
[53] Chapter 3 will further discuss what kind of social ethics are promoted in South African young adult literature.

traditional normative masculinity" and femininity are "made visible" (Pennell 56) in narratives for young adults can conventional gender stereotyping be subverted.

2.2 Homo- and Transsexuality

On 25 August 2014, the South African *Daily Maverick* reported on eighteen–year–old Gift Disebo Makau, a young black woman from Ventersdorp, who had been murdered because of her sexual orientation. Not only was she raped, but she was "strangled with a wire" and "a hosepipe [was forced] into her mouth, pumping water into her body" (Ngcowa). Recurring sensationalistic news reports inform us that such brutality is not the exception and is not confined to same-sex practising women (cf. Muholi). Such articles show that even though more than twenty years have passed since the country's new "Constitution" declared all South Africans of whatever decent or sexual orientation equal and their discrimination illegal (cf. Section 9.3 and 9.4), those whose sexual orientation differs from the heterosexual norm continue to be ostracized and in danger of violent attacks (cf. Brouard 64).

Discriminatory actions against so-called 'deviant' sexual practices have a long history in South Africa. Prior to the end of apartheid, a long list of laws not only forbade sexual encounters or marriages between different ethnicities, but promoted the ideology of a "puritan police state" (Hoad 2005, 16). Laws such as the Immorality Act of 1927, the Prohibition of Mixed Marriages Act of 1949, or the Mixed Marriages Act of 1950 played an integral part in the manifestation of heterosexism and homophobia prior to the end of apartheid. The passing of such laws shows that in the past, "the state imagined sexual control as central to the effective implementation and sustaining of apartheid politics" (Hoad 2005, 16). In 1969, the Immorality Act was further amended, including then a passage which "criminalized: 'any act by a male person … with another male person at a party … which is calculated to stimulate sexual passion or to give sexual gratification'" (quoted in Hoad 2005, 17). The advent of the HIV/AIDS pandemic further stigmatized "same-sex erotically inclined South Africans" (Hoad 2005, 21). In its beginnings, same-sex practices were thought to be responsible for the emergence of the pandemic. The history of the HIV/AIDS pandemic itself "is marked by a series of scandals and a few fragile victories for the millions of HIV-positive people in South Africa" and "under the apartheid regime and during the Nelson Mandela presidency is mostly one of silence" (Hoad 2007, 90). Controversial statements by South Africa's second president, Thabo Mbeki, and a counterproductive public health policy in the early 2000s (cf. Hoad 2007, 90–112; Lane 67) are some of the reasons why a critical public consciousness of the disease has arisen only slowly. In 2009, current president Zuma "initiated a National HIV Counseling and Testing Campaign aimed at mobilising South Africans to get tested regularly", which was declared a success in 2011 with "more than 13 million South Africans [being] tested for HIV between April 2010 and August 2011" (Grünkemeier 41, footnote 7). Initially connected only with male homosexuals in the early 1980s, the HIV epidemic was redefined "as heterosexual in the years around South Africa's transition to democracy" (Lane 66). Since then, cases of heterosexual transmission of the HI virus have outnumbered those among non-heterosexual couples by far (cf. Lane 67, Grünkemeier 29–30). One of the results of this turn is that today, women are more likely to be infected than men (cf. Grünkemeier 29). In his essay "From Social Silence to Social Science", Tim Lane (2009) points out that such redefinition bears the danger of excluding or rendering invisible other affected groups, such as black township men who have sex with men. It is thus necessary to discuss the pandemic across all types of sexuality.

Regarding the general literary market, responses to the pandemic only really began to emerge in the early 2000s (cf. Grünkemeier 42). Since then, literary texts for adults, such as Phaswane Mpe's *Welcome to Our Hillbrow* (2001), have contributed to making people aware that the HIV/AIDS pandemic affects not only the underprivileged and same-sex practising people, but also "the educated, the respectable, the normal" (Phaswane quoted in Hoad 2005, 21). The sociological redefinition of the HIV pandemic as a pandemic that predominantly concerns heterosexuals has also had an impact on the way HIV/AIDS is represented in the genre of young adult literature. When conducting her study of the field, Grünkemeier was "surprise[d] to find that a comparatively large number of books addressing the infection have been published for young readers, even dating back to the early 1990s" (186). As this is a topic often addressed in AIDS education, "the genre of teenage fiction is particularly prone to the production and circulation of meanings about HIV/AIDS", Grünkemeier concludes (186). Interestingly, none of the novels Grünkemeier analyses thereafter, UNICEF's *Sara – The Empty Compound* (2000), Lutz van Dijk's *Stronger Than the Storm* (2000), Jenny Robson's *Praise Song* (2006),[54] Gavin and Val Kruger's *A Story of Hope* (2006), or Nokuthula Mazibuko's *In the Fast Lane* (2007), discusses HIV/AIDS in relation to a homosexual character (cf. 190–220).[55] Nor do any of the novels to be discussed here – Biron Alnam's *No Problem, Man!* (2003), Robin Malan's *My "Funny" Brother* (2012), or Kasigo Lesego Molope's *This Book Betrays My Brother* (2012) – reference the pandemic in their stories about coming out while coming–of–age. A possible connection between HIV/AIDS and homosexuality is neither mentioned nor discussed in today's literary products although, obviously, the HI virus is still also a topic for non-heterosexual youth; but the fact that AIDS is not brought into explicit or direct connection with homo- or transsexuality also points to the 'communal' effort to remove the stigma and the fact that this has

[54] For an analysis of Jenny Robson's *Praise Song*, see also Inggs (2016, 72–73).

[55] *Dancing Queen* (2004) by Margie Orford, a novel examined in chapter 1, is a further example of the discussion of HIV/AIDS in a heterosexual context.

already worked to a significant degree. Instead, the recurrent theme in Alnam's, Malan's, and Molope's novels is homophobia. Showing the varying depths of the issue, these texts advocate diversity and the inclusive society originally promoted in the 1996 Constitution under the umbrella term 'rainbow nation', as we will see in the subsequent close readings.

If HIV/AIDS has not been a taboo topic in literary texts for young people, dealing withhomosexuality and other types of sexuality that 'deviate' from the heterosexual norm certainly has been until very recently. In 2005, Joanne Bloch and Karen Martin noted that "while there is a lot of very visible media for young people about making positive life choices, particularly around sexuality, none of it seems to be aimed at gay or lesbian youth" (6). Between 2000 and 2014 only six books were published which include characters that are attracted to the same sex: Biron Alnam's novel, *No Problem, Man!* (2003), accompanies Rashaad, a gay Muslim, on his way to accepting his sexuality. Robin Malan's *My "Funny" Brother* (2012) features a gay male character, whose story is told from the perspective of his younger sister. Marita van der Vyver's *The Hidden Life of Hanna Why* (2007) is the only novel to include a gay parent as a side-character. Kagiso Lesego Molope's *This Book Betrays My Brother* (2012) is the first text to include a lesbian side-character. Sonwabiso Ngcowa is the first author to create a lesbian main character in *In Search for Happiness* (2014). Before the publication of Molope's and Ngcowa's novels "[t]here ha[d] been so few South African texts of any kind representing female same-sex intimacies and desires, particularly between black women, that it is perhaps fitting that the figure who has emerged as the 'voice' of black South African lesbians is not a writer but a photographer", namely Zanele Muholi[56] (Munro 218–219).

The sixth novel is K. Sello Duiker's cross-over novel *Thirteen Cents* (2000), which is moreover the only one containing explicit and graphic details about sexual encounters between males. This novel shows that another kind of complication in one's sexual identity formation can occur in contexts of "structural violence – the violence of poverty, unemployment, powerlessness and lack of education" – as such an environment leads to "tensions, disturbances and insecurities in [one's] sexual subjectivity" (Lorway 277). Lorway came to understand that "[f]or many of [his] male informants, the pursuit of a life that is socially and economically more 'liberated' involves occupying multiple, partial and even contradictory gender/sexual subject positions" (277). Being sexually

[56] "Trained at the Market Photo Workshop, [Zanele] Muholi presented her first exhibition, *Visual Sexuality,* at the Johannesburg Art Gallery in 2004. She has a growing global reputation, although her images have also been used locally in pamphlets, posters, and publications by LGBT and women's rights organizations" (Munro 219). For more information, see Munro's chapter "Queer Citizenship, Queer Exile: K. Sello Duiker and Zanele Muholi" (218–233) in which she provides detailed information about Zanele Muholi's work, her growing international reception, and her formula for success.

flexible "allowed [these informants] mobility across seemingly diverse cultural spaces marked by multiple languages, ethnicities, ages and economic statuses" (Lorway 278). Here, I want to briefly return to thirteen-year-old Azure, the protagonist of *Thirteen Cents*, who was already introduced in the first chapter. The orphan and street child sells his body to strangers in order to get by (cf. chapter 1.2.1). Depicting the harsh circumstances under which the street child lives, the novel makes evident that the protagonist simply cannot afford to follow his own inclinations exclusively.[57] In the case of Azure, sexual subjectivity, "poverty and sexual-risk taking practices" (Lorway 277) are intricately intertwined. The more edgy and hungry Azure gets, the greater is the risk he is willing to take in his sexual encounters. In *Thirteen Cents*, sexual acts are also used as a means of gaining power over and even breaking a person. The gangsters, who are also not sexually attracted to men, force Azure to practise oral sex on the individual gang members as a form of punishment in order to break his will. The effects of these forced encounters between the teenage boy and grown-up men on the young street child's psyche have already been discussed in the previous chapter (cf. chapter 1.2.1).

The introduction to this chapter on gender stereotyping pointed to the limits of expressing gender linguistically, the tendency of Western scholars to describe masculinity and femininity with the help of certain schemata (cf. Stephens 1996; Russell), and the efforts of African scholars to declare these "Western" clusters unsuitable for African contexts (cf. Brouard; Lorway). In his article "Making Boys Appear" (2002), Perry Nodelman raised questions about the depiction of homosexual males after his analysis of *Bad Boy* (1989) by Diana Wieler, in which the gay character is portrayed as "lithe, quick-moving and mercurial, emotionally expressive, erratic, and passively masochistic in his sex life" and "the straight one is stocky, muscular, and deliberate, in control of his emotions, stolidly dependable, and aggressively sadistic as a hockey player and pursuer of women" (2002, 12). According to Nodelman, such a casting begs two questions: "Is the acceptance of gayness communicated here or are tired clichés about it reiterated? Indeed, is children's literature sometimes unintentionally but implicitly homophobic?" (2002, 12). In the novels selected for close reading in this subchapter, homosexual characters are cast according to gender schemata, yet neither of these texts is reiterating "tired clichés" (Nodelmann 2002, 12) about gayness nor can they be called homophobic.

[57] Azure is not attracted to males but his suitors are predominantly married men. When he has sexual encounters with men, he has to think of Tony Braxton, for instance, to become aroused (cf. *TC* 9). His blue eyes make him attractive to different types of men who belong to different social groups. There is the middle-class single, but also the rich white business type. With the selling of his body, Azure can momentarily alleviate his poor living situation. He realizes that it is important when and where to get his suitors as this results in better or worse payment (cf. *TC* 8, 10, 29–30). However, his own desperateness for money, too, leads him to accept better or worse clients and payment.

Biron Alnam, *No Problem, Man!* (2003)

Biron Alnam is one of the pseudonyms under which Robin Malan writes for *Siyagruva: A Series of Novels for South African Teens*, of which he is also the editor. Apart from being a writer, Malan is also well known for being the founding and current editor of *English Alive*, an annual anthology of writing from high schools and colleges in southern Africa. *No Problem, Man!*[58] is one of twenty-five novels published in the *Siyagruva* Series. The series is special not only because it is "non-sequential" (Grünkemeier 199), but also because it was the first to address the day-to-day issues of twenty-first century South African teenagers from mixed backgrounds (cf. Kaschula). The series is particularly valuable for second language learners. Short chapters, condensed plot structure, and a comparatively easy choice of words cater to the needs of this specific audience. Moreover, the series has a fixed set of characters which recur in the different novels. However, the protagonists of the individual novels change, with each novel focusing on the coming–of–age story of a different set of characters. Rashaad is part of this set of recurring characters in the series. In the rest of the novels of the *Siyagruva Series* he appears as a side-character, mostly featuring as a reliable friend and good dancer.[59] Only in *No Problem, Man!* (2003) do his identity issues concerning his sexuality take centre stage. *No Problem, Man!* contains three storylines, one of which follows Rashaad on his journey of self-discovery. Rashaad comes from a conservative Muslim family. He enters the story with the words "The thing is, I don't know if I'm gay" (*NPM* 9). With his first sentence, Rashaad has set the scene for the rest of the storyline. The reader learns that Rashaad is comfortable with his friends at the dance studio, which is why he does not hesitate to voice his doubts about his sexual orientation in that context. At the dance studio, but also at college, Rashaad appears to have found people to talk to about his situation. Trying to become more independent from his parents and to have more time to meet people, he registers at Odd Jobs, a company which "place[s] people in temporary jobs" (*NPM* 12). There he meets Theo, who openly voices his prejudices against "these gays" (*NPM* 28). Rashaad, who is still trying to figure out what being gay actually means, notes that "the way Theo said 'these' gays [...] was much too close to the way some white people referred to black people as 'these blacks'" (*NPM* 28f.).

In the short novel, Malan draws attention to the normality of homosexuality and homosexual behaviour and the fact that people with a gay orientation have been part of society for a long time. Despite the shortness of the storyline, which is narrated in only 28 pages, the narrative discusses stereotypes related to the looks of gay people (*NPM* 10, 28–30), touches on the difficulties of telling your parents about your sexual orientation (cf. *NPM* 68–69), includes a gay support group that

[58] The novel is hereafter cited as *NPM*.

[59] An exception is *Mom's Taxi* (2003) by Mteto Mzongwana, Onele Mfeketo, and Lamna Orbin, which contains homophobic verbal abuse against Rashaad.

talks about "what it's like to be gay [and] different ways of being gay [including] how being gay fits in with your religion" (*NPM* 67–68), and mentions the existence of a gay subculture in the city of Cape Town (cf. *NPM* 10, 64f.). This subculture is confined to places obviously advertised as gay bars or clubs, but the reader learns that these locations are also frequented by straight people (cf. *NPM* 70f.). When attending a gay support group's meeting toward the end of the novel, Rashaad can for the first time ask other gay people how they knew they were gay (*NPM* 84–87). Afterwards he is also able to acknowledge his sexual orientation in front of Theo. Rashaad's storyline ends with an exchange between Theo and Rashaad. Theo surprises Rashaad when he agrees to come with him to a meeting for gays one day, implying that Theo might be able to give up his prejudices and fall into step with the wider social project of de-stigmatizing homosexuality (cf. *NPM* 87f.).

Robin Malan, *My "Funny" Brother* (2012)

Malan published *My "Funny" Brother*[60] through his own publishing company, Junkets, which received the 2009 Excellence Award for Literature from the Arts and Culture Trust of South Africa. The novel is unique as it not only includes a homosexual character, but is also amongst the first to actually address same-sex sexual practices – at least in theory. In fact, the back cover warns the reader by using a red emergency triangle containing an exclamation mark in bold that this book "contains a biology lesson" (*MFB* back cover). The story of "Donovan. Called Donnie. And, also, Donna" (*MFB* 9) is told from the perspective of Missy, who is Donna's younger sister by six years. The story starts when Missy is nine years old, and Donna is fifteen years of age, and follows theirs and their seventeen-year-old brother Reginald's growing-up for roughly the next nine years. In order to cover this time span within 161 pages and 44 chapters, Malan uses numerous time lapses.

All the characters are constructed according to gender stereotypes regarding behaviour and appearance. Reginald represents the typical boy, who, "thundering in from school, hurl[s] his book-bag into a corner, kick[s] off his school shoes, rip[s] his tie off, [just to be able to] […] t[ie] the laces on his soccer boots" (*MFB* 8). Missy, the nine-year-old homodiegetic narrator, already knows well at her age that Reginald, who wants to be a policeman one day, sees his little sister not as "a proper person", but "'just' a girl" (*MFB* 6) with whom he cannot connect. On the other hand, Missy's "funny" brother, Donna, is introduced as "actually listen[ing]" (*MFB* 5) and willing to "spend hours on the floor in his room, or [her] room, playing with" (*MFB* 9) his younger sister. With both parents working, it is Donna,

[60] The novel is hereafter cited as *MFB*.

who, portrayed as having feminine, i.e. maternal, qualities and enjoying dressing up, becomes a substitute parent for Missy.

Malan's realist novel is the most overtly didactic one in the set of books including a homosexual character. In order to get its message of an inclusive and diverse society across, the story explicitly voices and reacts to persisting stereotypes of same-sex practising people, simultaneously trying to instill tolerance in the reader. The narrator is deliberately constructed as being very young, innocent, naïve, outspoken, and female, thus allowing the author to address more delicate topics, such as violent attacks against homosexuals in contemporary South Africa. Employing a homodiegetic narrator that is much younger than the protagonist allows the author to excuse potentially inappropriate straightforward questions, comments, or observations of the narrator with her age. Due to her young age, her inexperience and innocence – children at that age are not considered to have a social filter yet, i.e. an understanding of what should and should not be asked in certain situations – Missy can ask those delicate questions which children in their teens no longer dare to ask out of shame. "Donna, what's a 'moffie' and are you one?" is the opening line of chapter nine (*MFB* 27). Though a bit surprised about where such a question suddenly comes from, Donna answers, "yes, I am a moffie…" (*MFB* 28). This immediately prompts Missy's next question: "So do moffies stick their penises in other people's arses?" (*MFB* 28). In her analysis of Nokuthula Mazibuko's *In the Fast Lane* (2007), Grünkemeier showed that the use of a narrator that "does not speak from a supposedly superior position" or "moralis[e] or ridicule characters" (201) helps to get the novel's message across. If there is judgement, it is not passed from an authoritative position but from within the set of characters. Like in Mazibuko's *In the Fast Lane* (2007), the characters in *My "Funny" Brother* (2012) "are given space to inform themselves in order to recognize and reflect on their own assumptions" (Grünkemeier 201–202), as are the readers. The book is addressed to teenagers only and does not contain "paratextual signs for adults", as *A Story of Hope!* (2006) by Gavin and Val Kruger does, for instance (Grünkemeier 202).

Of course, this does not make Missy's question any less upfront and even the nonchalant Donna is startled by his sister's 'innocent' straightforwardness (cf. *MFB* 28). He nevertheless does go on to explain the difference between "vaginal sex" and "anal sex" and the difference between same-sex practices and sexual encounters between heterosexuals quite explicitly, yet with the fewest "graphic details" he can in order not to make Missy feel embarrassed (*MFB* 31). The reader only gets little hints at Donna's early phase of identity formation as a gay person. At a later point in the story, Donna confides that "[i]t was so painful" (*MFB* 48), but "[b]ecause [he] went through all this […] [he] reckon[s] that's why now [he] ha[s]n't got any hassles about who [he] is and what [he] is" (*MFB* 50). Donna's coping mechanism with other people's prejudices and scorn has been and still is humour. His older brother initially mistakes this attitude for thoughtlessness, however, Donna is very much aware that his family is also affected by him being gay, with him consequently changing, for instance, his "girlie" walk into a more masculine one (*MFB* 38). In contrast to *This Book Betrays My Brother* (2012), where Ole's family is mentioned only once in passing (cf. *BBB* 103), *My "Funny" Brother* (2012) addresses the effects that a homosexual family member has on his siblings and parents. Donna knows he is lucky to have a "Supportive Family" (cf. *MFB* 50). His father had fought with "his brothers and the old people" (*MFB* 50) about Donna, and both Missy and Reginald are repeatedly teased about Donna in school (cf. *MFB* 25–26, 37). Beyond the family circle, Donna encounters two worlds. One in which he is supported by both his fellow students "down to the little Grade 8s" and "most of the Staff" in his campaign to become Chairperson of the Students' Representative Council, and another in which he is denied the position "[f]or the sake of the school" as "it may be … um, a little early, to have someone … um, like you, as Chairperson of the SRC", the vice-principal tries to explain (*MFB* 67, 70).

After his matric, Donna encounters this second, homophobic world more often. However, when he and his boyfriend, Zadie, are insulted as moffies and faggots because they behave like a normal couple in public, Donna is proactive in that he makes the newspapers report about the incidents (cf. *MFB* 82–83). His aims are, however, not achieved as the tone of the article is "unctuous, and patronizing, and condescending", and thus counterproductive in establishing a culture of acceptance (*MFB* 84). A little later, Donna becomes the victim of a "queer bashing" (*MFB* 97) in which he is so gravely injured that he has to be in a wheelchair thereafter. Almost the entire second half of the novel is dedicated to Donna's recovery and him and his family coming to terms with his new condition, as well as with the "legal battle" (*MFB* 137) that ensues. This second part of the novel is written in fast motion, covering several years within a few pages. This technique allows Malan to conclude the book on a hopeful note: Eventually, Donna learns to walk again and three of his four attackers are found guilty. The last words of the novel are a reference to Pavlov's famous experiment with dogs: "PS. About the white mice … 'Conditioned.' That's the word. […] You make people behave in a particular way by presenting them with the same set of factors over and over again. In the end, they don't think for themselves at all. Not cool" (*MFB* 161). In these final sentences, the narrator points to the constructedness of conventional gender stereotypes and social norms. The endless repetition of these "factors" has a numbing effect on people, as they will lose or might have already lost their ability to think critically. Missy's "PS." to the novel is thus more than her conclusion of the previous events. With these last words, she raises a moral pointing finger asking the readers not to fall into the same trap, to reflect upon their own conceptions of others and society, and to opt for open-mindedness (cf. Inggs 2016, 80). Setting these last words off in an individual chapter further supports the final message and the conclusion that in *My "Funny" Brother* the didactic intention of the novel is very apparent for the reader.

Kasigo Lesego Molope, *This Book Betrays My Brother* (2012)

In 2014, Molope was awarded the Percy Fitzpatrick Prize for Youth Literature for *This Book Betrays My Brother.*[61] Her celebrated debut, *Dancing in the Dust* (2004), was the first novel by a black South African to be included in the 2006 list of outstanding books of the International Board on Books for Young People (IBBY). The novel has been translated into isiZulu and isiXhosa and is part of the recommended reading list of South African high schools, as is her second youth novel, *The Mending Season* (2005), the latter having also been translated into German (*Im Schatten des Zitronenbaums* 2009). Molope writes "stories [she] would have liked to have read when [she] was younger – coming of age stories about being young, African and female" ("Kagiso Lesego Molope"). In her most recent publication, *This Book Betrays My Brother* (2012), she includes a homosexual female side-character, Ole, short for Olebogeng. Ole's sexual orientation makes her one of the most prominent and remarkable characters in this novel, also because *This Book Betrays My Brother* (2012) was the first novel to include a young black lesbian within the examined timeframe 2000–2013. The fate of the side-character is usually meant to be quickly forgotten, as these figures are not intended to draw attention to themselves, with the actual plot being linked to the protagonist. However, in letting Naledi, the narrator of the novel, tell the story from an I–as–witness perspective, which puts the immediate focus of attention away from the narrating–I to the actions observed, the side-character can move into the centre of attention.

Ole is attracted to Moipone, who is the most beautiful girl in the township and the girlfriend of the aspiring and loved–by–all brother of the narrator. Ole becomes a decisive element in the story when Basi, Naledi's brother, Naledi herself, and their mother drive by Ole, who "wasn't just having a cigarette with a couple of boys – although that would have been scandalous and reproachful enough for Mama. She was smoking a cigarette in one hand, while her other arm rested comfortably around Moipone" (*BBB* 100). The narrator "knew from far away, from the second [she] had turned to see if it actually was Ole, [she] kn[e]w that this wasn't just like [her] putting [her] arm around Limakatso or Kelelo's waist" (*BBB* 101); and so did Basi, Moipone's boyfriend, who "hurriedly climbed out of the car" and "pulled Moipone away so abruptly [...] barely acknowledging Ole" (*BBB* 100). For Basi, Ole's affection for Moipone, although unrequited, is a threat (cf. *BBB* 129). Harsh responses to her actions and behaviour are not unfamiliar to Ole. Her being attracted to girls, or "cherries" (*BBB* 103) as they are called in the novel, instead of boys, and her acting like a boy had repeatedly led to fights during her childhood (cf. *BBB* 103). Her behaving "like a big brother" (*BBB* 113) confused people and they "didn't know how to talk about Ole. They called her a boy all the time. Those who didn't know her, with a little malice in their voices,

[61] The novel is hereafter cited as *BBB*.

would call her 'Transie'. 'Why does she want to be a boy?' they'd ask" (*BBB* 113). According to Ruth Morgan, Charl Marais, and Joy Rosemary Wellbeloved's glossary to their essay collection, *TRANS: Transgender Life Stories in South Africa*, "transie/trassie" is an "Afrikaans derogatory slang, similar to thc isiZulu term 'isitabane', meaning 'hermaphrodite' (see intersex)" (7). In the glossary the term is linked to "intersex", which means people "born with scx organs that are not clearly female or male" (Morgan, Marais, and Wellbeloved 6). Calling Ole a "transie" due to her boyish behaviour thus shows the lack of proper information of her surroundings as people are clearly unfamiliar with precise definitions of intersex or of transgender, the latter term identifying "[t]ransgender people [as] hav[ing] a very intense experience of their gender being different to that assigned at birth" (Morgan, Marais, and Wellbeloved 7). In the novel, there is no incident that would allude to Ole being transgender. Over time, Ole manages to grind out a place within her community; her "social standing seemed to have changed" (*BBB* 103) profoundly, the narrator observes. During the narrator and Ole's childhood, "there had been a fair bit of teasing, but now the boys seemed to waver between ignoring her, teasing her, and sometimes having a cigarette with her. What they never did was whistle and make comments about how pretty she was" (*BBB* 103). Interestingly, the narrator feels more comfortable and secure being with Ole instead of "just another girl" (*BBB* 103) when she walks along the street and receives compliments from young males. The respect Ole meanwhile gets from her male peers, "greeting her like she was one of them" (*BBB* 103), also protects her female company. Soon, however, it turns out that Ole's standing is restricted to a very small social realm, as she appears to be accepted only by people who have known her for a long time. When she walks by some guys who she has never seen before "one of them sa[ys], 'Eish, this one just needs to be raped. That will fix her'" (*BBB* 161). This comment makes Naledi realize "for a moment, and perhaps for the very first time, how terrifying it must be to be her, walking around Kasi every day [...] with the knowledge of unidentified bodies and [...] hearing people's contempt for her spoken out loud" (*BBB* 162). Given the narrative situation, the reader only gets minimal insight into the feelings and past of Ole. At one point she confides that "[y]ou don't know the things that have happened to me" (*BBB* 163), alluding to more abuse than the narrator could have witnessed and hence known and told about in the story.

It is most likely that it is her own history of violent encounters and the feeling of being misunderstood by her contemporaries that makes Ole the only person in the village to believe Moipone's story of having been raped by Basi, the narrator's brother. She is also the only one trying to help Moipone in the aftermath of the incident. The narrator knows that Moipone's claims are true. Naledi, who is also called Nedi in the book, witnessed how Basi raped Moipone, yet she does not tell anyone (cf. *BBB* 133–136). The reader, only having access to Naledi's observations, is left to speculate about Basi's reasons for committing such a crime. Utterly confused about what she has seen, Naledi tries to reason after the incident that "[e]veryone makes mistakes – […] It was only one time. Probably a misunderstanding. I'm sure … I'm sure he's very sorry because … That's not who he is, the type of person who would do that. I'm sure it's not what he meant … A mistake …" (*BBB* 164). Up until then, Basi had been his village's rising star, loved and respected by everyone – and apparently of greater value to his parents than his sister (cf. close reading in chapter 2.3). In the aftermath of being excluded from a game due to his skin colour, Basi had left the rugby team, in which he had been the only black member (cf. *BBB* 114, 116–118). With his retreat, his dreams of becoming the first "Black guy on the national team" were destroyed, but his friends and family were convinced that he was still bound for "greatness" (cf. *BBB* 118). After Moipone reports the rape, no one in the community except for Ole believes that Basi could do something like that to a girl: "'Not Basi' became the theme in subsequent weeks. 'Not our Bafana'" (*BBB* 139). A woman yells at Moipone "'You should feel lucky! Raped by Basimane? You should have said thank you'" (*BBB* 164). The love that people had felt for Moipone before the rape had gone with the incident: "no one gets more love than Basi" (*BBB* 164). When no one tries to speak up for Moipone, it is Ole who approaches Nedi to tell the truth about the incident. When her parents find out that Naledi knows more about the rape and has told Ole about it, they respond with anger and let Naledi know that she has shamed the family with her behaviour. The police officer also does not want to pursue the incident further and criticizes Naledi for her actions: "[I]t's a tough world for a Black man. He only has his family to count on" (*BBB* 167). Even years after the incident, people are "still shocked at what some women will do to one of our own men" (*BBB* 174). Ole's life, however, has turned out well, as the reader learns at the end of the story. In a brief look at the future, Nedi informs her readers that grown-up Ole teaches Political Science at Wits University. Moipone's reputation, by contrast, is never restored, the truth never publically acknowledged. Like Thando Mgqolozana in *A Man Who Is Not a Man*, Kagiso Lesego Molope draws on an animal metaphor to illustrate the codes of conduct of the social realm portrayed in the novel: Girls "move like impalas among hunting lions. Moipone knows it, so does Ole and so do I" (*BBB* 184).

Molope's play with the narrative voice and with the knowledge of the reader and the characters makes this novel not only a compelling read but a confession about social constraints and the careful maintenance of rules of conduct. Molope weaves contemporary South African gender stereotypes into the story without making them appear authoritative, repetitive, or shallow. The gender rhetoric Molope uses is particularly noteworthy and will be further discussed in the upcoming chapter on young females and their lives (cf. chapter 2.2.3).

Résumé

Before closing this subchapter, I would like to briefly point once again to the narrative perspective Malan, Molope, and Duiker choose in their books as these are particularly relevant regarding the intended audience of the novels. Since the majority of novels use a homodiegetic narrator through whom the gay character's development and actions are mediated instead of letting these characters tell their story themselves, *This Book Betrays My Brother*, and *My "Funny" Brother* are arguably intended for a heterosexual rather than a LGBT audience. In these novels, the coming–of–age and coming-out problems homosexual characters have because of their sexual orientation are mediated by heterosexual narrators, not by the homosexual characters themselves. Although *No Problem, Man!* employs an omniscient narrator to tell the story, this novel gets closest in the representation of a coming-out as Rashaad's discussions about his sexual orientation with other characters are mostly presented in direct speech. Whilst Molope's homodiegetic narrator recalls from her own memory the problems her homosexual friend, Ole, encountered while growing up due to her different sexual attraction and presents them in the third person (cf. *BBB* 103), Malan's heterodiegetic narrator gives much more space to direct speech acts, allowing Rashaad to state in the first-person that he does not know whether he is gay or not (cf. *NPM* 9). In *No Problem, Man!* the reader can subsequently follow the processes of Rashaad's homosexual identity formation more closely as these are transmitted from the character's own perspective. In *This Book Betrays My Brother* much fewer examples of direct speech acts by Ole can be found. In the few instances in which the narrator does quote her directly, though, Ole's utterances contain significant messages that hint at the complexity of her character and her difficulties in developing an individual identity, leaving the reader much room for thought. Analysing the novels' focalization shows that although the novels by Malan and Molope are progressive concerning the fact that they include homosexual characters in their texts, some of them remain conservative with respect to (not) giving a voice to the gay characters themselves. Not until August 2014 did South African publisher Cover2Cover publish Sonwabiso Ngcowa's *In Search for Happiness*,[62] the first novel published in South Africa to include a female lesbian main character and to be openly "dedicated to all young people who feel and know that they are lesbian, gay, bisexual, transsexual or intersex" (*ISH*, dedication). A year earlier Harmony Ink Press had published Suzanne van Rooyen's *The Other Me* (2013) in the United States, which is the first text to discuss a South African girl discovering her transsexual identity. Charmaine Kendal's *Miscast* (2015) is the first novel to focus on transgender published in South Africa (cf. Inggs 2016, 80–81). At this point it goes almost without saying that it is even more difficult to find fictional representations of transsexuality in South Africa's literature for young people,

[62] The novel is hereafter cited as *ISH*.

although once again the country's legislation is also quite progressive in this area. In 2003, "The Alteration of Sex Description and Sex Status Act" granted trans people the right to "change their identity number and bring it in line with their chosen gender", also "without having [had] genital surgery" (Morgan, Marais, Wellbeloved 9). The publication of Ngcowa's, van Rooyen's and Kendal's novels is significant and a necessary step towards instigating change in South Africa's attitude towards and acceptance of same-sex practising and transgender people.

2.3 Young Females and their Lives

At the beginning of this last subchapter on issues of gender in contemporary South Africa I would like to point to what Helen Moffet has called the "atrocious civil war between the genders" (Moffett 2006b) that continues to be waged in South Africa and beyond. Only in November 2014, we were once again reminded of the topicality of the issue in a meeting of the Ministry of Women in the Presidency in South Africa. When asked to comment on the current situation of women in the country,

> Mpumalanga Chief Moses Mahlangu […] announced to the crowd that women must be submissive to their husbands. Princess Dineo, from the Northwest Province, then stood up to tell us that feminism is un-African and encouraged the Minister to cut all funds for centers for abused women and children, as they should be dealing with these issues at home. Both speakers received nods from the Minister on the dais and applause from the audience. Others followed decrying women's abuse of men and women's aggression as the biggest challenges. (Thorpe)

Because of such "destructive discourse" being presented in a public meeting of the Ministry of Women, Thorpe is highly "concerned that the language used and the sentiments expressed in the meeting are an indication that a more conservative and frankly oppressive understanding and approach to women and social rights has emerged" and that this understanding is "supported if not promoted by State agenda" (2014). Such a development would gradually undo much of the progress made in the years after apartheid, indeed bringing "patriarchy […] back to the mainstream" (Thorpe; cf. Walker).

One of the difficulties that women's emancipation has faced in South Africa is its lack of achieving unity amongst all South African women. Sociologist Jacklyn Cock points out that since the early years after the democratic revolution, "[o]ne of the contradictions in this society [has been] that feminism is a discredited term and the people who claim the label – who call themselves feminists – tend to be white, middle-class women who are often leading very spoiled and affluent lives, supported by husbands and fathers and dependent on the labor of a domestic worker" (quoted in Romero 168). On the other hand, there is an "increasingly large category of black working class women – township women – who are leading lives quite independently of men[, w]ho are often quite contentious and rejecting of men: not in the sense of being lesbian but [they consider] men [...] irresponsible" (Cock quoted in Romero 168). Nevertheless, these women "refused participation in feminist movements because [...] [t]hey were convinced that virulent expressions of these sentiments intensify sexism" instead of achieving gender justice (bell hooks 267–268). Instead of the term "feminism", which is considered a Western model that is "not specific to our needs and situation and one [that] cannot [be] imported" easily, the preferred label has thus been "women's emancipation" in South Africa since the 1920s (cf. Cock quoted in Romero 169).

Since the beginnings of the new South Africa, the feminist agenda has been misused "to extend privileges [...] to the already privileged [i.e. for] making more room at the top for women in the professions, in the academic community", Cock further argues (quoted in Romero 169). This can be seen, for instance, in the fact that the number of female representatives in parliament has risen to 45% (cf. "Gender Statistics" vi). Recent data shows that almost twenty years after the end of apartheid, Cock's words from 1998 hold true: "it is that interconnection of class, race, and gender that has made [and continues to make] the situation so difficult for black, working-class women in South Africa" (Cock quoted in Romero 169). Till today, black, working-class women who live in rural areas are most disadvantaged (cf. "Gender Statistics" 30, 31, 41). Despite a progressive constitution, data from 2005 thus confirms that "progress has been much slower" on the ground than on paper (Morrell 2005, 273). Another nine years later, in 2014, there still appears to be only minimal progress regarding gender and social equality, as the utterances made at the public meeting of the Ministry of Women in November of that year confirm (cf. Thorpe). According to Cock and Romero, a "'democratic feminism,' which should be anchored in the needs and experiences of a majority of the women who are rural and poor" can only "emerge among a wider core of South African women when issues such as crime, violence, education, jobs, housing, and even basic needs such as running water and electricity have been resolved" (Cock quoted in Romero 169; Romero 30). Morrell moreover underlines the necessity of men contributing to gender transformation in South Africa, especially since inequality amongst South African males with different ethnic backgrounds is also a continuing issue (cf. 2005, 273; cf. chapter 3).

The issues that young female South Africans face today have found their ways into contemporary realist fiction. That the representation of topics such as teenage pregnancy, sexual abuse, the worthiness of females as opposed to men, or romantic love has not always been an easy task for authors of young adult fiction is underlined by Pennell's notion that "profeminist fictions, which make the feminine subject visible and reformulate feminine gender schemata, founder in their attempts to represent ameliorative engendering intersubjective experience"

(Pennell 56). Instead of developing new discursive patterns and narrative strategies that would redeem the classical power discourse between masculinity and femininity, "[t]hese narratives often remain tied to patriarchal coherences and closures which privilege the character who 'wins' or is triumphant and who, thereby, accrues symbolic and actual power" (Pennell 56). Pennell also found that "profeminist fiction which [does] regender – reformulate gender schemas – within patriarchal metanarratives [...] [is] often complicit in the maintenance of gender binarism and misandric in [its] resignification of the characteristics of masculine subjects" (56). One of the deficiencies of these narratives lies in their "demonizing of masculine subjectivities" in order to achieve visibility and empowerment for female characters (Pennell 56). In order to break out of the loop of gender binarism, the constructedness rather than the naturalness of the binary must thus be put at the centre of those narratives, Pennell argues (cf. 56). In a recent keynote lecture at the international conference on "Canon Constitution and Canon Change in Children's Literature" in Tübingen, Germany, Kimberley Reynolds observed that "for social change to be promoted one needs socially conscious novels. Novels that champion equal rights for girls and women, present the 'other' positively, and uphold the rights of minorities" (2014).

Sexuality has arguably become the most pressing topic in contemporary young adult novels that feature female main characters, despite the comparatively low number of "just over twenty" out of "more than two hundred English-language young adult novels published from 1989 to 2015 in South Africa" focusing on it (Inggs 2016, 65).[63] Vivian Yenika-Agbaw remarked in 2008 that this "is a delicate topic that must be approached with care lest we send the wrong message to our children, especially adolescent females" (56). The notion that authors need to be particularly careful regarding how to address sexuality with adolescent females is strongly felt in South African fictions. In this respect the country's authors follow a more general African trend when they "discuss danger and disease, pregnancy and rape and what to do to protect oneself from these things" rather than the pleasure of sexuality or romantic love (Sheffer quoted in Yenika-Agbaw 56). According to Yenika-Agbaw, the lack of treatment of romantic love stems from the fact that "in general [it] is not considered an important subject in African children's literature" (56) given that "traditional African culture does not encourage high school teenagers to have girlfriends or boyfriends, and it frowns on the dating among them" (Osa xxvi). In today's Nigerian fictions for teenagers, for instance, Virginia Dike found that although some authors have tried to address the topic of romantic love, "there is very little that is romantic about these novels" as they "describe dismal relationships characterized by infidelity, exploitation, and self-centeredness" (11).

[63] Other topics are, for instance, friendship, material desires, the significance of education, and patriarchal family structures.

South Africa's literary texts also predominantly focus on the negative aspects of teenage sexuality. In her article "Transgressing Boundaries? Romance, Power and Sexuality in Contemporary South African English Young Adult Literature", Judith Inggs examined publications from between 1989 and 2006. She found that

> adolescent sexuality, and even teenage romance, remain[ed] relatively unexplored in South African young adult fiction, and works that do depict sexual relationships generally do so in the guise of a didactic message that ultimately warns the reader of the potential danger of engaging in any form of sexual activity. (Inggs 2009, 101)

A first overview of the novels that comprise the corpus for this thesis, i.e. publications from between 2000 and 2013, leads to a similar conclusion. Women are for the most part portrayed as the weaker gender and shown as becoming victims of (sexual) assault or abuse more frequently than their male contemporaries. Young males are shown to experience violent abuse when their sexual orientation differs from the heterosexual norm. Furthermore, none of the female characters is depicted as taking pleasure in a sexual encounter, whilst men are repeatedly explained as having a natural right to the act. "[D]enying the characters any truly positive experience of their newfound sexuality" Inggs perceives as "potentially destructive as writers have largely failed to assist adolescent readers in understanding and adapting to their emerging sexuality in contemporary society" (Inggs 2016, 66). In books like *Young Blood*, *This Book Betrays My Brother*, or Kopano Matlwa's *Coconut* (2007)[64] it is predominantly older female characters who explain the subversive and potentially violent nature of heterosexual relationships in terms of irrevocable proclivities of the male and the female. In *Coconut*, for instance, Ofilwe's father repeatedly has sex with other women than his wife. When the protagonist's mother confides in her mother that she wants to leave her husband because of his betrayals, Ofilwe overhears her grandmother talking insistently to her daughter: This is how men are. She, Ofilwe's mother, will be "nothing" if she leaves her husband (*C* 13). The grandmother advises her daughter to "stop acting like a spoilt child" because her husband "is a man and [...] men do these things with other women" (*C* 12). Instead, Ofilwe's mother should realize that financial security and living in a safe area are more significant in life than romantic love (cf. *C* 12–13). Inggs shows that Phalime depicts a similar discourse in *Second Chances* (2013) (cf. Inggs 2016, 75). In Molope's *This Book Betrays My Brother* the privilege and naturalness of male proclivities becomes the central issue of the novel. In the book, older women and community members are shown to repeatedly reinforce this privilege when they declare that it is the fault of women when they are assaulted sexually as it is they who must have led the male on, not the other way around (cf. *BBB* 172). These older women and female friends of the protagonist, Nedi, reason that the male only follows his instincts, for which he cannot be held accountable: "Men

[64] The book is hereafter cited as *C*.

have different needs… It's natural. All men have those needs" (*BBB* 171). In both texts, the women's comments are not countered by contrary attitudes towards gender roles. In fact, the older women are portrayed as effectively silencing everyone who is trying to speak out against or trying to escape the realm of male privilege (cf. *BBB* 172). In *Coconut*, Ofilwe's mother does not leave her husband for fear of social decline. In *This Book Betrays My Brother*, Nedi becomes known as "the girl who betrayed her brother" (*BBB* 183) and shamed her entire family when she had admitted to Ole, who is not a family member, that she had witnessed the rape of Moipone. Moipone herself is met with public scorn and ostracism after reporting the incident to the police. At the end of *This Book Betrays My Brother*, Moipone's reputation is still not restored; even years later, "everyone said that she was a tainted liar" (*BBB* 184). Hence, both novels depict female characters that are either privately or publicly punished for complaining about the infidelity of their husband or for reporting their sexual abuse, respectively. Moreover, a simple romantic love is not portrayed in any of the novels in the corpus.

However, these and other fictions also deconstruct the male right to sexual encounters. Interestingly, in all of them it is younger women who speak out against the male privilege. This adds a further dimension to the discussion of an ongoing "civil war between the genders" (Moffett 2006b), namely that of a generational conflict. Young female characters like Goane in *Praise Song* (2006) by Jenny Robson, Mokgethi in *Untitled: A Novel* (2013) by Kgbetli Moele, Fikile in *Coconut*, and eventually also Nedi in *This Book Betrays My Brother* are examples of characters who promote a new self-esteem for South African women and achieve a certain degree of empowerment in the course of the novels. Contrary to the publications that Inggs examined in her article, today's fictions make the "[s]ilence in South African society" regarding the "discourse of sexuality which stigmatizes open discussion and silences voices which may otherwise transgress society's boundaries" the topic of their narratives (2009, 102). Evidently, today, authors are no longer "too cautious, or too wary of exploring territory that is so contested and so prone to transgressing society's multifaceted boundaries", as they were up to the mid-2000s (Inggs 2009, 112). This also means that South African authors have finally begun to use "the writing of adolescent literature as, in Trites's terms, an 'ideological tool […] to curb teenagers' libido'" and to decode the "strong link between sexuality and empowerment" (Inggs 2009, 112, 102).

Kagiso Lesego Molope, *This Book Betrays My Brother* (2012)

In *This Book Betrays My Brother*, witnessing her brother rape his girlfriend destroys Nedi's initially romantic perception of relationships between men and women. After the event, her

> interest in boys and relationships had gone from exciting to … well, confusing, at best. For years before going to varsity I avoided boys. I started wearing jeans and

> put away the short skirts and the sexy blouses. I started thinking really seriously about never kissing another boy, just in case we had a … "misunderstanding". You know, just in case we were not on the same page about things. Because I reckoned that if something did happen, I may not be in a good position to warrant support. (*BBB* 183)

After the incident, Nedi is torn between familial loyalty and fear of her brother. What prohibits Nedi from overcoming her trauma afterwards is that her family does not allow her to ever mention the matter to anyone and that Basi, too, never again mentions Moipone. Nedi realizes that because her brother is that "special" boy to everyone he can "pick and choose between what matters and what doesn't and sometimes, what's real and what isn't" (*BBB* 183). Consequently, "he has chosen to tuck away that chapter of his life in some safe, dark place and has [since] refused to visit it" (*ibid.*). She, however, cannot forget what has happened. When the narrator is eventually able to trap her brother in a situation where she can address the topic again many years later, Basi responds:

> 'Nedi, it was so long ago! I was young… You don't understand.' 'Tell me what I don't understand.' Basi stared at the ground for a very long time. When he finally looked up he said, 'It just… It got out of hand. It wasn't…' He bit his lip and blinked a few times. 'You're not taught to read women's minds. You're taught that they want whatever you want. […] I would never, never … even as a young man … She was my girlfriend and … She knew … she exp-' (*BBB* 179–180)

In contrast to other novels that thematize rape, Molope includes the rapist's voice in this short excerpt of the novel and gives insight into the male's perception of the situation in hindsight. Basi, raised in the consciousness that women "want whatever you want" (*BBB* 179) and that girlfriends "exp[ect]" their boyfriends to perform their masculinity (*BBB* 180), believes he has acted according to the codes of conduct he held to be true. Yet, he apparently did realize then that the situation had "gotten out of hand". However, he did not mean to assault her. His confession of his own confusion about the incident is the best that Nedi can get from her brother in this situation. Nedi herself has been in turmoil since the incident and is frustrated and in conflict with the fact that the incident itself has not influenced Basi's coming–of–age to the extent that it changed her and Moipone's development as young females. For one, this is due to the fact that their "parents 'made it all go away'" by sending Basi to a private school for boys in Cape Town and by "pretending that nothing had happened" (*BBB* 181). More importantly, however,

> Basi is a man […] but he is also more than that. He's the boy – the much-loved and adored boy – with luck and looks and brains. He manages to fend off misfortune (and his won struggles are, of course, not minor) with the ease of wiping dust off a shiny shoe. In many ways, as much as possible, he will always be cocooned in the loyalty of his parents, his friends and the women who love him, whatever he does.

> [...] I also know that my mother and his friends see him as infinitely faultless. Who hasn't heard of my brother or someone like him? (*BBB* 184–185)

The belief in the faultlessness of the beloved son and the parental tendency to protect and defend their male offspring against anything that is brought against them are what bring about Basi's easy way out of his situation. Nedi is aware of her being of lesser value to her parents in this respect, but her brother also knows of his prime position in the family. Similar notions are also depicted in Malan's *My "Funny" Brother* (cf. close reading of the novel). In *This Book Betrays My Brother*, Basi "can go anywhere he wants to go, be whoever he wants to be [...] He can be the *president*, if he wants to be" despite his actions (*BBB* 185). "You know [that]'s right" (*BBB* 185) are the words that follow and are also the last words in the novel. With this final address to the reader, Molope deliberately points beyond the book's pages, thus breaking the barrier between fiction and reality. *This Book Betrays My Brother* becomes a critique of contemporary social realities but also of politics in South Africa. It is no secret that current president Jacob Zuma was accused, tried, and found not guilty of the charge of rape in a controversial trial in the mid-2000s. The head of state's demeanour in the trial was found to be more than unfortunate. But also current statistics of gender violence and the many unreported cases of sexual assault show that the issue remains a highly topical one. Molope's novel illustrates a rape case from the perspective of a female family member who not only witnessed the crime, but is forced by social constraints to remain silent thereafter. Although the narrator herself is not raped, she has "always sensed a connection to Moipone, a feeling that [they] belong in the same corner of the room" (*BBB* 183–184). In *This Book Betrays My Brother*, Molope expresses the delicate decision-making process of those who have experienced such situations and empathizes with them. Even though the narrator condemns these practices, she herself is unable to break the circle of silence. Although Nedi finds herself in a no-win situation at the end of the novel, the narrative is a step towards the deconstruction of established codes of conduct, silence, and male privilege.

Kgebetli Moele, *Untitled: A Novel* (2013)

A specific type of female character usually accompanies the discussion of rape in recent teenage fiction, namely that of the 'rare good girl', who is without exception described as astoundingly beautiful, intelligent, and not afraid to openly voice her wish to save her virginity for a special partner. Representations of this type of character are, for instance, Nedi in *This Book Betrays My Brother*, Nana in *Young Blood*, Mokgethi in *Untitled: A Novel*,[65] and Sannah in *Praise Song*. The young females express openly to both their female friends and/or male relationship

[65] The novel is hereafter cited as *U*.

partners that they are not yet ready to have sexual intercourse. In most of these novels the girls' wish carries notions of a confession of misdeed, weakness, or crime. The girls are accused of being prudish and being uptight. In *Untitled*, Mokgethi gives the reader an explanation why she favours staying a virgin over having sex:

> Because I have seen all the girls that I know lose themselves, thinking that they understand their lives but only understanding the surface. They all blur into one. Once a girl loses her innocence, it becomes "My man this … My man that." They start identifying themselves with their man and judging themselves through the eyes of the man. Then they start to fight and quarrel over what they think are the best men available. At the end of it all one is left with a fatherless child and the realization that you have wasted your time. Hating all men because they have failed to find the right, the best man for themselves. They are on welfare, looking at "My man this… My man that …" from a very different angle. But they cannot start over again. They are caught in the tide. (*U* 6)

As we have already seen in other novels, engaging in sexual intercourse is here depicted as bringing about a woman's ruin. However, *Untitled* takes the debate one step further. In the novel, the wish of Mokgethi to remain a virgin is not respected but is in fact shown to incite the males' interest even more, while her female friends denounce the protagonist as arrogant or uptight: "Girl, it's going to rot between your legs" (*U* 166) is only one example of a female reaction to the girl's wish to retain her virginity. The males subsequently strive to conquer this type of girl by complementing her or presenting gifts, and they are mostly shown to succeed. In the majority of cases, their success is, however, accompanied by physical or emotional violence, often resulting in a form of rape, like in Mokgethi's case in *Untitled*. Of the above examples of 'special' girls, only Nana in *Young Blood* consents freely to having sex with Sipho. Yenika-Agbaw's findings on Nigerian youth fiction also hold true for South African teenage novels, which "suggest that when African girls engage in sexual activity or are being prepared for it, they suffer from some form of trauma or distress, be it emotional, physical, or cultural" (58). Sex is moreover shown to have "nothing to do with romantic love or with pleasure" (Yenika-Agbaw 58). Consequently, sexuality is for the most part connected to the disempowerment of women in South African young adult fiction. The mere wish or intention to remain abstinent is, however, no solution to this problem, as the sexual act is often a forced encounter. How then can young females regain power over their lives in such violent environments?

As distinctive as Molope's, Moele's, Snyckers's, Robson's, or Mzobe's female characters are, they all share a will for self-empowerment despite adversary circumstances. This will for self-empowerment exercises itself both within and outside of the fictions' realms, with different results for both characters and readers. This means that although the female characters remain marked by their negative experiences and the novels end at best on a hopeful note given the circumstances, the deconstruction of the issue in the fictitious realm decodes the very real issue of female sexuality and violent abuse in South Africa in a highly realistic manner. The realist depiction of such coming–of–age stories is a profound step in the transition of the young adult genre in South Africa as these novels encourage their readers to reconstruct the difficult processes behind a person's empowerment.

Kgebetli Moele's *Untitled: A Novel* is a book full of firsts and thus obtains a special place in the contemporary South African canon. Hailed as one of the new young voices of South Africa, Moele received the Herman Charles Bosman Prize for English Fiction as well as the University of Johannesburg Prize for Creative Writing for his debut novel *Room 207* (2006). In 2010 he furthermore received the South African Literary Award for *The Book of the Dead* (2009). *Untitled* is his third novel, yet the first to discuss issues that concern young females and their lives in current South Africa. In his novel Moele depicts the social reality of seventeen-year-old Mokgethi from a poor, small rural place called Teyageneng in an uncompromising manner. Letting her narrate her story in the first person and in the format of a diary, Moele takes away the barrier that usually remains between reader and protagonist and confronts his readers "intimately and directly, often uncomfortably" (Rosenthal). This is the first time that a black female character, who is raped in the course of the novel, is depicted in the immediacy of the first-person voice by a male black author. The novel deconstructs and simultaneously reinvents the fictional representation of an issue that primarily concerns women in South Africa, namely rape. Moele's narrative is an answer to Irigaray's call to "represent women 'otherwise'", to deform "language and discursive structures" as "[l]inear reading is no longer possible" (Irigaray quoted in Wilkie-Stibbs 40). Moreover, Moele proves wrong Irigaray's thesis that women are the better authors when it comes to representing femininity in fiction. Irigaray believes that "if we [the women] don't invent a language, if we don't find our body's language, it will have too few gestures to accompany our stories [...] asleep again, unsatisfied, we shall fall back upon the words of men" (1985c, 124). Yet it is the words of a male that create the story of Mokgethi's journey in *Untitled.*

The story is told in a frantic, non-linear way, playing with conventions of genre, time, as well as layout. The cover of the book is coloured in a washed-out, faded blue and designed after a conventional school exercise book that has been frequently used. There is no blurb or any other text on the back cover, just some black spots from ink that was also used to write the title on the front cover. The font of the title mimics the handwriting of a young person. The text of the story itself is kept in regular font for the most part, with occasional sentences in italics for emphasis. The novel starts with the narrator's emotional response to her rape immediately after the event. The reader learns quickly that the event that has led Mokgethi to sit down and tell her story has shattered her very understanding of reality and herself. The reader experiences her confusion, her struggle to put it into words, and her loss of a sense of personality first hand and struggles in turn to try and make sense of this unconventional form of writing. "*I now pronounce myself deflowered*" (*U* 1; emphasis in the oiginal) are the words at the bottom of the first page. They are meant to become the final words of a poem Mokgethi intends to write. She explains: "Usually, expressing myself in a poem helps me to see a way forward, but now I am in difficulty" (*U* 1). For lack of words that could head the poem she calls it "Untitled" (*U* 5). She is in complete disarray, observing her transformation as if being outside of her own body and, moreover, speaking about herself in the third person. "Though physically this Mokgethi and that Mokgethi are one and the same, they will be very different in character. I do not know how much the character of the Mokgethi that I so loved being will remain with me after today. The difference between them is what scares me" (*U* 5). Before Part I of the novel begins she explains the purpose of her writing. She is "[t]rying to find a way for her to live comfortably with herself [as s]he will have to enjoy being this Mokgethi first, just as the murdered Mokgethi enjoyed being Mokgethi" (*U* 6). Although she has not used the word rape so far, her non-sequential and confused manner of writing as well as her wish to remain a virgin – which she utters in the conditional perfect, "she would have wished to remain Mokgethi the virgin" (*U* 6) – strongly point to the fact that her "deflowering" has not been a positive experience. She furthermore states that her former personality has been "murdered" (*U* 6) in an act she had long seen coming, realizing that she will now have to become somebody else. Yet, she is scared of that process. Part I follows this untitled and immediate beginning of the novel. This part is structured in individual non-sequential subchapters in which Mokgethi introduces the reader to those people whose actions influenced her earlier identity formation: absent parents and frustrated relatives, precocious girls and sugar daddies (cf. also Ros Haden's *Sugar Daddy* 2011, or Margie Orford's *Dancing Queen* 2004), as well as pedophiles. Part I ends with a sort of summary which is presented in the form of eight poems, one for each impressive character or situation she has experienced in her short life (cf. *U* 132–139). Thereafter, Part II is the exact to the minute protocol of the day on which Mokgethi was raped, Saturday, 7th of August. The worst thing for Mokgethi is that she "knew it all along, since [she] was eleven. Ever since that age [she] ha[s] been running, ducking, hiding and looking behind [her] to avoid this situation. It had to happen, yes, but [she] wanted it to happen after [she] turned twenty-one and never like this" (*U* 208). One must not misread *Untitled* as a young woman's cry for help, because Mokgethi has come to realize that no one would answer this cry:

> I know that there is no woman who can help me. Even if there is one, she will be between the men and if she even suggests any action, they will look at her with manly eyes because they are the ones doing this to us. Yes, this woman feels my pain because she has been me […]. How can I expect a man to come and help me if he is the one doing this to me? The people who lead us are these men, the people who write the law are these men, the people who administer justice are these men, and the people who police us are these men. (*U* 209)

In light of such adversity and socially inscribed gender relations many women before have lost their courage and succumbed to the given circumstances. Mokgethi decides not to be one of them. She "wipe[s] away [her] tears because [she] ha[s] just discovered that this is a very old, very big subjugation. And though we pretend to breathe, we are not breathing" (*U* 209). She draws on the struggle that South Africa has been through, concluding that "this struggle has not changed its face. This struggle's face is the same as it ever was because it lacks a woman to lead it" (*U* 209). This observation leads Mokgethi to end her story with a promise: "However, now I am taking centre stage and after I die no woman will ever suffer as I have" (*U* 209). She has come to realize that what she perceived to be the end of her "cannot be a conclusion; it is and can only be an introduction to another life…" (*U* 209). "*I pronounce myself deflowered*" (*U* 210; emphasis in the original) subsequently heads the final page of the novel, symbolizing the narrator entering a new phase in her life.

In her book review in the *Mail and Guardian*, Jane Rosenthal recommended that this book should be read

> at schools, in youth groups and, perhaps best of all, in private, by young girls like Mokgethi; and by young men like her friends James and Mamafa – but most especially by teachers, parents and whoever else has contact with those whose brains have "completely decayed". However unused to or inept they may be at reading fiction, some beneficial residue of understanding and compassion may remain. (2014)

With her clear recommendation that this book be read in educational frameworks as well as in private, by both boys and girls and above all adults, Rosenthal speaks in favour of the direct message of the novel. In light of the novel's graphic content and explicit language, its plain accusation of parents of being hypocrites, and the denunciation of the decayed minds of authority figures, as well as its open discussion of poor character judgement and materialism of young females, one cannot necessarily attribute a subtle tone to the novel. Yet, due to Moele's different style of writing, which is "difficult to endure [contentwise] but fluent and easy to read" (Rosenthal), this didacticism does not come across as condescending or disempowering. *Untitled* is a sweeping blow at both older and younger generations, men and women alike. The novel holds every character accountable for the present situation and leaves it in the hands of them all to achieve change.

Another reason why *Untitled* is such a valuable contribution to the contemporary canon is that it reworks both gendered violence and materialism from a female perspective. *Untitled* can thus be seen as a form of antithesis to Mzobe's *Young Blood*, the novel examined in the previous section on machoism and masculinities. In Moele's novel, cars are also a marker of South African masculinities. Only males are portrayed as owning cars and again the female characters are shown to be more attracted to car owners (cf. *U* 161). Evidently, the disposition to materialism has never been exclusive to men. In the new South Africa, clothes, smartphones, and other material objects have become a significant marker of female identity formation, as well. Interestingly, *Untitled*, but also other novels like Ros Haden's *Sugar Daddy*, Maria Phalime's *Second Chances*, Kagiso Lesego Molope's *This Book Betrays My Brother*, or Sello Mahapeletsa's *When Lions Smile* (2003) and *Tears of an Angel* (2007) (cf. Inggs 2016: 73–75), shows that the material objects that younger women desire are bought for them by "their" men since they cannot afford them themselves (cf. *U* 145, 151). The difference between *Young Blood* and *Untitled* is that the latter deconstructs the supposed tendency of "poor, young girls [to] target well-off men" (*U* 100–101), while *Young Blood*, due to its focalization, is an uncritical reflection of the unspoken code that men are granted sexual favours in return for paying women's expenses in the form of money for mobile phones, chocolate bars, or cool drinks. "The truth is that [...] [men] use money as bait" (*U* 101), Mokgethi declares, and no one in the community is speaking out against their actions:

> They [i.e. the members of the community] know what [they are] doing to us, all the young girls, but they still speak to [them] [...] They never tell [them] that they know to [their] face and make [them] shameful for [their] acts. And yet they, this community, made Mokgethi shameful for things that I had not even done. (*U* 88–89)

The reason why young girls are always automatically accused of misconduct by the community is because they are "just" young girls (*U* 87). But even if these young girls provoked males, Mokgethi argues, the men, who are almost always older than the girls, "should have reprimanded and punished [them] for doing what [they] did" (*U* 87) and not react to the provocation. Mokgethi's tale is convincing because she lets the reader see that she, the homodiegetic narrator, is not immune to her social surroundings or the bait of money and so she too is shown to almost fall prey to all the talk about sex and her bodily instincts, to stay in the animal metaphor (cf. *U* 44, 181). In these moments, she starts believing that she might miss out on something, yet so far she has always been lucky to be in the company of her good friend Mamafa, who has not taken advantage of her although she played with his desire. How dangerous it is for a girl to live in her community Mokgethi illustrates with the following statement: "I don't like to be found anywhere after eighteen hundred without [my two friends, James and Mamafa], as after that I do not trust anyone else. Even my girlfriends will sell me. They have been trying to set me up with whoever [...] since forever" (*U* 41). During the day, Mokgethi also appears to play the game of the streets and slips into the role of the pimp of her female friends, advertising them to the interested male passers-by, as is shown in Part II of the novel (cf. *U* 156–158; 168–171).

What eventually leads to Mokgethi's apparently unavoidable rape is only one unconsidered action. She gets into the car of a male friend, Thabakgolo. Her previously displayed eloquence and cautiousness are lost in the situation. With her taking a seat in his car, Mokgethi is entering his sphere of power, where she no longer has a say. Consequently, Thabakgolo does not consider her objections to the following rape to be meant seriously (cf. *U* 190–197): "Just come inside for a bit, Mokgethi. There is no harm in coming inside for a bit" (*U* 194), Thabakgolo asserts at an abandoned house. Mokgethi herself is not sure "whether it is out of fear or respect" (*U* 193) that she entered the car in the first place, apparently knowing from the start what is about to happen. She is intimidated by Thabakgolo and his physical strength. She "wrest[les]" with him but her muscles get "tired and bruised", which is why Thabakgolo can subsequently "dra[g] [her] through the door" (*U* 194). Thabakgolo does address the protagonist three times while having his way with her: "Mokgethi, am I hurting you?", "I love you", and "Mokgethi, I am sorry" (*U* 196–197). As the incident is reported from Mokgethi's perspective, we do not gain insights into Thabakgolo's thoughts. However, we do get to know that Thabakgolo is not just anybody in the community:

> Everybody likes Thabakgolo […]. They all love and respect him so much that he has become a kind of Mandela in the community. He is the yardstick that older people use when they are making a point to people of our generation. They always say "Why cannot you be like Thabakgolo?" or "This is what makes Thabakgolo better than you!" He has become a point of reference. (*U* 192–193)

As Thabakgolo is the "Mandela" of the community and "because he has money" (*U* 206), he is untouchable and the police will not act against him. He thus thinks "he can do what he likes to people" (*U* 206), Mokgethi's brother, Khutso, explains. When he learns about the incident, Khutso insists that: "You [i.e. Mokgethi] do not tell anybody about this. Okay? If you accuse him, he'll buy the docket and everybody will be looking at you, pointing fingers at you" (*U* 206). Mokgethi knows that Khutso is right; no one will speak in her favour:

> Thabakgolo is thirty-nine and I am seventeen. Does he care? He told me that he loves me but I know that love is not sex. Today I was raped but I cannot do anything about it. I cannot go to the police because they will call him before opening a case against him. And even if they do not call him, which they will, I do not believe that my case would see a courtroom; it will disappear into thin air and I will be left to be victimized by my community. (*U* 208)

Moele's *Untitled* thus ends on a similar tone to Mgqolozana's *A Man Who Is Not a Man*. As long as there is no change in the codes of conduct and silencing practices of local communities, as well as in the behaviour of parents and other authority figures towards acting responsibly according to their societal position, nothing will change for the young women: "We have come to accept that there will never be an end to this. We have come to love it because there is nothing we can do about it but extract some joy out of it. The community will victimize us, no matter the reality of the situation" (*U* 208). As mentioned before, Mokgethi is not crying for help as she is aware that there is no one to help her but herself. She moreover knows that "if [she were] a man" she could act differently, "shoot [him]" or "cut [his] balls off right now. If [she were] a man… If [she were] a man…" (*U* 197). But being a woman, she presently only has her writing pen to help her open a new chapter in her life.

Resumé

I have previously referred to Pennell, who argued that in order to transform the discussion of gender binarism, its constructedness must be put at the centre of narratives (cf. 56). The previous pages have shown that twenty-first century adolescent novels have in fact begun to deconstruct the naturalness of gender binarism. Both *This Book Betrays My Brother* and *Untitled* depict gender binarism as being a formative force in the lives of young females. The books follow the female protagonists in their attempts to decode their surrounding social landscape and the status of gender. They are shown to falter and to be in need of a strong will for self-empowerment in order to transcend the prevalent discourses. Often this self-empowerment comes at a price: social acceptance. Both Nedi and Mokgethi fight their wars against the silence surrounding the issue of rape alone and with their pens. The latter has become their only chance to get at least some form of closure as an open dialogue between the generations and the genders about the events appears not to be an option in their cases. Their first-hand experience of the effects of silence ultimately leads to their written testimony. At the end of the novels, Nedi and Mokgethi can no longer remain silent as this silence causes greater damage to them than the social ostracism that awaits them when they speak out. Both narratives are supportive of an ideology that fosters open discourse and demands the re-evaluation of established forms of reaction in the area of gender-based violence. They signal that silence can no longer be an option.

Conclusion

Gender stereotyping is frequently represented in contemporary young adult literature. Simultaneously, we are witnessing a slow move towards the liberation of gender and social norms as many novels have started to decode these norms. More and more issues that have been neglected so far, such as homophobia, male circumcision, rape, and above all the methodical silencing of victims, are now being debated and, most importantly, have become represented in twenty-first century adolescent novels. Significantly, all these narratives are careful not to introduce new methods of demonizing. Moreover, neither male nor female characters are shown to be resistant to stereotyping of the other gender, and both are shown to be responsible for the perpetuation of social norms. Processes of resignifying gender binarism are so far only shown to happen on the individual level, and not within the broader social space. South African narratives have become part of "new hybrid realism" as they promote their ideology "in ways that are less obviously one-sided and seductive" (Pearson and Reynolds 72).

3 Adapting Socio-Economic Issues: From Race to Class

Ever since "the basis of disadvantage shifted from race to class" in the late twentieth century, the debate on socio-economic issues has been amongst the hottest in contemporary South Africa (Seekings and Nattrass 4). According to South Africa's Constitution (Act No. 108 of 1996) and its Bill of Rights,

> all South Africans [have] certain basic socio-economic rights such as the right to have access to healthcare services; social security; sufficient food and water; adequate housing and a safe environment. Over and above these rights, additional protection afforded to children includes the right to basic nutrition, shelter, basic healthcare services, social services and protection from abuse and neglect. ("Social Profile of Vulnerable Groups" 1)

Although the Constitution grants all South Africans a legal right to "basic socio-economic rights", these have not become a social reality for everyone. In 2001, Pundy Pillay counted "six key socio-economic challenges" that needed to be addressed by the South African government: "1. Macroeconomic Policy; 2. The Labour Market; 3. Poverty and Inequality; 4. The Social Sector; 5. Globalisation and the South African Economy; and 6. Fiscal Decentralisation" (3). "With almost 25% of the population (and 65% of young people [between the ages of 15 and 24]) without work", Kumo, Rieländer, and Omilola found unemployment to be "South Africa's largest social challenge" (2). "Poverty and inequality" are usually added to this list of challenges that need to be addressed most urgently (Chabane 1). All of the fields Pillay (2001) identified are interconnected and relate to the rate of unemployment, poverty, and inequality: For instance, when a sub-national government lacks a concise "Co-ordination Framework" for local skill development, the "Efficient and Equitable Distribution of Resources" is not guaranteed (Pillay 2001, 25). Consequently, a potential shortage of skills aggravates a region's level of inequality, poverty, or rate of unemployment. Simultaneously, inequality, poverty, and unemployment are factors that correlate with developments in the "social sector", including the degree of education, the availability of social services, and whether people can afford adequate housing and health care services (*ibid.*). Macroeconomic policies regarding "growth", "investment", "savings", and "inflation", which are themselves ever more dependent on and influenced by global developments, frame the local decision-making processes (*ibid.*). Pillay points out that "[t]he nature and direction of policy making will determine whether th[e] relationships [between globalisation, macroeconomic policy, fiscal decentralisation, and the social sector] will have a positive or negative dimension" (2001, 24). To him, "[o]ne of the most important lessons from the emerging market crises is that there is more to life than macroeconomics. Sound monetary and fiscal policies may be vital to economic success, but good government, robust financial systems and effective social provision also matter" (Pillay 2001, 24).

So far, the democratically elected governments of the new South Africa have not done enough to achieve the substantial change in the country's social profile which citizens had envisaged in the mid-1990s. The scholarly verdict on contemporary South African politics is far from benevolent: Seekings and Nattrass, for instance, argue that even though "democratization brought to power (in 1994) a government with a clear public commitment to, and a political interest in, mitigating inequality [...] no significant policy shifts have occurred" to counter the further consolidation of socio-economic inequalities (3). A more recent study by Lawrence Hamilton (2014) concludes that although South Africans were liberated from apartheid's legal oppressions twenty years ago and have since been free to participate in the elections of a government, they have not necessarily been able use this freedom to empower themselves in the time period:

> [F]reedom from poverty and inequality depends, at least in part, on the power to control the economic and political environment via meaningful control over one's political representatives. Freedom in South Africa, as elsewhere, therefore depends on the relatively equal power of influence that all South African citizens wield over macro-political and macroeconomic decisions via meaningful control over their political representatives. This is not possible under prevailing economic and political conditions and orthodoxies, an electoral system that privileges the interest of parties above the needs of citizens and a debt management system that puts economic stability and the interest of creditors before redistribution and empowerment. (Hamilton 130–131)

Hamilton shows that it is due to "[r]ampant poverty, inequality, unemployment, and poor education, together with a macro-economic policy trajectory which subordinates development to growth and a macro-political structure which dissuades rather than encourages accountability to voters" that for the great majority of South Africans the freedom which they have been granted in their 1996 Constitution has not automatically resulted in "social, political or economic benefits" (quoted in Maserow 2014). Hamilton's (2014) approach and observations are not new. Burger had already argued in 2005 that "in addition to the completed political transformation" "[t]here is the need for economic and social transformation" (3). He was convinced that the "political transformation was the simplest part of the total transformation process" (Burger 2005, 3). Burger also pointed to the complexities connected to "[e]conomic and social transformation" processes as these not only "affec[t] the interest of different interest groups", but also touch on delicate topics such as "property rights and the restitution of such rights where they were violated in the past, the establishment of equity in living standards, jobs and educational opportunities and policies of affirmative action and, in general, a change in attitudes" (Burger 2005, 3).

In an attempt to find reasons for the failure of the South African governments to promote socio-economic development, Michael Chapman points to Ivor Chipkin's "highly provocative" political analysis "Citizenship, Knowledge and the Nationalist State" (2009), which offers the following explanation:

> The goal of the ANC government—like that of Mugabe's Zanu-PF—is not primarily the cementing of liberal democracy, but the transformation of the state according to the values, norms and visions of the ruling party still in its garb of a revolutionary African national liberation movement. Whatever the Constitution might enshrine as nonracial, the task of the ANC is to position itself as the dominant state apparatus able to orchestrate change in the instantiation of the black African subject. (Chipkin quoted in Chapman 2011b, 66)

What is more important in the context of this chapter than whether or not Chipkin's contentious verdict is correct or whether or not the ANC-led governments of post-apartheid South Africa have so far been primarily preoccupied with "position[ing] [themselves] as the dominant state apparatus able to orchestrate change" (Chapman 2011b, 66) is that the country has meanwhile turned from "a society of control" into a "society of consumption" (Mbembe 2014). This shift, Mbembe points out, "has exacerbated the old contradiction at the heart of South Africa's history", which comes down to one basic question, namely who owns what. Mbembe explains that

> [a]t least since the wars of dispossession of the 19th century, citizenship and rights of personhood have been constructed in relation to a particular regime of ownership. Whites owned property and blacks sold their labour at a cheap price on a captive market. The end of apartheid has not meant a repudiation of this axiom. Today, the construction of self still depends upon the possession of a certain quantum of property. If anything, democracy seems to have exacerbated the confusion between the rule of the people, the rule of law and the rule of property. (2014)

Neoliberal economic policy has added substantially to what Mbembe calls the "confusion between the rule of people, the rule of law and the rule of property" (*ibid.*) and supported the quick establishment of a "society of consumption" (*ibid.*) and the persistence of socio-economic inequalities. Neoliberalism is "characterised by fiscal austerity, deregulation and privatisation" combined with "a distinct withdrawal/shrinking of the state and a transfer of competence to the private sector" while the areas that were "previously [in] the competence of the state are subsumed under a capitalist mode of production" (Narsiah 3). The effects of neoliberalism on the country's social economy have been so widespread and comprehensive that they have become a subject of academic research across the disciplines (cf. Marais; Saul). An observer of the influence of capitalism on the development of South African individuals and their nation, Achille Mbembe informs us that "[t]oday, we have reached a stage where it is increasingly apparent that *capitalism is not naturally compatible with democracy*" (2012, 20; emphasis in the original). He explains that "[f]or capitalism to be compatible with democracy, capitalism would have to be subjected to extensive political control and democracy protected from being restrained in the name of market power" (Mbembe 2012, 20). Due to the neoliberal agenda, neither of these scenarios has been the case in South Africa according to Mbembe (2012). He as well as Seekings and Nattrass (2005) and Ashman, Fine, and Newman (2011) find capitalism and global market forces to be responsible for the country being amongst the most unequal societies in the world to the present day. The government's decision to change the country's macro-economic strategy and follow a neoliberal approach to economic development, which meant moving away "from the nationalisation and redistribution basis of the Freedom Charter to free market capitalism" (Everatt 319), has also had drastic effects on how South Africans have lived their lives after 1994. As Everatt puts it:

> Fetishising market forces is not simply a policy shift but a lifestyle choice. The new ruling elite adopted many of the unsavoury habits of their predecessors, most notably conspicuous consumption. Black empowerment deals have created a thin stratum of black multi-millionaires who live like their white counterparts. (319)

The ethnic component of socio-economic inequalities is – next to the persistence of "[l]arge income gaps and pervasive unemployment" (Burger 2005, 17) – the third reason why it has been so difficult to improve social cohesion in present-day South Africa. Inter- and intraracial violence remains a recurring problem in the new South Africa.[66] In an acute observation, Mbembe explains that

> [b]y boosting difference and by reinserting this difference into the cycles of its reproduction, contemporary global capitalism, as with its earlier incarnations, relies more than ever before on a reconfigured version of the "racial subsidy". This is probably what explains its renewed violence and the extreme disorders it is engendering worldwide. (Mbembe 2012, 25)

Two years later, the critic points out once more that "race is still a crucial marker of privilege", but this time he also asks his readers to consider that "the forms of social polarization, inequality and exclusion are becoming increasingly complex" (Mbembe 2014). Most importantly, Mbembe finds that twenty years after the formal end of apartheid, economic structural inequality can no longer be explained exclusively along the lines of the

[66] At this point it is worth noting that "[w]hile we observe a decline in the importance of between-race inequality, within-race inequality has risen sharply and this has been strong enough to stop South Africa's aggregate inequality from falling" (Leibbrandt et al. 67). Leibbrandt et al. also point out that "while the between-race component of inequality has fallen, it remains remarkably high by international norms and its decline has slowed since the mid 1990s" (67).

> two generic blocks of blacks and whites. In ways hardly experienced before, it now cuts through both categories and in between. The expansion of a black middle class goes hand in hand with the crystallization, at the margins of black society, of a mounting army of those who, having been expelled from formal work, are condemned to a wageless life. (2014)

This means that today, South African capitalism not only "relies for its operations on racial subsidies in the form of low skill levels, inadequate nutrition, poor health, bad housing, social instability and an increasingly authoritarian ruling elite", but also "depends on the institution of migrant labour, a highly unequal and racialised partition of land and a thoroughly extractive economy" (Mbembe 2014). As part of a global market economy, the characteristics of South African capitalism resemble those of global capitalism, which "is attempting to squeeze every last drop of value out of the planet by increasing the rate of innovation and invention or through an active refiguring of space, currencies, resources and time itself" (Mbembe 2012, 25). This is why Burger's observation that "[u]nemployment and the distribution of income both have racial, gender and spatial dimensions" also holds true twenty years after apartheid officially ended (2005, 17; cf. Kumo, Rieländer, and Omilola). Still, "African women in rural areas are the worst off" in the social strata (Burger 2005, 17; cf. "Social Profile of Vulnerable Groups"). The continued publication of opinion pieces such as Verashni Pillay's "Six Things White People Have That Black People Don't" (2015) – namely generational wealth, social capital, early childhood development, the benefit of the doubt, a financial head-start, and self-sufficient parents – underlines that the discussions about a "racial subsidy" (Mbembe 2012) are far from over. According to Pillay, the economic imbalance between different ethnic groups continues to be so severe that growing up black in South Africa still means for these children literally having to work harder to achieve the same as their white contemporaries. "[J]ust because we're (sort of) equal now", Pillay explains, this "in no way erases the after-effects of centuries of economic structural inequality that are largely racial" (2015).

If changes and improvements in the socio-economic sector were not brought about, Burger anticipated "a breakdown in the social fabric" of South Africa as a whole already in 2005 (17). Although the social fabric has not broken down since the publication of Burger's essay, it has acquired substantial cracks. The rise in the number of xenophobic attacks against foreign nationals, which supposedly reached a peak in May 2008 but have frequently reoccurred thereafter – most recently in April 2015 in Durban and Johannesburg after a speech by Zulu King Goodwill Zwelithini in which he reportedly said "foreigners must pack their bags and go home" (cf. Jennifer; Karimi; Raborife; Westcott) – is but one example of the failure to enforce necessary socio-economic improvements, such as enhanced income distribution or better living standards.[67]

However, not only foreigners are perceived as potential threats to social cohesion in South Africa. In recent years, youths have also once again come to be seen "as threats rather than as victims and survivors of grinding, systematic poverty" (Samara 7; cf. Swartz 3). I say 'once again' because already during the apartheid years, young people had been "conceived as communists and terrorists" when they first joined the struggle (Samara 7). Then they were applauded and heroized for making "townships ungovernable throughout the 1980s" (Samara 59). Now, especially "black youth have reemerged at the intersections of security and development in the context of urban governance" in this early twenty-first century (Samara 7; cf. Swartz 3). Everatt found "[W]hat's wrong with the youth?" to be the "most frequently asked question among former activists and the media" in the years after the end of apartheid (2). During this period, an image of the "so-called lost generation of black youth" (Samara 62) was created with the help of, for instance, regular media reports on the high number of juveniles in prison.[68] This discourse of a juvenile counternation has made itself felt not only across the media and in political and private discussions (cf. Samara 54–89), but also in contemporary literary texts for young South Africans (cf. Inggs 2007; Barnard 2008).[69]

Methodologically, this chapter on social economics is framed by the concept of community or social profiling (cf. chapter 3.1.) and the question whether literary publications can, when approached as *witness documents*, give insight into the zeitgeist of their period of production concerning socio-economic development and consequently provide a literary social profile of contemporary South Africa. Before attempting to answer this question, I will first debate the challenges that come with methods such as social profiling and then go on to discuss to what extent social segregation, a phenomenon which is prevalent in South Africa's social reality, is represented in narratives for young adults. In the second sub-chapter, I will discuss what kind of social ethics pervade literary texts for young people. We will see that social cohesion is a recurrent topic in the novels discussed below. Significantly, South African authors use different narrative perspectives, a diverse range of characters, and settings in both offline and online spaces to debate social cohesion. While the majority of texts for young adults addresses traditional

[67] It has to be noted that socio-economic issues are but one reason for the rise in xenophobic violent attacks in the late 2000s. Patel (2013) names the "lack of trusted and effective conflict resolution mechanisms", a "culture of impunity" in communities, as well as "competition for community leadership" as further reasons for xenophobic violence. Jason Hickel (2014) also points to globalization and neoliberal politics, as well as witchcraft.

[68] Samara states that "[b]y 2006, almost half (42 percent) of the prison population was under the age of 25" (62).

[69] The notion of a juvenile counternation is also discussed in the introduction and in the close reading section of Sifiso Mzobe's *Young Blood* (2010) (cf. chapter 2.1).

socio-economic issues, such as poverty, unemployment, and the lack of role models and nuclear families, there are also texts that discuss the socio-ethical implications of using new technologies and media.

3.1 Community/Social Profiling and the Novel

In their monograph *Theory from the South*, Jean and John Comaroff "posit that, in the present moment, it is the global south that affords privileged insight into the workings of the world at large" (2012, 1). Their argument is based on the understanding that scholars from the southern hemisphere theorize the spatial and social mechanisms at work in their societies through a transnational lens and in relation to influences which capitalism and economic policies have on individual lives. They inform us that the South African Ministry of Higher Education and Training in South Africa, for instance, has deliberately called for the development of "social theory" and "critical thinking" which integrates current transformation of the economic world order (Comaroff and Comaroff 2012, 48). Scholars like Nuttall (2009)[70] and Mbembe (2008, 2014, 2015) have worked to describe African modernity in terms that have steadily moved away from "establish[ing] similarities with something else while at the same time inventing something original" (Mbembe 2008, 38f.).

Mbembe describes the "current theoretical moment as one of cacophony" (2012, 23). The Comaroffs even observe "something of a flight from theory, a re-embrace both of methodological empiricism and born-again realism; also a return to the ethical and the theological" (2012, 47). Mbembe is convinced that in an age in which "theory" as such is under scrutiny, theory will only survive if it "helps us, in any way, to make sense of the times we live in; whether it helps us to assess with some degree of plausibility various intuitions about what is going on, what is possible, and the odds against it" (2012, 22). At the same time, however, "[t]he need to interrogate the workings of the contemporary world order – to lay bare its certainties and uncertainties, its continuities and contingencies, its possibilities and impossibilities, its inclusions and exclusions – has be[come] increasingly urgent" as this new world order not only "holds out the promise of new ways of knowing, new means of control, new techniques of accumulating wealth", but also "yield[s] rising inequality and inequity, joblessness and homelessness, poverty and disempowerment, corruption, criminality, and xenophobia" (Comaroff and Comaroff 2012, 48). The Comaroffs argue that what this globalized and hence radically open and simultaneously entangled world needs is so-called

[70] For a discussion of Sarah Nuttall's *Entanglement* (2009), see chapter 1.2.1.

> *grounded* theory: the historically contextualized, problem driven effort to account for the production of social and cultural 'facts' in the world by recourse to an imaginative methodological counterpoint between the inductive and the deductive, the concrete and the concept; also in a different register, between the epic and the everyday, the meaningful and the material – and, here in particular, between capitalism and modernity, the fitful dialectic at the core of our present concerns. (Comaroff and Comaroff 2012, 48; emphasis in the original)

The sociologists Barney Glaser and Anselm Strauss had already argued "for grounding theory in social research itself – for generating it from the data [...] rather than verifying it" (viii) in their book *The Discovery of Grounded Theory: Strategies for Qualitative Research* in the 1960s. Glaser and Strauss consider the collection of current sociological data necessary for "arriving at theory suited to its supposed uses" (3). One way of collecting such data is community profiling,[71] which is understood as "a tool of community development" used, for instance, by local authorities, but also by voluntary or community organizations "to inform decision making about the allocation of resources" in predominantly disadvantaged areas (Hawtin et al. 1–2). The profile is intended to be

> [a] *comprehensive* description of the *needs* of a population that is defined, or defines itself, as a *community*, and the *resources* that exist within that community, carried out with the *active involvement of the community* itself, for the purpose of developing an *action plan* or other means of improving the quality of life in the community. (Hawtin et al. 5; emphasis in the original)

Social profiling is a derivative of community profiling. Rob White informs us that a social profile "involves constructing a matrix of variables and matching individuals to the variables described in the [...] matrix" (157). Ideally, community or social profiles include both hard data and soft data analyses. This means that statistical data collected by state officials on housing, living conditions, socio-economic status, and class (i.e. hard data) is evaluated alongside interviews of community members who would have been asked about what they believed their community needs to be (i.e. soft data). However, in reality soft data is seldom included in the compilation of a social profile (cf. Hawtin et al. 3). As a result, the "action plans" (Hawtin et al. 3) developed by the compilers of the profiles may not always be adaptable to the reality of the affected, which is why the results of community profiles have come to be seen as highly controversial.

In 2012, *Statistics South Africa* published its second "Social Profile of Vulnerable Groups in South Africa", using hard data from the General Household Survey (GHS) of the country as a basis for the report. The "Social Profile" is based on the following variables: "household characteristics and living arrangements[,]

[71] "Community profiling" is also known as "needs assessment", "community consultation", or "social auditing"; for more details on terminology, see Hawtin et al. (2–5).

vulnerability to hunger and access to food[,] health[,] poverty and social grants[,] economic participation[,] education[,] and finally housing and access to basic services" (ii). According to the report, children and youth, who comprised "40% and 37% of the total population in 2011", as well as women, the elderly (9% of the population), and disabled persons account for vulnerable groups ("Social Profile of Vulnerable Groups" ii). The study shows that it is particularly difficult for these population groups to free themselves from their (potentially disadvantaged) social backgrounds. Social mobility is not common for these groups of people. The strength of this "Social Profile" is its condensed display of information about the living conditions of South Africans; yet, this is also its weakness and disadvantage as it does no more than provide naked data. As White argues, social profiles "tend to be descriptive and do little to provide a basis for understanding *why* and *how* specific groups of young people experience problems or find meaning in their lives" (157). However, this is the precise strength of literary texts. Particularly fictions written in the realist mode are all about the *why* and the *how* and aim to give insights into different concepts of life, as will become evident in the close reading sections later in the chapter.

Despite its drawbacks, the method of social profiling has also been used in research concerning youth. As the results of the profiles have frequently been reproduced in the media, they have in fact nurtured a discourse that has come to describe the younger generation as lost, vulnerable, and a counternation. One must know that in South Africa "youth are [perceived as] a lens that reflects society in sharper detail: the negative trends are amplified, as are the positive" (Everatt 320). As youths represent the largest group of South Africa's population, they have been a "focal point for policymakers, mainly because of their potential to be a major resource for national development. Another consideration may also be that they have the potential to create social upheaval, unless their needs are adequately addressed" ("Social Profile of Vulnerable Groups" 1). Since the end of apartheid, national youth policies have been in place that are intended to foster but also to guard the development of this most significant age group:

> Currently, the National Youth Policy 2009–2014 governs work related to the youth. This policy relies on information of the particular needs and circumstances of the country's youth to address identified gaps and challenges (National Youth Policy, 2009: 5–6) and relies on the National Youth Commission Act, No. 19 of 1996, the White Paper for Social Welfare, 1997; the National Youth Policy, 2000; the National Youth Development Policy Framework, 2000–2007; and the Draft National Youth Policy, 2008–2013 for its implementation. ("Social Profile of Vulnerable Groups" 1)

The many policies initiated especially for South African youth show the significance that the country places on its youngsters. The policies speak of high hopes pinned on the young persons and of great efforts undertaken to make sure that the youth is heading in the right direction. But what is the 'right' direction?

By 2001, only seven years after the end of apartheid, a decisive gap had emerged between how adults expected their youths to behave and the ideas that youths had for themselves, according to Everatt. Then, "'What has happened to the youth?' really mean[t] 'why aren't they like I was?' – but in the democratic South Africa, struggle has been replaced by consumption" (318). Given their history of struggle, "South African adults [...] kn[e]w about politically engaged 'youth'" (Everatt 324). However, they were "unused to 'teenagers'", leading to major problems "in the way older people interpret the behaviour of youth" (Everatt 324). Consequently, well-intended political initiatives seldom found response with the youth (cf. Everatt 318).

Notably, those who are identified as "at risk" experience social ostracism and stigmatization because of the designation "at risk", which further "add[s] to their sense of difference and marginality" (White 157). Thus, political intervention in the form of an increase in policing and security measures has further encouraged what one wanted to keep at bay: the criminalization of specific spaces as well as the marginalization of those 'at risk'. Rob White (2008), for instance, informs us about the composition of social profiles in relation to ethnic gang groups. In so-called risk analyses, social profiles of youths were used to assess the risk of them joining a gang. Such risk analyses have proven to be "difficult and problematic" not only due to the "multilayered nature and dynamics of youth associations and affiliations", but also because of the so-called "fluid identities" of young people, which allow them to "be simultaneously gang members and non-gang members" (White 149). Social profiling is ever more problematic when it is "heavily dependent upon racial and ethnic markers" and when these markers are "linked to a crime control agenda rather than one where the emphasis is on social inclusion, access and equity" (White 158). Such negative forms of social profiling also influence "police assumptions that some ethnic groups are more likely to commit crime than others, and to target such groups accordingly" (White 159). White's research shows that

> youth gang intervention premised upon particular gang identifiers can in effect create the very problem allegedly being addressed. That is, the intervention itself can serve to consolidate and concretize gang formation and gang identity. This is especially so if accompanied by aggressive forms of policing and street regulation. (149)

The same processes hold true for other groups of the population who have been termed vulnerable or 'at risk' by South African authorities, namely children, the youth, women, and the elderly (cf. "Social Profile of Vulnerable Groups"), but also the urban poor, and of these particularly "young men" (cf. Samara 2).

In light of these opinion-forming outcomes of social profiling, the questions of concern in the following pages are: As all the variables considered in the "Social Profile of Vulnerable Groups" in South Africa – namely "household characteristics and living arrangements[,] vulnerability to hunger and access to food[,] health[,] poverty and social grants[,] economic participation[,] education[,] and finally housing and access to basic services" (ii) – feature to a greater or lesser extent in literary texts for young adults, what kind of social profile of South Africa and particularly of its young people do we encounter in South African adolescent literature? Are youth depicted as being "at risk", "lost" (cf. Everatt; Seekings), vulnerable, "marginalized" (Perrow), or a counternation? In order to be able to establish what I hope to be a literary social profile of contemporary South African narratives for young adults, I will draw on both distant and close reading. In more general terms, I will read the results of South Africa's social profile, i.e. hard data on housing, living conditions, socio-economic status, and class (cf. "Social Profile of South Africa"; "Social Profile of Vulnerable Groups"), against what I would call literary hard data, which I understand to be socio-economic background information and living situations of characters. Character development, ideological implications, values, morals, and responses to societal codes of conduct are understood as literary soft data. The two subsequent subchapters focus on the representation of (hard) socio-economic facts (cf. chapter 3.2) and discuss what kind of social ethics, values, and social attitudes are conveyed in literary texts for young people (cf. chapter 3.3).

3.2 Social Segregation Continued?

Bond (2000), Budlender (1996, 1997, 1998), Marais (2001), Morrell (2005), and Seekings and Nattrass (2005) are but a few of the scholars who have already discussed the persisting interconnections between class, gender, and race in South Africa and how these influence societal development. Samara's study on *Crime and Governance in the Divided City* (2011) of Cape Town is particularly interesting with regard to this subchapter's focus on social segregation. In chapter 1, I pointed to spatial segregation as a continuing phenomenon in present-day South Africa. In her study, Samara adds a social dimension to this spatial segregation, showing that "Cape Town, like many cities, is a city divided, both socially and spatially" (Samara 2). According to her, "contemporary urban governance" is shaped by a belief in the connectedness of "security and socioeconomic development" (Samara 2). This perception influenced local governance after an ever greater number of incidents of crime had occurred, leading to an increase in "progressive social development initiatives", such as "conflict management and intervention training", but also to a rise in money spent on security measures, such as "safety gates, burglar bars, barbed wire, mesh wire, alarm systems with armed response, and secure fencing" (Samara 1). Not only criminals became an item on the agenda. A "new 'quality of life' bylaw approved by the Cape Town city council in May 2007" prohibits "begging, washing clothes in public, and failing to move along when ordered to do so by a security officer" and thus specifically targets the urban poor. Interestingly, these

> have been routinely demonized by local press, downtown business interest, and city authorities for years as manifestations of urban blight and threats to urban revitalization, primarily because of the crimes they allegedly commit and the fear they induce in the more affluent classes with whom they share this contested space. (Samara 2)

What is often overlooked in studies of urban sub-spaces, Samara argues, is that "crime and its victims are highly localized" (3). In the case of Cape Town this means that "the majority of the city's crime happens on the Cape Flats, far from the tourists and wealthier residents clustered in and around the city's core" (Samara 3). These ruptures within urban areas have led to a two-fold image of the city,

> one is a well-connected global brand that attracts tourists and investments from all corners of the globe, the other an underdeveloped urban periphery that has more in common with expanding ghettos across the global South than with the glittering Euro-themed downtown just kilometers away. (Samara 3)

The twofold image of the post-apartheid city has its origins in the authorities' market-driven, neoliberal approach to city governance, which "means for all cities under its sway renewed and reinvigorated tensions between the demands of 'free markets' and those of populations" (Samara 4). Samara observes that "the city today is governed through a complex network in which local and global forces clash and combine to reproduce the fractured urban spaces inherited from apartheid but which are also found in other cities with very different histories" (3). Her exemplary study of Cape Town thus shows that social and spatial segregation continue to shape life in post-apartheid cities. As a result, the socio-economic situation of citizens greatly influences how and where people live in urban spaces and whether or not they feel socially included.

The relevance of having access to socio-economic resources is frequently debated in fictional accounts of young South African lives. South African authors of young adult fiction are aware of the (often constrained) socio-economic situation that their target audience grows up in and thus have started to integrate the topic into their narratives. A statistical assessment of those 147 literary texts written in English in the realist mode in the years 2000 to 2013 found that the corpus is heterogeneous with a variety of social contexts and social realities portrayed in these literary texts (cf. Stadler 2015). These texts can be described as "a nexus of economic, political and social influences" (MacKenzie 1990, 127). I found that "the spectrum of social backgrounds represented in the novels is comparatively representative of the social reality of South Africa, i.e. the majority of [...] fictions (41%) are set in poor areas" (Stadler 2015, 52). The 2012 "Poverty Profile of South Africa" shows that 47.1% of South Africans live below the international poverty line of 2.50$ per day (cf. Lehohla 2012b, 5). When referring to South Africa's own national poverty line, which is drawn at R557, the number of people living below that line is even higher, namely 52.3% (cf. Chabane 30). Collins Chabane's research shows that "[t]o date, unemployment remains age, gender and racially biased, with young people (16–34 years old) making up more than 70% of the unemployed at the end of 2012; and more women than men are without work and a larger proportion of Africans are unemployed than whites" (21). These numbers are proportionally represented in narrative texts. Black characters coming from a poor social background feature in 32% of the 147 texts that were assessed in the analysis (cf. Stadler 2015, 53). The category white/middle class is the only other one which is represented in more than 10% of the titles, while characters of the other nine categories (rich/black, middle-class/black, mixed/black, rich/white, poor/white, mixed/white, rich/coloured, poor/coloured, mixed/coloured) are represented in 5% or less of the cases (*ibid.*). All in all, protagonists coming from a middle-class background (23%) are represented almost twice as often as main characters coming from a rich background (13%) (cf. Stadler 2015, 52). Seventeen percent of all novels include sets of characters that come from different social backgrounds, discussing either "a family's fall or rise on the social ladder" or "the building of friendships across the imaginary borders between social groups" (Stadler 2015, 52). Such novels intend to foster social cohesion and tolerance across the social strata by the use of different narrative strategies.

Throughout the thesis the texts which were selected for close readings were chosen with regard to content and not according to authorship. This means that the socio-economic and ethnic background of the characters was considered more important than the background of the author, as the focus of this study is on the discussion of fictional realities. It is nonetheless interesting to note that the great majority of novels examined for the statistical assessment were written by white authors (cf. Stadler 2015, annotated corpus). The close reading sections of the previous chapters discussed narratives which contain characters from different social backgrounds: We have read the coming–of–age tales of poor black females (cf. *Untitled* and *Dancing Queen*) as well as of poor black males (cf. *Young Blood*, *Thirteen Cents*), middle-class black children (cf. *This Book Betrays My Brother*, *A Man Who is Not a Man*), middle-class white children (cf. *Spud*, *E Eights*), and a rich coloured girl (cf. *Trinity Rising*). In the following we will gain insight into the lives of a poor white male in *Back to Villa Park*, a poor black boy (cf. *Heist Wind*), a poor coloured girl (cf. *Katy of Sky Road*), a middle-class white girl (cf. *Dark Poppy's Demise*), and a middle-class black girl whose family experiences social decline (cf. *Tears of an Angel*).[72] As easy as these classifications – 'poor

[72] I have stated elsewhere that "the research categories were termed 'poor', 'middle class', 'rich' as these classifications better mirror the social reality in twenty-first century South

black', 'middle-class coloured', 'middle class white', 'rich black', etc. – sound, they are also highly problematic and in danger of one-dimensionality as the different labels are tied to stereotypes and thus liable to misreading. Labelling a novel as depicting a black character from a poor social background initially pre-defines the character according to that classification. A character's attempts to participate in other social environments during the course of the novel or his or her social mobility are not apparent from such a preliminary description. Also, due to the country's history of racial and continued social segregation, such labels remain contested. Hence, close readings of fictional texts are necessary and valuable additions to distant reading approaches, which may otherwise be at risk of one-dimensionality.

Youth novels draw on this public discourse and include those stereotypes that are typically connected to, for instance, 'rich blacks' or 'middle-class coloureds' in their storylines. While it is true that only a few characters in South African novels written in the realist mode are able to change their socio-economic situation within the novel's pages, this is mostly due to the age of the protagonists. The novels depict what it means to be born *into* poor, middle-class, or rich socio-economic environments. As the great majority of characters are under age, required to attend school, not yet entitled to have a regular job, and dependent on their parents or other figures of authority to see to their accommodation, their options for changing their living situation before they have finished school or come of age are comparatively limited. Nevertheless, character empowerment and knowledge play a decisive role in the novels, even though empowerment no longer necessarily means political, but rather economic empowerment. Whilst politics feature only to a marginal extent, socio-economic issues pervade contemporary narratives. With regard to social economics, a great number of novels depict adolescents who do not want to wait to earn money until they are of age. Both males and females are eager to live a good life now, not later, and are shown to go to considerable lengths to enhance their current living situation. Often, this means that the characters have to rely on criminal methods to achieve their aim. In these instances, juvenile characters are shown to stretch their definition of what they consider right or wrong to fit their current material desires.[73] Generally, a lack of trust in authorities, especially in the police's capability to ensure a safe life in the township (cf. analysis of *Tears of an Angel*), as well as in the moral authority of adults, permeates narratives published after the year 2000. Last but not least, it should be noted that a character's striving for a good life does not depend on their

Africa than the traditional four categories of social class, i.e. 'upper', 'middle', 'working' and 'lower class'" (Stadler 2015, 54, footnote 7). The former categories are also those used in the documents published by *Statistics South Africa* (cf. "Social Profile of Vulnerable Groups").

[73] The concept of right (and wrong) will be further discussed in the subsequent subchapter on social ethics. Generally, adolescent characters are depicted as responding flexibly to their surroundings and to the pre-established codes of conduct (cf. chapter 3.3).

background: Everybody is trying to (further) improve their current socio-economic status.

Rita Barnard has called the nuclear family one of the new "normative" (563) elements in contemporary South African youth novels, which is used as a means to "reassert […] power over […] threatening youth" (*ibid.*). While nuclear family structures are represented to a growing degree in twenty-first century fiction, they are not depicted as harmonious entities. The family's happiness is usually shown to be disrupted by socio-economic constraints. In *Tears of an Angel* by Sello Mahapeletsa, unemployment is shown to lead to alcohol abuse on the part of the father, who subsequently turns violent, jealous, and insecure in response to his fears of losing his empowered position in the family. Not only crime and violence are shown to result from socio-economic setbacks, but also the willingness to risk one's health and compromise one's convictions in exchange for financial relief. We have seen this already in the analyses of *Thirteen Cents* and *Dancing Queen* in chapter 1. This chapter's novels, *Katy of Sky Road* (2007), *Tears of an Angel* (2007), and *Back to Villa Park* (2013) were chosen in order to reconsider some of the spatial and gender issues raised in the previous chapters through a socio-economic lens. Katy in *Katy of Sky Road* comes from a poor background. *Tears of an Angel* follows the rise and fall of Dikeledi's family on the social ladder of a mining township. Lastly, *Back to Villa Park* is a story about familial disruption and socio-economic setbacks.

Dianne Case and Yvonne Hart, *Katy of Sky Road* (2007)

Katy of Sky Road[74] by Dianne Case and Yvonne Hart won the Maskew Miller Longman Award in 2007 and appeared in its second impression in 2012. In a recently published essay collection on *Authors and Illustrators of Children's and Young Adult Literature*, Lisa Kimble and Barbara A. Lehman point out that "[w]ork by authors like Dianne Case is crucial to incorporate in young readers' experiences with books because they will have opportunities to read books portraying children of color" (45). The story is told in 37 chapters, which are usually no longer than three or four pages, and is narrated by the homodiegetic narrator Katy. The novel includes a notes and activities section aimed at learners and teachers as well as a list of themes. One theme the novel deals with, according to this section, is "how important it is for Katy to develop her individuality and gain her independence. Hector [i.e. Katy's father] has to learn to let Katy make her own choices and be her own person" (*KSR* 158). Further themes are listed as follows:

[74] The novel is hereafter cited as *KSR*.

- Addiction and its effects: cigarettes, "tik" alcohol
- Communication between parents and children/The "generation gap"
- Secrets/Lies and deceit/Trust and betrayal/Appearance and reality
- Crime
- Race and racism
- Relationships
- Love and infatuation
- Jealousy
- Religion/Moral values
- Dreams/Aspirations

(*KSR* 158)

Socio-economic issues relating to variables considered in the "Social Profile of Vulnerable Groups", such as "household characteristics and living arrangements[,] […] social grants[,] economic participation[,] education[,] and finally housing and access to basic services" (ii), are not named as distinct topics even though they feature prominently in the novel and have a bearing on all of the above-named themes. The socio-economic specificities of the novel thus not only serve the purpose of establishing a background to the story, but also help to construct a social profile of the social milieu portrayed in the story. In the case of *Katy of Sky Road*, this means that information about the family's socio-economic situation is presented alongside the situation of the community as such.

The reader is informed that Katy and her family's socio-economic situation is not precarious but that they are not well-off either. Katy, Hector, and Auntie Rose inhabit a house on the Cape Flats, an area of Cape Town where, as the notes and activities section informs us, "many 'coloured' people were forced to live during apartheid" (*KSR* 156). Auntie Rose receives a pension and Hector is working full-time at the nearby international airport of Cape Town. Despite their income sources, there is hardly any money for extras and Hector has to save up before he can afford a new dress for Katy, for instance (cf. *KSR* 62–63). Toward the end of the month, all resources are usually exhausted. Even food and electricity become scarce goods by that time (cf. *KSR* 123–124). It appears to be this way throughout the area they live in and businesses also struggle to make ends meet because of the payment practices of customers, who only want to settle their bills at the end of the month (cf. *KSR* 107). When people get their money at the beginning of the month, queues in front of the cash machines are long. Katy's family usually celebrates payday with a full take-away meal to compensate for the meagre meals of the previous days (cf. *KSR* 62). Katy is used to her family's financial situation and has arranged her wishes accordingly. Still, like every other teenager in the novel, she likes to go shopping and would like to have a mobile phone. In order to fulfil their wishes, Katy's best friend, Melissa, steals from her mother to buy clothes for herself and Katy. While Katy feels this to be wrong, Melissa explains her actions as a form of revenge because her mother is never around due to her working various jobs.[75]

Katy of Sky Road covers delicate topics, such as drug abuse, the selling of drugs, stealing, and the value of friendship and family, leaving the reader with the ultimate socio-economic question: How far would you go for money? This is not the first time that money is described as playing a decisive role in young people's lives in this thesis. Previous close readings of *Young Blood* and *Untitled* (cf. chapter 2.3) showed the tendency of young males to become gang members or to engage in dubious activities which allow them to make money more quickly than if they stayed in school. These adolescents are shown to have a vested interest in economic empowerment rather than in political empowerment. Moreover, both *Young Blood* and *Untitled* debate the inclination of young females to expect 'their men', i.e. their boyfriends, to provide for them as well as their habit of 'selling' their female friends to interested men for their own benefit. This area of discussion is once again taken up in *Katy of Sky Road*. Using the plot line of the love triangle Case and Hart play with preconceived notions of young males and females and illustrate that young people's understanding of human relationships is shaped by notions of consumption and material desire.

The story in *Katy of Sky Road* unfolds with Katy developing feelings for Ricardo although she is expected to be Wesley's girlfriend. Wesley is depicted as a determined, well-respected, well-behaved but impulsive and slightly obsessive young man who is convinced that he and Katy are meant to be together, stating repeatedly that he will one day marry Katy. His opinion is supported by Katy's father, Hector, who already considers Wesley his future son-in-law, lauding him as "a fine young man" who will "go places one day. Comes from a nice home [with] decent people" (*KSR* 11). The reader soon learns that Katy does not see herself with Wesley, but also comes to understand that she is torn between what her father expects from her and what she herself wants her life to look like. Throughout the novel, Katy is careful not to raise Wesley's hopes for a relationship and insists on paying for her snacks herself, signalling that there is no need for Wesley to "protect her" or to take care of her (*KSR* 84). Katy's reactions show that she knows what it means when a boy pays for a girl's expenses, namely that he expects something in return. Wesley also thinks this to be the regular pattern of relationships and is convinced that if he had enough money and a car, there would be no debate about Katy's affection for him.

Ricardo's arrival at Katy's school marks a turning point in the protagonist's life. Initially portrayed as Wesley's unreliable and thoughtless other, Ricardo turns

[75] Melissa has a change of heart toward the end of the novel. She declares that she "want[s] to earn money so [she] can help" (*KSR* 155) her mother after she has finished school. So far, her mother has been the sole breadwinner: "Food, cigarettes, beer – she pays for all of it" (*KSR* 155). Contrary to Katy, she will therefore not begin tertiary education (cf. *KSR* 155).

out to be a respectable young man, who is eager to make something of himself the honest way (cf. *KSR* 30). By contrast, Wesley turns out to be an example of a well-educated and cared for youth that has nevertheless gone astray despite his good upbringing. Without anyone noticing, Wesley has started dealing drugs at school and socializing with criminals (cf. *KSR* 123–131). When Katy runs into Wesley while on an errand for her aunt, he offers to take her back home in the car of his friend. Being drunk and/or high and increasingly jealous of Ricardo, Wesley takes advantage of the situation and refuses to let Katy go again. When Katy asks him about the drugs, he tries to reason with her, saying that "Tik's no big deal [...]. It's not as if I'm selling heroin. They'd *tog* buy it from someone else. Plus I have money now, Katy. I can buy you anything you want. I'm going to buy a car so I can take you out. But you must come back to me. Be my girl again" (*KSR* 130). Katy tries to make it clear that she "never [was] his girl" (*KSR* 130) and money will not change this, but Wesley is not listening to Katy, ultimately trying to force himself on her. Luckily, Katy is able to escape, shocked but unharmed.

When Wesley's parents find out that their son is a drug dealer and that he was capable of kidnapping Katy, they, too, are in shock: "'I don't know what got into him,' Wesley's father says, biting his lip. 'We are not that kind of people. We taught him right'" (*KSR* 143). Nevertheless, when they come to Katy's house "to see Hector and Auntie Rose, to apologise on Wesley's behalf, [t]hey ignore [Katy] as if [she's] the bad one. Then Wesley's mother asks Hector to withdraw the case" (*KSR* 143), which Auntie Rose quickly refuses. When Wesley's mother finally does address Katy, she asks her for "*the marks*" (*KSR* 144; emphasis in the original) which her son must have left on her. Katy is dumbstruck and only able to respond in her thoughts: "*Where are the marks?* I don't know what to say. How do you measure pain? What counts? Isn't betrayal pain? Are all wounds visible?" (*ibid.*).[76] The novel thus shows to what lengths parents would go to protect their children. Even though Wesley has disappointed his parents and committed several crimes, his parents ask the victim not to press charges. This parental attitude is addressed and problematized by both Katy and Auntie Rose.

In light of the easy availability of drugs like tik, the desire of young men to possess money to impress their girlfriends, and young females' wish to indulge in consumerism, parental figures appear to have lost their children to new market economies and a new materialism. Throughout the novel adult characters complain that youth "suffer from a lack of direction" (*KSR* 99). Auntie Rose, like the majority of adult characters in the novel, is aware of the generation gap, which

[76] The father of Zeke, a friend of Katy's and a customer of Wesley's who had to be hospitalized because of his addiction to tik, also comes to the house "telling Hector that he does not want Zeke to be involved in police business, and please to tell [Katy] to stop mentioning Zeke's name to the investigating officer" (*KSR* 144). Not Hector but Auntie Rose is the one to say "in disgust": "You can't protect your children forever" (*KSR* 144). However, she says this only after Zeke's father has left and insists that Katy "hold [her] head high" (*KSR* 145) despite people gossiping behind her back.

according to her originates from "watch[ing] too much violence on TV" and the growing importance of "American values" like consumerism and wasting food (*KSR* 99). Generally, adult characters are shown to be overwhelmed by the "many challenges, [...] HIV, tik, gangsterism" that "youth of today face" (*KSR* 99). Katy, on the other hand, has long since become used to, and hence indifferent to, the generalized, ill-conceived, and media-driven views that adults have of the younger generation. Her character development is motivated by a desire to grow as a person. She perceives herself as a teenager of the new South Africa whose problems are results of the present situation, and not of bygone struggles of the adult generation. Thus, *Katy of Sky Road* addresses the contemporary perception of the youth as a "lost generation" (cf. "Social Profile of Vulnerable Groups"; Everatt), but also decodes the many double standards persisting amongst the adult generation and points to a mental gap that has emerged between the generations. Moreover, the concept of 'lost' children is shown to be double-edged, with people looking for scapegoats in the wrong people. Nobody believes Wesley to be capable of his actions. In this novel, the well-respected and well-behaved are revealed to be two-faced criminals, while those who were assumed to be involved in shady business turn out to be upright and morally sound.

Before moving on to the next case study, this analysis must briefly point to a dispute fought between Auntie Rose and Katy's father which runs through the entire course of the novel and concerns their attitudes toward the new South Africa. Like in *E Eights*, it is the father figure who has not yet arrived in the new South Africa and is still "thinking in terms of race" (*KSR* 10). Auntie Rose is presented as a moral counterpart to Hector's tirades about the failure of the new South African government to enforce social equality between the different ethnicities. Hector repeatedly complains about the disadvantaged position of his social group in the new South Africa, arguing that the government favours black people over coloured people: "Before we were not white enough: now we are not black enough" (*KSR* 11). His case in point is the N2 Gateway Project, which provided new flats for black people who had formerly lived in squatter camps (cf. *KSR* 10). Auntie Rosie informs him that the N2 Gateway Project was started "to get rid of the eyesore before twenty-ten [, i.e. before the 2010 Soccer World Cup]", explaining that while coloured people are not well-off either and every one of them has "backyard tenants in a Wendy house", these tenants are, in contrast to poor black people, "neatly tucked away in [...] backyards" and do not squat openly (*KSR* 10).[77] Contrary to her intentions, Auntie Rose's explanation substantiates Hector's belief in the discrimination of "his" people, who have been waiting for these N2 flats "for the past thirty odd years" (cf. *KSR* 10). In order for coloured people to be heard, Hector argues, they should consider making themselves more visible so that politicians realize that they have to be cared for as well. Auntie Rose

[77] Interestingly, Katy's backyard tenants are a homosexual couple. However this is not further addressed in the story.

continuously confronts Hector with his outdated, apartheid perceptions and asks him to change his convictions, but it is only toward the end of the novel that Hector is becoming more open-minded. When his former favourite future son-in-law, Wesley, abducts Katy, Hector realizes that he does not always make the best character judgements. Brenda, Ricardo's mother and Hector's new partner, likewise challenges Hector's outdated attitudes and they start to "have very regular, very comfortable debates around the goings-on in the world", which make Hector also "a bit more understanding towards" Katy (*KSR* 146). The protagonist informs us that her father "has finally given permission for [her] to dance with Ricardo [in a dancing competition], though half-heartedly and with many conditions" (*ibid.*), suggesting that Hector is, eventually, beginning to understand that one cannot measure the present with the yardstick of the past. By contrast, Hector's mindset has always been too narrow for Katy, making her feel "shrink-wrap[ped]" (*KSR* 155), i.e. as if being kept way below her best. Her notions of identity have never hinged on being coloured, or on belonging to a certain social milieu, but on her curiosity for life beyond the parental home. At the end of the novel, she utters the wish to see the world as soon as she has finished school and to become "a journalist for a big magazine" or an "air hostess", as her friend Melissa suggests (*KSR* 155). Her wish implies that Katy not only aims to improve her socio-economic situation in the future, but is eager to further outgrow her father by getting to know more about this "wide world" (*ibid.*).

Sello Mahapeletsa, *Tears of an Angel* (2007)

Tears of an Angel[78] is Mahapeletsa's second novel after *When Lions Smile* (2005). Both novels have appeared in second and even third impressions, indicating their success with young readers. *Tears of an Angel* is narrated from an omniscient point of view. So far we have mostly encountered novels with homodiegetic narrators. While the latter perspective is valued for making it easy for the reader to identify with juvenile protagonists and their formative processes, the heterodiegetic narrator can also shed light on the feelings and thoughts of other characters in the novel, a capacity which is exploited in *Tears of an Angel*. The reader gains insight not only into Dikeledi's, but also into the other family members' thoughts and feelings – the father, Moroko, the mother, Mahlodi, and their children, Dikeledi and Palego – and gets answers as to why these characters develop the way they do and how they justify their decisions. Using variable internal focalization, Mahapeletsa is able to make the reader comprehend how a happy ending can come about despite the terrible events that precede it.

[78] The novel is hereafter cited as *TA*.

The cover of *Tears of an Angel* is designed like the front cover of a comic, which is rather unusual for novels written in the realist mode.[79] Within the 139 pages and 15 chapters of *Tears of an Angel*, Sello Mahapeletsa covers the rise and fall of Dikeledi's family on the social ladder of a township community. From chapter 2 to 13, the family's story is told chronologically from when Dikeledi's parents led a good life in the township of Lepareng as a young couple until the socio-economic collapse of the family. Chapters 1 and 14 serve as a frame to this storyline. Chapter 15 is set six years after these events on Dikeledi's wedding day.

The novel touches on a great variety of socio-econimic topics, namely unemployment, homelessness, drug abuse, patriarchal social structures, traditional belief systems, violent abuse in families, the inefficiency of the police, life in a township, sugar daddies, and sexual violence against young women. Significantly, the novel not only mentions these problems but – due to the omniscient narrator's perspective – the reader gains insight into both the perpetrator's and the victim's points of view. As the novel follows the rise and fall of a family, it illustrates a variety of socio-economic situations and shows how the status of the family varies accordingly in the community. For instance, when Dikeledi's father is still employed and earns well, the family enjoys a well-respected position in the community and gives away clothes to poorer families in the township as a gesture of social cohesion and social responsibility. When Moroko loses his job, Dikeledi realizes that the family will no longer be able to give away clothes because of their now constrained financial situation and she is afraid of the consequences.

Moroko struggles most to come to terms with the new situation, as he had drawn his entire self-confidence from his well-paid job at the mine. Moreover, his religion and a patriarchal family structure are central for Moroko's identity (cf. *TA* 13–14; 80–81). When he is "retrenched" (*TA* 22) and the family loses its "breadwinner" (*ibid.*), Moroko's concept of identity is destroyed and he is not able to form a new one. Instead of working on his new business as a fruit and vegetable vendor, he takes to the bottle and wallows in self-pity, which soon clouds his judgement. He starts to mistrust his wife and follows her around instead of looking after his new business. He finds out that Mahlodi meets up with her former boyfriend Stanley and is quick to draw the wrong conclusions (cf. *TA* 55). His drinking partner, Lelofa, nourishes his fears of losing his family to this more successful businessman. Then, "Moroko staggered home. He had to take control.

[79] The most prominent characters in the novel – the main character, Dikeledi, Dikeledi's best friend Lerato, Dikeledi's neighbour MaLetsogo, and Dikeledi's intimidating boyfriend Sting – are drawn in the manner of comic characters. The colours used for the images of the different characters reflect character traits, as do their posture and facial expressions. Dikeledi, or Dike as she is also called by her family and friends, is presented in a self-confident position with one hand in her pocket, bright eyes, and a faint smile on her face, for instance. All the characters displayed on the front cover are standing in front of a mine in an otherwise bleak and sandy landscape. The back cover shows some township houses illuminated by the setting sun.

Lelofa's words echoed in his ears and he nodded in agreement. Mahlodi needed to know that he was still the man of the house even if he wasn't working" (*TA* 60). In the following, Moroko is not to be convinced that his allegations are wrong and that Mahlodi has never intended to leave him. What is more, due to his constant drinking, his failure to bring home money, and his growing ever more violent against their mother, his children gradually lose respect for their father. This lack of respect eats Moroko up and further encourages him to be violent towards his wife (cf. *TA* 61–62). One afternoon, when "he had been drunk like he had never been drunk before" (*TA* 88), an argument with Mahlodi turns into a crime of passion. He kills his wife as "[i]t would be better if she were dead" than her being "with another man" (*TA* 89).

Throughout the novel money is linked to respect and esteem. The employed enjoy social acceptance while men who are unemployed perceive themselves as "loser[s]" (*TA* 60). Whether they are on the payroll or not, the primary thought of both parents and children is how to cover the everyday expenses. In *Tears of an Angel*, male characters are depicted as weaker than their female counterparts when they get into a situation where they are no longer the sole breadwinner. Both Lelofa and Moroko never recover from losing their jobs as miners and turn their anger towards their wives. Lelofa's wife has already left him and Moroko, too, is quick to sabotage his relationship through jealousy. By contrast, Mahlodi and Dikeledi adjust to the less advantaged life situation more quickly. Whilst the male characters lose themselves in the local shebeen, the female characters actively try to improve their situation and do not let themselves get distracted by alcohol or self-pity.

Mahlodi, for instance, is depicted as a supportive wife and mother. She backs her husband's notions and acquiesces in the patriarchal arrangement as long as the family is able to lead a good life because of it. When the family's situation deteriorates after Moroko has lost his job, Mahlodi starts to look for ways to improve the situation. She does so in secret and lies to her husband about her going to a business advisor, as he happens to be her former boyfriend (cf. *TA* 54). Even though the meetings are helpful and Mahlodi "knew she could start her own business with ease if she followed [Stanley's] advice" (*TA* 54), she does not tell her husband or children of her intention to open a catering business because of Moroko's jealousy. "[T]he happiness of her family c[o]me[s] first" she states (*TA* 55). However, this alleged happiness comes at a high price. Her remaining the obedient wife ultimately drives her daughter Dike into the arms of a dangerous man, Sting, who promises to cover her family's expenses if she becomes his girlfriend. When Mahlodi finds out about Dike's boyfriend, she is worried about her daughter and senses that "something is wrong" (*TA* 77). She wants Dike to talk openly to her about her boyfriend even though this is regarded as "shameful" (*TA* 76) and "disrespectful" (*TA* 77) in their culture. Despite her attempts to get through to Dike, her daughter thinks it better not to worry her mother with the fact that Sting has forced her to become his girlfriend and that it is fear and the difficult socio-economic situation of her family, but not love, that binds her to him (cf. *TA* 77–78). The omniscient narrator does not switch to Mahlodi's perspective again after this, leaving the reader to speculate about her thoughts about the fact that her daughter is receiving so much money from her boyfriend that she is able to support the entire family. The narrator only tells of Moroko accusing Mahlodi of "throwing away this child's future" (*TA* 81) and of leading "Dike down the path to prostitution" (*TA* 88). "We must always support one another" (*TA* 81) is Mahlodi's ambiguous last sentence in direct speech in the novel: Is she implying that it was Dikeledi's responsibility to do whatever was necessary to support the family? Or is she talking about herself, meaning that she has to be supportive of her daughter's decisions whether she likes them or not? In either case, the novel addresses the fact that Mahlodi is closing her eyes to the fact that her daughter is 'selling' her body to support the family, yet again pointing to the uncompromising socio-economic atmosphere of the township space.

The great majority of the novel is told from Dikeledi's perspective. From the beginning, Dikeledi is aware that her father's unemployment will have severe consequences on their lives as a family, but also her own future:

> For Dike, it wasn't just about what they were going to wear or eat, but about her tertiary fees. She had no intention of letting her dreams fall from her hands. Dike knew it wasn't going to be easy for her father to pay her tuition fees from the money he would make from selling fruits and vegetables. (*TA* 22)

The protagonist is described as intelligent, beautiful, and determined to achieve her dreams. The previous chapter on young females and their lives (cf. chapter 2.3) has shown that young females who have no interest in having a boyfriend before coming of age nevertheless still excite the interest of males. This is no different in Dike's case: "Almost every boy of her age wanted her, for she was a tall, slender, beautiful girl. Even some of the educators had tried their luck with her, but Dike didn't like any of them" (*TA* 46). Both her best female friends, Thuli and Lerato, cannot understand why Dike does not want to become Sting's girlfriend when he asks her. After all, "Sting could be the answer to your family's financial problems", Thuli reasons (*TA* 67). To her, things are clear: "I agree. It's not easy to date guys like Sting, but we all need money to survive, Dike. Do you think I enjoyed dating Letsogo? At first, I thought I was making a huge mistake, but now I think I love him and he takes good care of me" (*TA* 67). Dike is shown to struggle with herself and even though she despises Sting and knows he is dangerous, she debates with herself whether she should just give in to him because of his money. But every single time she argues with herself she decides against becoming his girlfriend because the costs are too high (cf. *TA* 68, 71). Simultaneously, she has "felt" for a long time that "[t]he man would hurt her one day […] for she saw he really wanted her" (*TA* 46), a line of thought we have also encountered in Moele's *Untitled* (cf. chapter 2.3.). And indeed, when Sting realizes that nice talk is not getting him anywhere with Dike, he turns to death threats to reach his goal – and he does (cf. *TA* 71). Significantly, a violent threat is what marks the beginning of their relationship and not Dike's wish to extract money from Sting. However, after her consent, Dike is determined to make as much of the situation as possible for her family and uses her position as girlfriend of the most feared gangster in the township. She becomes the "man of the house" (*TA* 81) and loses "all the respect she used to have for Moroko" as "she was the one who was bringing money home, while he was doing nothing but lying around in the city's parks all day" (*TA* 80). Only after her mother's death does the protagonist find the strength to stand up to Sting and to tell him to leave her alone. Unwilling to accept the breakup and in order to take revenge on Dike, the gang leader sends Letsogo, one of his underlings, to kill his former girlfriend. Dike survives the attack only by chance.

Money also plays a role in the aftermath of Letsogo's attack on Dike. Letsogo is the son of Dike's neighbour, MaLetsogo. As a means to make amends for her son's crime, MaLetsogo offers to pay for Dike's tertiary education. Her deed marks the beginning of Dike's new and better life. Both Letsogo and Sting are eventually convicted of attempted murder (cf. *TA* 132–133). Hence, *Tears of an Angel* as well as *Heist Wind* by Willem van der Walt (cf. chapter 3.3) convey the notion that money earned by crime does not lead to a happy life. Like in *Katy of Sky Road*, honest work and education are rewarded and thus promoted as 'good' ways of living, while criminals end up socially ostracized in this set of novels. Thus, *Tears of an Angel* and *Katy of Sky Road* highlight notions that foster social democracy and the ideal that those who are good will have good done to them (cf. chapter 3.3).

Tears of an Angel ends happily. This is a rare case in South African youth novels, which in the majority of cases end on a hopeful note but do not draw on the happily–ever–after motif. The novel concludes on Dike's wedding day, which is also the day when her father's prison sentence ends. When he shows up at the wedding to beg his children for forgiveness, Dike's wish for her wedding day to signal a fresh start into a happier life helps her to meet her father halfway and she accepts his apology (cf. *TA* 139). Concluding with a gesture of forgiveness and the image of the family reunion, the novel invokes a community profile of the township that speaks of acceptance, inclusion, and cohesion but also disruption and loss as characters must find the strength to overcome prejudices and to forgive those who caused them pain. The novel debates the effects that a decline on the social ladder can have on the psyche of family members, showing that men and women approach such a situation differently. The nuclear family structure becomes disrupted as a result of socio-economic constraints and it takes all the characters a considerable amount of time to adjust to the new living situation and to develop the strength to get back on their feet. Thus, the social milieu of the township is largely portrayed as merciless, but there are noteworthy exceptions: MaLetsego's decision to right her son's wrongdoing by paying for Dike's tertiary education ultimately enables Dike to reverse her former social decline.

Jenny Robson, *Back to Villa Park* (2013)

Back to Villa Park[80] is a narrative about disrupted family structures, the difficulty of making something of oneself when coming from a disadvantaged background, and a topic that is usually glossed over, namely white poverty and the place of whites in post-apartheid South Africa. In 2012, "[a]pproximately 64,5% of children lived in households that fell into the bottom two income quintiles and that had a per capita income of less than R765 per month" ("Social Profile of Vulnerable Groups" ii). Of these 64.5% of children living in low-income households, "only 4,4% [were] white children" compared to 70.5% who were of "black African" decent (*ibid.*).

Jenny Robson is the winner of five Sanlam Awards for South African youth literature and is known to not shy away from delicate topics in her writing. *Back to Villa Park* (2013) is no different. Addressing a South African taboo topic (cf. Evans 2008; Bottomley 2012), the book depicts a male protagonist who is poor, white, and speaks up about inequality on the labour market.[81] Writing about such delicate topics as "racism and ideas of privilege and fairness" in *Back to Villa Park* caused Robson many "sleepless nights and panic attacks", as she admits in an interview conducted by Lindsay Callaghan in 2013. The author is moreover aware that her being white just like the main character makes her vulnerable to accusations of political incorrectness (cf. Chris). However, given the country's unique historical context, Robson believes that "South Africa is the only country where this specific story could be set. It would not make sense anywhere else" (Chris).

Robson's novel is doubly significant in the context of this chapter: firstly, because of its discussion of the anxieties of youths about their future and the logic of Black Economic Empowerment (BEE) (cf. Warnes 2014, 155), and secondly, because of its treatment of social ethics. The novel confronts the reader with a wide spectrum of people from quite contrasting social backgrounds and provides insight into different lifestyles as well as their socio-economic opportunities and constraints. The story features white characters from poor (the protagonist, Dirk), middle class (e.g. the Camerons or Dirk's sister, Fat Sonja), and rich (Bethany and her father, Mr Lawrence) backgrounds, black characters from poor (Aggis), middle class (e.g. Mr and Mrs Mogwera, Jenny September), and rich ("these Double As"[82]) backgrounds, and one poor coloured character (Rosie). In the

[80] The novel is hereafter cited as *BVP*.

[81] Eight percent of realist novels published between the years 2000 and 2013 feature poor white protagonists, amongst these are Anoeschka von Meck's *My Name Is Vaselinetjie* (2011) and S. A. Partridge's *Fuse* (2009) (cf. Stadler 2015, 52).

[82] "Double A" is a derogatory term for those black persons who have benefited from the introduction of affirmative action (AA) legislation, which was introduced in 1998 as "measures designed to ensure that suitably qualified people from designated groups have

narrative, the socio-economic status of a character is defined by his or her job situation, which in turn identifies the character as either a member of the new South African society or just a bystander.

Since the end of apartheid, "policies designed to promote 'affirmative action,' 'employment equity,' and 'black economic empowerment'" (BEE) have been "core aspects of the postapartheid state's attempts to transform South African society" (Warnes 2014, 158). Though well intended, BEE as well as its 2003 replacement, the Broad-Based Black Economic Empowerment Act in 2003 (BBBEE) and the 2013 amendment to the act, lag behind their goal of ensuring equal job opportunities for both genders and all ethnicities and of undoing past discriminations. Local businesses call BBBEE

> an imposition that generates needless expense and inefficiency; for foreign businesses, it may be simply another form of tax and possible corruption, for some whites, it is an enormous wellspring of dissatisfaction; for some blacks it is perceived as benefitting only the well connected. (Warnes 2014, 160–161)

The 2014 report of the "Commission for Employment Equity" admits that

> [w]hat the real numbers reveal is that the 'cake' has been expanding/increasing over the past ten years, but it has not transformed at the same rate as it has been increasing. We then have the biblical situation of even more being added to those to whom more representation had been given, whereas from those whose representation was less, lesser still will be added. To continue the cake analogy, the black raisins on the cake remain scattered here and there even as the cake continues to enlarge. (52–53)

In other words, white males still hold 62% of Top Management positions in 2013 while Africans hold less than 20% ("Commission for Employment Equity" 52). The representation of coloured people in Top Management positions is also unsatisfactory: "the only solid and consistent progress in the percentages of representation at Top Management level, between 2003 and 2013, takes place in the Indian sub-category of designated group members" ("Commission for Employment Equity" 52). As a matter of fact, "[f]emales constitute 20.6% of Top Management. Their actual figure is 4 646 employees. So, in real terms, there are more females in Top Management (4 646) than all the Africans in Top Management (4 464)" ("Commission for Employment Equity" 52). Regarding its set of characters, Robson's novel turns these numbers around and includes one

equal employment opportunities and are equitably represented in all occupational categories and levels in the workforce of a designated employer" (Edigheji 1; cf. Burger and Jafta). Burger and Jafta were able to show that "[t]he effects of affirmative action policies in reducing the employment or wage gaps have been marginal at best, and were much less significant in bringing about changes in labour market outcomes" (abstract).

white male character who obtains a Top Management position, namely Bethany's father, Mr Lawrence, but two "Double As" in senior positions, namely Mr Mogwera and an interviewer at Kagiso Holdings, and four "Mega–mega–Double As" (*KSR* 85). By reversing the number of representatives, the novel gives the impression of a significantly greater number of black males in senior positions than white males. Notably, each of the above-named men features only briefly in the novel, but neither of them treats the main character, Dirk, fairly. These notions feed the novel's debate of white *angst* and the fear that white people no longer have a place in the new South Africa, ideas which are most explicitly expressed by the side-character Bethany.[83]

Telling the story of a young white male who is looking for a job to start a new life, *Back to Villa Park* takes up a public discourse which abounds in discontent with BEE and related policies intended to tackle social inequalities, and debates to what extent racial discrimination continues to shape people's lives. The story covers the events of one day only, namely Dirk Karel Strydom's eighteenth birthday. Due to many flashbacks, the reader also learns about Dirk's childhood. The narrative is told by Dirk and opens *in medias res* with Dirk being thrown out of Kagiso Holdings by "this Double A" because he cheated on a test that preceded a job interview (*BVP* 14). Dirk is devastated and "so angry, [he] smashed [his] fists against the fancy egg-shell-painted wall [...] until there was blood and pain" (*BVP* 18). He had thought the job interview would be the beginning of his new life as a real man and earning employee. After all, the interview was on his eighteenth birthday, the day that "mark[s] that you've become a man. That you can drive and go to a bar and vote and earn a proper living. You're not a boy any more and so things will never, ever be thc samc for you" (*BVP* 20). Instead of his birthday

[83] Bethany is a rich white girl who heads a group of young white males who meet at her mansion to discuss what they can do to change the now – as they perceive it – underprivileged position of whites in the new South Africa: "We whites have to hold our heads up high, you know. Especially you men. We can't let them think we are, like, beaten", Bethany explains to Dirk on the day of their first encounter (*BVP* 53). Puzzled, the main character asks, "Them?" to which Bethany responds: "The blacks. The Double As. Listen: you are the descendent of proud, powerful men. Men who, like, conquered a whole continent. So stand tall and be a hero" (*BVP* 54). The character of Bethany, whose views are clearly problematic in terms of their ideological basis, represents those voices in present-day South Africa who remain stuck in apartheid thought patterns of racism and imperialism. Dirk is confused about Bethany's harsh attitudes, but does not speak out against them in the first half of the novel when he is still living on the streets of Johannesburg because he does not want to risk losing access to her house and its amenities. However, when Bethany and her group brainstorm ever more violent schemes to reverse a system which they perceive as "tilted against" whites (*BVP* 67), the protagonist parts company with them, also because he by now understands that not all black people are like "those guys with their Rolexes and Mercedes Benzes and bodyguards" (*BVP* 66).

marking the beginning of his future, better life, Dirk finds himself back on the streets of Johannesburg without any prospects.

In *Back to Villa Park*, Robson plays with people's tendency to make hasty judgements and to think in stereotypes, only to prove them wrong in the very last pages. The protagonist is a character who at the start of the novel appears charmless, lost, violent, and unlikable. Moreover, Dirk's frantic style of narration leaves the reader with more questions than answers about the protagonist's situation. Why does he think it is unfair to be thrown out of a test when he was caught cheating? Is there anything more to what clearly must be perceived as biased perceptions about "Double As" (14), "Zed[s]",[84] and "political correctness" (15) in the beginning of the novel? What further adds to the reader's confusion is that the storyline is frequently interrupted by the protagonist's thoughts and memories of his childhood. Mimicking the natural process of remembering and thinking, Dirk's narrations of past events are triggered by events in the present. Yet Dirk does not narrate his past chronologically, leaving the reader to speculate about what might have led to his improper behaviour during the job interview. Only as the story unfolds does the reader find out that the source of Dirk's anger and frustration is not his exclusion from the interview, but the suicide of both of his parents six years earlier after finding out that their application to migrate to Australia had been denied, which left Dirk seriously traumatized (cf. *BVP* 110–111). Moreover, the reader learns that Dirk's outcry against "this Double A" in the beginning of the novel is not racially motivated, but originates in his having been treated unfairly by all kinds of people throughout his life. In fact, it turns out that Dirk is not even sure what exactly "this Double A" means, which becomes apparent when he asks "Must I really call [all black people] Double A[s]?" (*BVP* 67).

A few months prior to his eighteenth birthday Dirk decides to return to Johannesburg from Port Alfred, where he had lived with his older sister ever since the death of his parents. Having dropped out of school and arriving without any certificates, papers, or money, Dirk gets stranded on the streets of Johannesburg the minute after his arrival in January. In April, Dirk is allowed to move into the "maid's quarters of 5 Groenewald Street, Villa Park" (*BVP* 18), the property which formerly belonged to his parents but is now owned by Mrs Mogwera's husband. Mr and Mrs Mogwera represent the growing black middle class in the novel, who can now afford to move into those areas of the city which were formerly exclusively white. History is reversed when Dirk moves into the little shed in the backyard of the house, where he can stay for free in return for helping in the garden. Mr Mogwera is clearly uncomfortable with the situation, but agrees to his wife's wish to let Dirk stay with them, as we are informed by Mrs Mogwera. Mr Mogwera speaks to Dirk only once, when he first finds him in front of his house: "He stared across at me like I was maybe a criminal or a burglar. He shouted,

[84] That is, young white males.

'What do you want? Go. Voetsek! Go Away!'" (*BVP* 34). Scenes like this one clearly play on the notion of a juvenile counternation and the stereotype of young (black) males being potential criminals, which we have already come across in the above chapter on machoism and masculinity (cf. chapter 2.1). "Looking to South Africa", Jones argues,

> constellations of crime and victimhood remain tied to race and class, "the proclivity to pin lawlessness on young black men – to situate it, that is, at the confluence of race, gender, and generation – [and] the 'fact' that violence is highly enclaved plays into a mass-mediated view of the townships as breeding grounds of brutality." [Novels such as *Young Blood*] go some way in contesting the reification of townships as sites of violence and suffering, but they reiterate the destruction of poor black bodies as symptomatic of their social exclusion. (220)

Tellingly, Dirk's body is not destroyed in the course of *Back to Villa Park*, nor is the protagonist socially excluded. In the roughly three months that he is living on the streets, Dirk is granted regular access to Bethany's house to clean and feed himself at her cost. Moreover, he is quite successful at begging (cf. *BVP* 38), showing that it is much easier for Dirk as a white person to survive on the streets than it is, for instance, for the immigrant Aggis. In fact, the novel shows that it is not really possible for him as a young white person to become excluded, because as soon as people – and notably people of different ethnic backgrounds – realize that he is 'at risk', they give him money and provide shelter because "[t]hey will feel too sad to see a nice-looking white boy in trouble" (*BVP* 34). Except for one scene in which Dirk is insulted and spat at for begging (cf. *BVP* 91), the novel's portrayal of life on the streets is markedly different from the depiction in *Thirteen Cents* (cf. chapter 1.2.1). A reason for this certainly is that Dirk is only temporarily living on the streets, as he is allowed to move into the backyard house of Mr and Mrs Mogwera's property after three months.

Employment, money, and the prestige connected to both play a significant role in *Back to Villa Park*. Yet in both the novel and in the real South Africa, these are granted to only a few. The "Social Profile of Vulnerable Groups" informs us that in 2011 "[a]pproximately 32,4% of children lived in households without any employed members, and social grants and remittances were vital to improve the access to food and education" (ii). Therefore, it is not uncommon for young people to try to find work themselves in order to support the family with their income. The "Social Profile of Vulnerable Groups" moreover found that "[o]lder youth[, aged 25–34], were much more likely to engage in business (7,7% cited non-farm income as their main source of income) and to cite salary and wages as their main source of income than younger youth[, aged 15–25]" (ii–iii). The results of the profile also show that "[f]emale-headed households were consistently more likely to be poor", namely 57% "compared to 36% of male-headed households" ("Social Profile of Vulnerable Groups" iii). The overwhelming majority of literary texts in the corpus feature adult figures who work but nevertheless do not earn enough to rise on the social ladder. Child-headed households are only seldom represented.[85] Because of their constrained living situation, many teenagers are shown to be eager to work and try to earn some kind of money. In the novels that I have selected for close reading in this thesis, young males are more likely to look for work than young females, who are either rather more interested in their education or expect men to earn money and to pay their expenses.[86] Such an image is also presented in *Back to Villa Park*. Dirk had learned from his father at an early age that getting a job was a man's business. Throughout the novel, males are presented as providers of the family, while women are portrayed as living off their husband's income. Dirk's mother, Mrs Mogwera, as well as Mrs Cameron and Dirk's sister are all housewives who take care of raising the children and all the housework while their husbands have a steady job. Interestingly, the same pattern occurs throughout all social classes: Aggis, who lives on the streets, begs in order to be able to provide for his Rosie; Mr Mogwera and Mr Lawrence work to ensure a good life for their wives and daughter. When Dirk's father loses his job and is not able to find a new one, he does not tell his wife, who is already suffering from depression, but his son. Dirk's father takes it upon himself to find a solution for the family and expects Dirk to understand – because he is a young male – why he will not be getting a birthday present. Contrary to the male protagonists in *Young Blood*, *Take Me to the River*, and *Heist Wind*, Dirk did not try to find work during his childhood although his family was never wealthy and although his sister repeatedly reminded him of how much he cost her when he moved in with her (cf. *BVP* 34, 62). The reason for this is certainly Dirk's trauma after his finding his parents in the midst of "a giant lake of blood" (*BVP* 102) and his closing himself off mentally from his surroundings thereafter.

Back to Villa Park shows that school education has become a prerequisite for success in the world of work and for getting a job in the first place. Due to learning difficulties after his parents' death and his dropping out of school, Dirk does not have any certificate or accredited qualification to his name (cf. *BVP* 38). Hence, not even Bethany's influential father and top manager, Mr Lawrence, dares to give Dirk a job: "How would [it] look", he asks, "me employing him? It just wouldn't be fair, would it? It wouldn't be honest" (*BVP* 58). To the present day, Dirk has problems with spelling, which is believed to be rather uncommon amongst white children, who normally "all get *mos* properly educated", as Aggis puts it (*BVP* 38).

[85] In their "analysis of the 2006 General Household Survey" Meintjes et al. "found 0.67% of children living in child-headed households[, which] is equivalent to roughly 122 000 children out of 18.2 million children in South Africa" (1). Critics must know that research on child-headed households is scarce and that "[s]tatements about child-headed households are often not based on evidence", leading to "[c]ommon but inaccurate assumptions about child-headed households" (Meintjes et al. 1). For instance, the assumption that "most of the children in child-headed households [are] AIDS orphans" is invalid (*ibid.*).

[86] An exception is *Trinity Rising* in which Trinity is shown to be even more eager to earn money than her male peers.

Bethany is moreover convinced that because of Dirk being a "pale man" he "do[esn't] have an ice cube's hope in hell" of finding a job in the new South Africa (*BVP* 63). These notions collide with Dirk's own attitudes toward work: "I am ready and able and willing. That's for sure" (*BVP* 71), the protagonist states and hopes for a salary which would allow him "to get a little flat somewhere" (*BVP* 71). In light of his ambition, why did Dirk cheat during the test at Kagiso Holdings and destroy his chance at a job?

During the test situation the main character recognizes Jenny September, the daughter of his parents' former help, Dorcas, who had taken advantage of the family's situation by repeatedly stealing meat, or more precisely mince, from the Strydom's. Caught up in his anger and unable to think straight, Dirk reasons that it must be because of this lack of protein during childhood that his brain has not grown as much as Jenny's, who appears to have no trouble completing the test (cf. *BVP* 100). The main character is frustrated and stressed because of the unexpected test situation and fails to understand that it is his lack of qualifications and his psychological trauma and not necessarily his skin colour or a lack of protein that keep him from getting the job. When asked why he cheated on the test, he explains to Mrs Mogwera: "I was just taking back what Dorcas stole from me in the first place. You know, like the people taking back their land that got stolen by apartheid? I mean, all I was trying to get was a little fairness. A little justice. That's all I ask for. Just a little fairness in this world" (*BVP* 101). This sense of being treated unfairly goes back to his parents' suicide, which he has always felt to be highly unfair toward him and which has triggered IEA, an "Intermittent Explosive Anger" syndrome (cf. *BVP* 112). Not until he returns to the exact location of the suicide, namely the kitchen table in their former house in Johannesburg, is Dirk able to overcome his parents' deaths and to let go of his anger against them. It is at that table that Mrs Mogwera responds to Dirk's explanation of taking back what belongs to him:

> I must warn you – now that you are an adult, you are ready to hear. This world is not a fair place. Mostly it is very unfair. If you keep hoping for fairness, it will make you upset and disappointed. It will drive you crazy. [...] But you know what else, Dirkie? It isn't all hopeless, because you know what else? [...] Well we have the power to treat others fairly. That's what I think. We have to create our own fairness and justice in the world. (*BVP* 117–118)

Having confronted his childhood trauma, Dirk finally understands that fairness has nothing to do with taking back what one thinks belongs to oneself. At the end of the novel, the character changes from an angry youth to a sensitive, self-conscious, and understanding young man who agrees to return to school and to work on his anger management. Making conscious decisions about his future life, Dirk feels self-empowered for the first time in the final pages of the novel. Robson's novel thus responds to Pennell's call for a "rejection of the concept of the unitary masculine subject" in literary texts in favour of "a diverse range of self-reflexive masculine subjectivities" (56), making *Back to Villa Park* a prime example of a novel that explains *how* young people experience life and make meaning and *why* the young male protagonist acts the way he does (cf. White 157). In broader terms, the novel discusses the tendency to not ask for the individual story, illustrates how long it can take to uncover the real reasons behind a person's improper behaviour, and shows the complexity of an individual's socio-economic situation. Despite setbacks in his attempt to find his place in Johannesburg, Dirk never falls prey to Bethany's ideologically motivated talk about the place of whites in the new South Africa. Engaging with a variety of people from different backgrounds and accessing different social milieus, Dirk learns to see beyond racial stereotypes and ideas of privilege and to ponder the real reasons for his socio-economic situation.

Résumé

The previous close readings of Case and Hart's *Katy of Sky Road*, Mahapeletsa's *Tears of an Angel*, and Robson's *Back to Villa Park* have shown that social segregation primarily results from persisting socio-economic inequalities. *Katy of Sky Road* and *Tears of an Angel* depict how young people experience life in a coloured community on the fictionalized version of the Cape Flats and a black community in a fictional township. The novels show that these spaces are inhabited by people with different socio-economic resources and are thus socially segregated in themselves. *Back to Villa Park* is the only novel of the three that shows a character transgressing the invisible boundaries between ethnicities. Simultaneously, Dirk moves through poor, middle-class, and rich environments and experiences each way of living. As a young white and poor male he apparently elicits compassion from his contemporaries, and people from different ethnic backgrounds help him to get back on his feet. Johannesburg is thus presented as a multiethnic space which is socially divided but also as a city in which this divide can be overcome. All three novels show that the teenagers are aware of the importance of socio-economic resources for their future. Thus, all the characters show an ambition to be economically successful. This drive for money initially exceeds a character's push for education or their appreciation of friends and family, but is overcome in the course of the novel. These books thus end with a "normative conclusio[n]" (Jones 211), namely that money should not be sought at any cost. Eventually, education, friendship, and family supersede its value.

3.3 Social Ethics and the Adolescent Novel

In the preceding chapters, we have accompanied adolescent characters through their coming of age and we have seen that every one of them is concerned with finding his or her place in the surrounding space and social community. Fictional texts written in the realist mode document young people's struggles to decode the codes of conduct of that space and community and discuss the relevance of sticking to these rules in order to become accepted as full members of society. The novels seldom subscribe to a specific code of conduct. Rather, the literary texts negotiate individual developmental processes alongside societal expectations and communal living and outline the meaning-making processes of young people and their (counter-)reactions to pre-established social norms. Generally, a juvenile character in South African youth novels feels empowered and accepted when he or she is respected both as an individual and as part of a community. Some novels, like Jayne Bauling's *E Eights* (cf. chapter 1.2.1), depict the formation of new social ethics amongst the young. Others, such as *A Man Who Is Not a Man*, make the consequences that individuals face when they do not follow the community's rules, namely social ostracism and stigmatization, the topic of their narrative. The analyses in the previous chapters have shown that South Africa is made up of numerous social sub-spaces, each of which has its own code of conduct. Moreover, we have seen that these rules differ for male and female characters.

While they are still learning the pre-established codes of conduct of their surrounding space, juvenile characters appear to already have quite an elaborate sense of what they consider right or wrong. In a qualitative study containing hard and soft data, Sharlene Swartz was able to show that youth have developed a sense of right and wrong which they tend to relax when it fits their purpose. When Swartz asked 18 males and 19 females between the ages of 14 and 20 what they thought of substance use, crime, and violence, they clearly understood them as wrong (cf. 15, 54). However, when asked in greater detail, it became apparent that the youth had established a set of "rules to govern violence", which differentiated "between types of violence, hierarchies of crime, and better or worse kinds of substance use" (Swartz 56). They also "differentiated between drinking alcohol and getting drunk, and between smoking *dagga* and merely experimenting with it" (Swartz 54, 55; emphasis in the original). Moreover, "[y]oung people's construction of the wrongness of crime was also not in keeping with their practice. Despite a strong consensus that crime was wrong, young people were involved in it at multiple levels [...] delineat[ing] a hierarchy regarding *types* of crime" (Swartz 56). For instance, "[m]ore young people said it was wrong to steal from your parents (33 out of 35), than from white people (28 out of 36) or from the rich (20 out of 36)" (Swartz 55–56). Interestingly, crime, substance use, and violence are moralized and judged in a similar manner in young adult novels such as *Katy of Sky Road*, *Untitled*, or *Young Blood*.

What all novels in the corpus share is a didacticism that intends to foster a social democracy in spite of, or rather in response to, the different value systems and cultural specificities that are portrayed in these rural, urban, suburban, boarding school, and township novels. In her study, titled *The Moral Ecology of South Africa's Township Youth* (2009), Sharlene Swartz points to the failure of scholars to "trea[t] young people as 'transcultural knowers'" who are "able to interpret morality and provide insight into society rather than only be objects of study whose values and psychological processes are investigated" (4). By contrast, literary texts for juveniles depict South African youths as being significantly more open to negotiating cross-cultural relationships than adult characters. The process of negotiating cross-cultural differences is never presented as straightforward or following a romanticized ideal. Its outcomes, whether negative or positive, are the result of complex meaning-making processes and the result of debating personal and communal expectations (cf. *E Eights*; Robson's *Monday Evening, Thursday Afternoon*).

Social ethics remain a delicate topic in contemporary South Africa as notions of race, class, gender, religion, and politics intersect in this area of discussion. Research into social ethics is above all concerned with questions of the individual's position in society and his or her chances to lead a 'good' life in that society. In relation to these questions, this area of research looks, for instance, into whether politicians see to the eradication of poverty and the creation of new jobs, and discusses the accessibility of media, the relevance of family structures, and the importance of values, freedom, and tolerance for social cohesion. An area that has been frequently discussed in South Africa is the relationship between employers and employees, i.e. work ethics and corporate social responsibility (cf. Hamann and Kapelus; McWilliams, Siegel, and Wright; Dawkins and Ngunjiri). As a multicultural hub South Africa is a conglomerate of different belief systems and cultural idiosyncrasies. Yet there are values that transcend all these differences, namely the wish to be accepted, to be treated humanely, and to be able to lead a 'good' life.

As early as 1902, Jane Addams (1860–1935), the first woman to win the Nobel Peace Prize in 1931, argued that "we can only discover truth by a rational and democratic interest in life" (11). She also noted that "each generation has its own test, the contemporaneous and current standard by which alone it can adequately judge of its own moral achievements" (Addams 1902, 2). Her works have recently been rediscovered and re-evaluated (cf. Elshtain; Knight; Seigfried; Shields 2006), leading to the republication of her most famous works, amongst them her monograph *Democracy and Social Ethics* (1902). The blurb of the republication praises Addams for "put[ting] forward her conception of the moral significance of diversity" almost "a century before the advent of 'multiculturalism'" (Addams 2002, blurb). Jane Addams opened *Democracy and Social Ethics* with the following clarification: "It is well to remind ourselves, from time to time, that 'Ethics' is but another word for 'righteousness,' that for which many men and women of every generation have hungered and thirsted, and without which life becomes meaningless" (1902, 1). To her, "ethics" or "righteousness" need to be at the core of a functioning social democracy. Addams firmly believed that

> [w]e are [...] brought to a conception of Democracy not merely as a sentiment which desires the well-being of all men, nor yet as a creed which believes in the essential dignity and equality of all men, but as that which affords a rule of living as well as a test of faith. We are learning that a standard of social ethics is not attained by travelling a sequestered byway, but by mixing on the thronged and common road where all must turn out for one another, and at least see the size of one another's burdens. To follow the path of social morality results perforce in the temper if not the practice of the democratic spirit, for it implies that diversified human experience and resultant sympathy which are the foundation and guarantee of Democracy. (1902, 6–7)

Though written in a different time and space, Jane Addams's observations resonate with the kind of social ethic that is being promoted in twenty-first century South African literature for young adults. Interestingly, whilst literary texts discuss social ethics on three levels, namely with regard to local, global, and digital developments, scholarly discussion of social ethics for the new South Africa has so far revolved predominantly around a redefined version of ubuntu, in which both African and European ideals of living are combined.[87]

The original idea of ubuntu "was developed in very different circumstances from contemporary South Africa, in the pre-scientific, pre-industrial Africa of the past" (Shutte 32). Both Desmond Tutu and Augustine Shutte draw on these original notions of ubuntu to conceptualize a version of ubuntu that resonates with contemporary societal developments in South Africa.[88] In order for a reconciliation of the different social classes and ethnic groups to be achieved, Emeritus Archbishop of Cape Town Desmond Tutu argues that South Africa needs both "a strong group feeling" in the traditional sense of ubuntu and the appreciation of each individual's "inalienable uniqueness" (quoted in Battle xiii). Arguing in a similar manner, the South African scholar of philosophy Augustine

[87] Swartz also points to "the Truth and Reconciliation Commission, the Moral Regeneration Movement, [and] Race and Values in Education" as three further initiatives which "have contributed in some measure to the discourses around moral renewal and rebuilding in post-Apartheid South Africa. Their actual impact on moral behaviour is relatively unknown, and certainly uninvestigated" (25). For further information on the different initiatives, see Swartz (20–25). In the present study, I confine myself to the discussion of ubuntu.

[88] Swartz adds that "[a]lthough not called ubuntu by other postcolonial leaders, African humanism has [also] been described by Julius Nyerere (Tanzania), Jomo Kenyatta (Kenya), Kenneth Kaunda (Zambia), Milton Obote (Uganda), and Seretse Khama (Botswana)" (cf. 194, footnote 12).

Shutte believes that in order to fill the "moral vacuum" that has characterized the early years of the new South Africa, and to put an end to

> [i]ncreasing crime, callous and often gratuitous violence, corruption in public office and in private financial affairs, self-centred retreat into private security or the equally self-centred "culture of entitlement", [and] materialistic consumerism taking the place of traditional family values (Shutte 1)

people need to be reminded of "values of humanity as such" (*ibid.*). The term ubuntu, Tutu and Shutte argue, subsumes this demand for a new understanding of ethics in South Africa. Tutu's theology is based on both "African Insights and the Old Testament" (*ibid.*).[89] By "embrac[ing] the notion of ubuntu and link[ing] it to Christian theology", Tutu "provides a basis whereby 'black' people can forgive 'white' people for the atrocities of apartheid, based on transcendent authority" (Swartz 106). Shutte also perceives "African and European ethical ideas [as] complement[ing]" (viii) each other and has taken up the concept of *Ubuntu [as] An Ethic for a New South Africa.* Shutte explains that "[t]he European idea is the idea of freedom, that individuals have power of free choice. The African idea is the idea of community, that persons depend on other persons to be persons" (10).[90] Moreover, Shutte describes South Africa as "a society where the dominant culture is *European*, not African, and where many other cultures from other parts of the world exist together" (10; emphasis in the original), as well as a country shaped by "a history of continuous inter-group and inter-cultural misunderstanding, leading to conflict and eventually disintegration and chaos in a state of permanent, sometimes open, sometimes hidden, war" (Shutte 223). Tutu's and Shutte's new version of ubuntu aims to help overcome cultural misunderstandings and avoid further disintegration between different groups. Government initiatives and concept papers which investigate social cohesion draw on the notion of ubuntu (cf. Cloete and Kotze). In their "Concept Paper on Social Cohesion/Inclusion in Local Integrated Development Plans", Cloete and Kotze argue, for instance, for "[t]he promotion of a community spirit, where commonality in place of a notion of 'us' and 'them' is accepted" (45). Moreover, they propose that "[t]he interest of the

[89] Swartz points to Coertze (2001), "who shows how many of the qualities found in Galatians 5 and Colossians 3 of the Bible have found their way into the concept of ubuntu as 'the Christian faith became part of the cultural heritage of many African individuals'" (Swartz 106).

[90] More explicitly, this means that "European culture has taught us to see the self as something private, hidden *within* our bodies. [...] The African image is very different: the self is *outside* of the body, present and open to all. This is because the self is the result and expression of all the forces acting upon us. It is not a thing [as the European concept of self is], but the sum total of all the interacting forces [....] [P]ersons exist only in relation to other persons. The human self is not something that first exists on its own and then enters into relationship with its surroundings. It only exists in relationship to its surroundings [...] As African philosophers are fond of saying, 'I am because we are'" (Shutte 22–23; emphasis in the original).

broader community should be promoted above sectional interests but according to values of justice and equity" (Cloete and Kotze 45). Moreover, they are convinced of the impetus arts and culture can be for the promotion of social ethics as they provide a "space for communication and a better understanding of people not part of your own group" (Cloete and Kotze 45).

Interestingly, South African youth literature of this early twenty-first century finds itself precisely in the midst of this debate of balancing personal growth and community development. Tutu's and Shutte's arguments for the combination of European and African ideas about the ethics of communal living as well as Swartz's findings on *The Moral Ecology of South Africa's Township Youth* (2009) echo in a great number of young adult novels of this early twenty-first century. *Heist Wind* (2003) by Willem van der Walt is a prime example of such meaning-making processes. However, literary discussions of social ethics do not stop there. An analysis of *Monday Evening, Thursday Afternoon* (2013) by Jenny Robson makes clear that it is not enough to promote a new version of ubuntu in South Africa, as the country inhabits not only communities with European and African origins but also people of Asian and Middle Eastern heritages. Robson's novel shows that with progressing globalization, foreign events have come to deeply affect local decision-making processes and the lives of young adults. The author thus calls for a reconsideration of preconceived notions and the necessity of tolerance across belief systems. Lastly, a close reading of *Dark Poppy's Demise* (2011)[91] by Sally Ann Partridge spells out the relevance of expanding our discussion of social ethics not only from a local to a global level, as becomes apparent after reading Robson's novel, but of extending this debate to the digital sphere as well. It should go without saying that, generally, social ethics should be considered relevant not only in social reality but also, for instance, in the virtual realities of online spaces. Such notions become increasingly relevant when considering that communication between individuals increasingly takes place online. *Dark Poppy's Demise* tackles problematic issues related to this field of discussion.

Willem 'Thembalethu' van der Walt, *Heist Wind* (2003)

Van der Walt's *Heist Wind*[92] is a novel that examines a specific phenomenon of adolescent life in African countries, namely "the rise of a 'hustler's mentality' among the African youth" (Ekema-Agbaw and Yenika-Agbaw 188). Stephen

[91] Though *Dark Poppy's Demise* was published two years earlier than *Monday Morning, Thursday Afternoon*, Partridge's novel will be discussed after Robson's book. This order was chosen for the purposes of argumentation.
[92] The novel is hereafter cited as *HW*.

Ekema-Agbaw and VivianYenika-Agbaw describe the everyday life of African youth as

> a 'hustler's culture.' This 'hustler's culture' arises from a dilemma facing African youth. On the one hand, African youth are at a stage in their lives where they greatly need their independence; they are young adults who are ready to leave or are just leaving home for the first time. On the other hand, African youth have incredibly limited resources afforded to them – specifically, money. These youth are forced to get by day–to–day on remarkably limited budgets. Moreover, because of the struggling economies of most African countries, job prospects are poor for most youth, and they are unable to turn to their parents for help, because they too are struggling under the difficult economic circumstances. (188)

Growing up with a restricted set of resources and finding themselves in the midst of the socio-economic dilemma of African countries, African youth understand money as a symbol of opportunity and social success from an early age, because

> money quite literally permeates every decision throughout their day. The result of this dilemma is the rise of a 'hustler's mentality' among the African youth. In any action or exchange in which money is involved, there is always a barter that takes place and a bargain to be had. African youth are remarkably savvy in how they are able to stretch their money as well as make money. (Ekema-Agbaw and Yenika-Agbaw 188)

Sharlene Swartz's research supports Ekema-Agbaw and Yenika-Agbaw's findings, showing youth to have "a mixed morality of money" (Swartz 56). Although most youth "displayed conventional and traditional values around not stealing and advocated 'working hard' for your money […] they exhibit strong modernist materialistic values – loving material possessions (boats, cars, cellphones, clothes, big houses, swimming pools, and a desire to live in the suburbs)" (Swartz 56). Due to the significance young people place on the fulfilment of these materialist desires, they suspend their prior intention of "working hard for [their] money" when it comes to buying stolen goods, or lying to save money or to get a job (cf. Swartz 56). Close readings of *Heist Wind*, *Young Blood*, or *Untitled* support the understanding that juvenile characters relax their otherwise clear notion of 'right' and 'wrong' behaviour with regard to the fulfilment of material desires.

Heist Wind's type of main character as well as storyline can be compared to Sifiso Mzobe's *Young Blood* (cf. close reading in chapter 2.1). Both novels feature male black characters who are crucially aware of their constrained socio-economic background and eager to do something about it. They see how their parents struggle to make a living and that their small incomes barely feed the family. They have grown up living with the bare minimum and without 'little' extras, like regular access to cool drinks, sweets, mobile phones, or brand-name clothing. Simultaneously, they see what more money could buy them and that more money often translates to receiving more respect from people. Hence, they are eager to differentiate themselves from their peers with new clothes, smartphones, and extra cash. Both main characters, Sifiso in *Young Blood* and Branson in *Heist Wind*, believe that school is keeping them from making the money that would buy them these things, and drop out or attend school only irregularly as a consequence. The notion that money can be made much more quickly on the streets than in a classroom is supported by their male friends who have enough money to show off with after they have engaged in street crime or become members of a gang.

Growing up in a capitalist, consumerist environment in which everybody is "put[ting] money into their pockets or spending" it (*HW* 5), Branson Ntsikelelo Mtombeni, *Heist Wind*'s protagonist and Grade 11 student, becomes obsessed with making money now, not in one and a half years when he would receive his matric. On the novel's opening page, Branson possesses only a R5 coin. This coin means that

> [h]e had enough money for a chocolate. He had enough for chewing gum. But he didn't have enough for anything else. A R5 coin is that kind of coin. It smiles at you and says, *Hey man, I'm here, but you can't do much with me. You can't go to movies with me. You can't take me to the Club. I look nice, but that's about all.* (*HW* 5; emphasis in the original)

The protagonist is raised by his mother, who works three jobs and spends much of her time in busses and taxis that take her to her jobs on the other side of town, leaving Branson alone during most of the day. A few years previously, Branson's father had left him and his mother to live with a white woman in a more affluent area of Cape Town. Although his father is working for the government, drives a big car, and lives in an affluent area, he does not share his money with his former family, and despite working three jobs, Branson's mother struggles considerably to make ends meet – a situation Branson is acutely aware of and angry about. Despite her many absences Branson's mother tries her best to raise her son to be a good person and insists on him finishing school properly before he starts looking for a job: "Times are hard. School is the only way of getting somewhere. Don't you understand that?" she asks (cf. *HW* 6). She warns her son to stay away from gangsters and "bad money" (*HW* 45), but due to her many jobs she cannot really influence how her son spends his days.

In a moment of weakness and opportunity, Branson gives in to his urge to have more money and steals a bike when its owner leaves it out of his sight (cf. *HW* 7). Excitement and joy about his stolen goods soon give way to fear of being detected and a growing unease about how he is going to explain where the bike came from. He decides to hide the bicycle outside of the city and makes his way to an abandoned warehouse. Soon, however, Branson has to worry about more than a stolen bike when he gets involved in a car chase and witnesses a man, who turns out to belong to a gang of bank robbers, fleeing the scene with a big black bag containing the heist money. While trying to find a hiding spot for his bike, Branson runs into the apparently wounded bank robber again, who persuades him to get him food and to help him escape from his fellow bank robbers and the police in return for more money than Branson has ever possessed. In the following, the main character has to weigh the value of money against the value of the lives of a stranger and of his friends and family. Stealing the bike signals Branson's entrance into what he had believed to be a better life, namely a life with money. However, the first instalment of the money he was promised by the bank robber for taking care of him does not bring him the happiness he aspires to. Buying himself new shoes, he can only enjoy them a few minutes before people start asking where he got the money for them: "If you have money, it shows. People know you have it. If you're not working, you have a hard time explaining where things come from" (*HW* 43).

Branson's personal development is paralleled by an introduction to gang life, an illustration of gang hierarchies and of the lack of social ethics amongst gangsters. Movu is the head of a gang of criminals who rule over Branson's township and the mastermind behind the bank robbery. Branson has met the gangster boss before and knows about his "reputation of ruthless cruelty" (*HW* 28). When Branson once heard about Movu killing an undercover police officer, "he had felt sick for days afterwards" (*HW* 28). His strong reaction implies that Branson is not the typical young male soon–to–be–criminal many people in the township had anticipated. Branson himself comes to understand that money is not the only thing one subscribes to when entering a gangster's life; murder in cold blood, corruption, death, and lethal envy are elements that accompany the desired money. This is best illustrated by Movu, who only cares about making money and his own profit. He never shares the profits from his schemes with his partners in crime equally, always taking the bigger part for himself (cf. *HW* 107). "[S]haring in fairness" (*HW* 105), as suggested by his partner Vapi, is simply not in Movu's interest. Movu's arrogance and opinion of himself as the smarter and thus worthier man in the gang are the reasons for his downfall (cf. *HW* 106, 108).

Constructed in the manner of the *Entwicklungsroman*, Branson's character development is similar to Sifiso's in *Young Blood*. The more Branson gets involved with criminals and the more he understands how unforgiving, lethal, and uncompromising this environment is, the more uneasy Branson feels. Yet, at the same time, the protagonist wants to have money and even briefly considers killing the fugitive bank robber to secure the stolen money for himself (cf. *HW* 67). But he resists the temptation: "Branson shuddered. He shook his head to get rid of the terrible tempting voice [telling him to kill for the money]. [...] He hated the temptation, the money" (*HW* 67). Branson realizes that he is in danger of "becoming a savage, with a lump of cement for a heart" (*HW* 114), and subsequently tries to resolve the situation, deciding that money is not worth the potential loss of his loved ones. Branson's decision against money is rewarded both emotionally and monetarily. Firstly, Branson finally earns the respect of his girlfriend's father, who concedes that anybody would be tempted by that amount of money (cf. *HW* 114), and secondly, the bank that had been robbed rewards Branson's report to the police financially by paying for his tertiary education. Having heard of his son's involvement in solving a crime, Branson's father moreover promises to help the family from now on and agrees to pay Branson's mother a monthly alimony to alleviate her situation. *Heist Wind*'s ending is thus similar to *Young Blood*'s as the 'stray' child is successfully incorporated into the social fabric of the new South Africa (cf. Barnard 563).

In *Heist Wind*, Branson's 'incorporation' is explained as resulting from his growing awareness of the significance of human relationships, i.e. from a growing appreciation of the ubuntu ideal which combines European and African ideas of identity and social ethics. *Heist Wind* shows that this ideal cannot be easily attained, but is the result of conscious decision-making and value adjustment. At first, Branson is primarily drawn to the concept of self-determination, as he is only concerned with fulfilling his own wishes and material desires. Only in the course of the novel does he learn to adapt his focus and to include the (African) "idea of community, that persons depend on other persons to be persons" (Shutte 10) in his concept of identity. More specifically, this means that Branson eventually places more value on his relationships to other persons than on the fulfilment of his individual (material) desires.[93] Van der Walt's novel, however, shows that not every character development is as straightforward or balanced as Branson's. The novel includes both characters who believe exclusively in African ideas of community and characters who prefer notions of European individualism, as the following excerpt illustrates:

> Nathi had no belief in such things [, i.e. the old African traditions]. 'We're in the twenty-first century, *mfethu*,' he boasted. 'We don't need things like that anymore.' Siyabonga didn't say anything about the old traditions. It was possible that he did believe in some of them, but he was too embarrassed to say so. Oscar was a bhuti: he'd been to the bush; he'd been circumcised, and even though he was quiet about it, he said that he believed that *izinyana* – those who have gone before us – are with us, that our ancestors stand by us in our times of difficulty. (*HW* 44; emphasis in the original)

Generally, admitting to one's belief in spirits and in the relevance of a cultural rite of passage appears to have become rather unfashionable amongst the youth in the new South Africa, and Branson's peers are indecisive about their relevance. Oscar is thereafter the one who encourages Branson to believe in his secret second name, Ntsikelelo, which means "*The Protected One*" (*HW* 106; emphasis in the original).

[93] Relationships to other humans, whether alive or dead, are central to the idea of ubuntu. "[T]he maxim 'a person is a person because of other persons'" specifically includes "ancestors. Dying is an ultimate homecoming. Not only must the living and the dead share with and care for one another, but the living and the dead depend on one another", Bangura explains (219).

Branson never speaks openly about whether he treasures his mother's religion or not, yet he lets us know that the meaning of his name resonates with him throughout the novel. Branson's choices and decisions are presented as not solely individual but guided by an ancestral presence: "Inside, somewhere, he heard a voice: *We are with you. You are the Protected One*" (*HW* 44; emphasis in the original). Branson knows he is not alone, not even in the most dangerous situation, when "[s]omewhere in the wind he heard, *It's bad money. It's no good*" (*HW* 111). The notion that nothing good can come of "bad money" frames van der Walt's novel and is proven to be right as the story proceeds. Significantly, Branson is not the only one to profit from the solving of the robbery. At the moment of Movu's death, about half of the heist money is blown away by the wind toward the township (cf. *HW* 109). Once again, Branson is tempted and "almost automatically grabbed at [a R100 note], but he missed, and it went whoozing off into the air. Somewhere in the wind he heard, *It's bad money. It's no good*" (*HW* 111; emphasis in the original). The next day, hundreds of township inhabitants "were telling each other that a miracle had happened during the night: money had fallen from heaven" (*HW* 114–115). They "find money stuck in trees, blowing about on school playgrounds, in car parks, on soccer fields" (*HW* 115). Branson's mother's statement that "[a]t last, what was bad money has become good money" grants a form of absolution to those involved in the heist as their crime eventually benefits the township community. The novel comes full circle in the final pages, when Branson treads the path his mother had already pointed to in the first pages: He choses to pursue education and thus a slower path to money. Most importantly, Branson's decision evokes in him a feeling of hopefulness toward the future, something which he had not felt before. In the final paragraphs of the novel, Branson wants to cleanse himself of the last remnants of his short career as a criminal and buys his young neighbour a brand new bike from what he has left of the bad money from the fugitive bank robber. Thus, in *Heist Wind*, Branson's 'incorporation' into his social environment does not come across as a surrender to the system (cf. Barnard 2008, 560), but is the result of conscious value adjustment.

Jenny Robson, *Monday Evening, Thursday Afternoon* (2013)

Robson's novel *Monday Evening, Thursday Afternoon*[94] adds a so far neglected dimension to the idea of ubuntu, namely the idea that a social ethic of South Africa can not only entail African and European elements, but in order for a new South Africa to emerge, its codes of conduct must also integrate aspects of Asian and Middle Eastern cultures. *Monday Evening, Thursday Afternoon* is the story of Faheema Majait and Louise van Rensburg's friendship, which is told by Louise in the form of an extended letter to Faheema. This is the first novel in the corpus to

[94] The novel is hereafter referred to as *META*.

discuss a cross-cultural friendship between a dark-eyed, Muslim girl with "thick black hair" and "beige arms" (*META* 16) and a white, Christian girl with "wild blonde curls" (*META* 18) – a physical and visual difference continuously reinvoked throughout the novel. In this novel, socio-economic details retreat into the background, providing a loose framework for the narration. Both girls grow up in nuclear families with working fathers and stay-at home mums. Louise has an older brother, who emigrates to England, and Faheema an older sister, who marries the son of an imam after having completed her hairdresser's exam. Neither of the families has financial problems and both Louise and Faheema grow up well protected.

The title of the novel refers to two moments when the girls' friendship is put to an acid test: "Suddenly", Louise writes,

> bad events happened far, far away. Not even in South Africa but in other countries. Not even on the same continent as us. Bad events caused by thoughtless, uncaring people. And for some strange reasons that I don't properly understand even now, these events drove a massive wedge between us. (*META* 124–125)

The bombing of the London underground on a Thursday afternoon, and a few months later the publication of the Danish cartoons of the prophet Mohammed on a Monday morning scare Louise's and Faheema's parents to the extent that they forbid a friendship between their daughters. Both girls fight for their friendship vigorously and repeatedly, but "[i]n the end", Louise concludes "it's what parents want that counts. They have their reasons and their explanations and they give them over and over. As though repetition will make them right and fair" (*META* 97). Despite their efforts to convince their parents of the value of their friendship, the novel ends with the two girls finding themselves separated.

In both *Monday Evening, Thursday Afternoon* and *Back to Villa Park*, Robson discusses fairness and what is considered fair by adults and by children. Both texts speak of a significant gap between the two generations regarding their concept of fairness. Both Dirk in *Back to Villa Park* and Louise in *Monday Evening, Thursday Afternoon* consider it unfair when their parents make decisions that interfere with their lives over their heads. Dirk's parents committed suicide after receiving their letter of refusal to immigrate to Australia; years later he still cannot understand why his parents did not ask him about his stance on the emigration. If they had, Dirk could have told them that he was indifferent to it because he liked their life in South Africa (cf. *BVP* 112). When Faheema's and Louise's parents forbid the friendship in the aftermath of what each of them interprets as unforgivable cultural transgressions, both of the girls find their reactions utterly out of proportion and label it "unfair" (*META* 69, 88). According to Louise, these events have "NOTHING to do with Faheema" (*META* 69; emphasis in the original), and Faheema argues that Louise "would never, ever insult" (*META* 88) Faheema's religion. Though the two girls recognize their differences and have argued about them before, their parents' approach of ending their friendship because of their cultural differences has never been an option for them. Even when they are no longer allowed to speak to each other, the girls try to find a way around their parents' prohibitions and look for options that could satisfy both them and their parents. They start to write to each other instead of exchanging words orally, and Faheema even organizes a secret renaming ceremony during which they give new names to each other which they can use thereafter in conversations with their parents. Louise christens Faheema "Victoria Walker" and Louise is named "Najmah Khan" (cf. *META* 104–105). The two girls pick these names deliberately, as their parents will only accept a friendship with a girl from the same culture. The fact that they willingly exchange their cultures underlines the value that Louise and Faheema place on their friendship, which they perceive to be able to defy cultural difference. But neither of their ideas work, and one day Faheema does not show up for school. Her extended absence is what prompts Louise to write down their story. She still has to figure out a way "to get these notebooks" to Faheema, as her parents have blocked all communication and Louise only finds out from fellow students that Faheema must have switched to Habibia College, a school for Muslims (cf. *META* 122).

In the final pages Louise asks Faheema for a favour:

> It is a hard thing I am asking of you. It will need all your courage. But I want you to take your father to the telephone table in your passage. I want you to stand in front of the Qur'an verse and recite the words. Slowly and clearly. *Ya ayyuha allatheena amanoo koonoo qawwameena lillahi shuhadaa…* And then I want you to repeat the words in English, the way your mum did for me all those years ago. Slowly and clearly. *Oh ye who believe, stand out as witnesses to fair dealing, and let not the hatred of others make you depart from justice.* […] I'm not asking you to shout and throw a tantrum the way I did. […] But can you speak to him quietly? Respectfully? […] Can you fight to the end, my very best friend? (*META* 126–127; emphasis in the original)

Prior to this final scene in the novel, Louise had "exploded" (*META* 113) after attending a church service with her parents during which the pastor had asked the congregation, "do we treat all people with kindness and compassion? *All* people?", even "those we disagree with[?]" (*META* 114–115; emphasis in the original). When her parents nod in agreement, Louise can no longer swallow her anger. Once at home she wants to know:

> "How can you sit in church and nod about loving people and caring for people? […] And meanwhile you are so mean. […] I'm talking about Faheema, the way you've treated her. You banned her from our house like she's a leper or something! And for what? She never did anything wrong! She never did anything except be my best friend. And make me laugh. And care about me. Why are you so horrible to her? Why do you blame her for stuff other people did – people she doesn't even know? And then you sit nodding while Pastor Drayer talks about loving people! You're hypocrites, that's what! HYPOCRITES!" (*META* 116; emphasis in the original)

After her outburst, Louise's parents change their views about Faheema and welcome her back in their house (cf. *META* 117). Yet Louise is never able to tell her best friend about this turn of events because from the next day onwards Faheema no longer attends Louise's school. Told from Louise's perspective, *Monday Evening, Thursday Afternoon* only gives the reader insight into how the narrator was able to solve the situation with her family. Thus, Robson's novel ends with a powerful, yet unanswered, call for friendship and a social ethic that promotes tolerance and acceptance across religions.

Social Ethics, Social Media, and Online Communities

In this day and age, social ethics have to be considered not only along the lines of social encounters in real life, but also in relation to social behaviour in online communities and in the media as such. As distinct as offline and online spaces may appear, they share the danger of being misused. I have previously shown that the media is obtaining a powerful and at the same time an ambivalent position in present-day South Africa. Its influential role in public discourses, such as the fostering of the image of a juvenile counternation, underlines its significance in the identity formation of this young nation. Zegeye and Harris describe the current situation in South Africa in the introduction to their 2003 monograph *Media, Identity and the Public Sphere in Post-Apartheid South Africa* as follows:

> South Africa is undergoing a complex, far-reaching and multifaceted process of social transformation. The country's media of mass communications are playing an important role in this process. They are not only important sources of public information and channels of communications; they also serve as important conveyors of the identities and interests of the different social groups within South Africa[n] society. In this capacity, the media help to determine the relative power, status and influence of these groups. In addition, they provide an important forum for public debate and opinion formation in South African society. Thus, they are an important element in the on-going democratization of the political system. (1)

This introductory quote gives an impression of how the role of media is perceived in South Africa by both its people and the critics, namely as a liberating force. In this sub-chapter, I limit myself to the analysis of one particular medium of mass communication, social media – also known as Web 2.0. Facebook, MySpace, and Flickr are but three of the many platforms where online interaction between acquainted and unacquainted people takes place. More generally, social media are understood as a means to express oneself, to participate and "to 'talk back' and send a message instantly, whereas previous media had wielded power over their one-way publishing or broadcasting channels. [In essence, these] new interactive platforms [...] [have] promised to make culture more 'participatory,' 'user centered,' and 'collaborative'" (van Dijck 10), all of which are characteristics that contribute to the attractiveness of the internet and social media sites. These attributes are the reason why young people are particularly fond of social media and online communities and why they use them extensively. The youths experience them as as active and vibrant as they are themselves. Hence, the internet in general and online platforms and smartphones in particular deserve our attention as literary critics because they are so tremendously appealing to children and young adults. Ekema-Agbaw and Yenika-Agbaw's research shows that

> African youth bring a unique reality to social media. Through their online profiles and behavior, they show the same 'hustler's mentality' that is present in their lives offline by hiding their economic conditions while exaggerating their independence. Based on their profiles, African youth convey a sense of freedom that is antithetical to their reality offline. Moreover, even more amazing is that these youth have an understanding of the 'good life' or the 'nicer things in life,' as their profiles tend to show off their most glamorous activities and their most in-style items. What is most unique about the reality that African youth bring to social media is that they exhibit first-world materialism while stuck in a third-world reality. (189)

This discourse has not yet been tackled in twenty-first century English South African fictions for juveniles. While the wish to possess a mobile phone is omnipresent in literary texts for South African young adults, smartphones with which one can go online do not yet feature in literary texts. So far, mobile phones are only used in narratives to make calls and for text messaging. Hence, while twenty-first century young adult novels debate the contrast between Western materialism and African realities in their narratives, they have not yet discussed the issue in relation to the use of social media or new technologies. Partridge's *Dark Poppy's Demise* (2011)[95] is to my knowledge the only English-language young adult novel that tackles the dangers of social media. However, it does so not in relation to consumerism or specific South African realities, but in broader terms, namely with regard to online identity development and online perpetrators.

Dark Poppy's Demise is a story about a young, awkward teenage girl who finds escape from real life as her online persona, Dark_Poppy. According to Kerry Mallan's definition, the main character, Jenna, uses Dark_Poppy as "a hybrid identity whereby online and offline identities and worlds merge. […] To understand the dual nature of identity in this instance is to acknowledge virtual and physical selves as not distinct aspects of a personality, but as how an individual is differently situated both within and outside a distributed network" (74). In *Dark Poppy's Demise*, the chat room is understood as an experimental space where you can live the one identity you do not show in public. Having moved to the city with her father and her brother after her parents' separation, Jenna grows up feeling left alone and misunderstood by everybody, including her friends at school. Her computer becomes her sanctuary (cf. *DP* 12). Chatting with her online friend,

[95] The novel is hereafter referred to as *DP*.

Twiggy, and later RobertRose, as he calls himself in the online community, becomes the only relief from the uneasiness Jenna feels in real-life surroundings. Van Dijck reflects in his analysis of *The Culture of Connectivity: A Critical History of Social Media* that "[o]riginally, the need for connectedness is what dr[i]ve[s] many users to [social media] sites" (4). In order to escape her unsatisfying real life and in search of acceptance, Jenna enters various social media sites, such as MySpace (*DP* 14), Flickr (*DP* 29), and Facebook (*DP* 13). Her search for somebody with whom she can connect and who accepts her the way she is drives her into the arms of an online predator, RobertRose. Pretending to be the perfect young male, Robert lures Jenna into a relationship and gains her trust, before he shows his real face. Jenna soon confides in her online friend Twiggy that she is "scared" (*DP* 140) because Robert has changed since they started dating in real life. However, she does not trust her intuition enough to end contact with Robert altogether. Only shortly afterwards, Robert abducts Jenna and threatens to abuse her in an abandoned house somewhere in the city of Cape Town. Luckily, Jenna can escape from the house and she returns home, shocked but physically unharmed.

The remaining chapters of the novel show that Jenna has been able to recover from the terrifying experience with the help of her parents, who have reunited, and her offline friends. The title of the novel predicts the demise of Dark_Poppy, not that of Jenna. The advantage of an avatar is that it only exits online and can be deleted. Jenna regains power over her life as she continues to chat online, albeit with different intentions and under a different name, Emogrrl (cf. *DP* 180). "Emo" derives from "emotional hardcore", which is "a style of rock music that developed from punk, but has more complicated musical arrangements and deals with more emotional subjects" (Oxford Learner's Dictionary 2015). Moreover, according to the Oxford Learner's Dictionary, "[e]mos are typically supposed to be emotional and sensitive and full of angst" (2015). The suffix "grrl" is a transformed version of 'girl'. Giving preference to a second 'r' over the 'i' in grrl leads to two impressions: While the user is still a young female person, the second 'r' strikes a more distanced and aggressive tone which stands in contrast to the innocence of a 'girl'. Thus, Jenna's new avatar is as ambiguous as her previous one, Dark_Poppy. The latter flower image had pointed to a fragile, innocent, and potentially weaker and melancholic user, who the online predator RobertRose then took advantage of. With her new avatar, Emogrrl, Jenna discards the implicit connotations of innocence attached to her former online persona, and admits a certain amount of insecurity via the prefix 'emo', while also asserting a form of strength via the suffix 'grrl'. Moreoever, by creating a new avatar the protagonist denies the online predator his ultimate success, her degradation as a young female. Emogrrl allows Jenna to enter the online space from a different and fresh perspective. Subsequently, Jenna uses social media to connect with friends whom she already knows from school and thus manages to merge her online and offline lives. Having combined both lives the protagonist no longer has to slip into an alternative online personality, marking the end of her search for acceptance and a sense of connection.[96]

The novel's message is that it does not make sense to hide from the real world in the virtual one, thus arguing for the integration of both. The book discusses the difficulties which are associated with the alleged divide between the virtual and the real worlds and asks us to renegotiate this binary and declare it redundant. There is no denying the fact that our personal and professional lives "have gradually become inundated with social media platforms" (van Dijck 3) and the internet as such over the past twenty or so years. In South Africa, the arrival of the digital age coincides with a profound social transformation and the restructuring of an entire country. More twenty-first century young adult novels will need to debate the growing significance of new media and technologies in young people's lives and engage in discussions regarding the extent to which social media and new technologies have already transformed personal lives.

Résumé

Heist Wind, *Monday Evening, Thursday Afternoon*, and *Dark Poppy's Demise* address socio-ethical questions on a local, a global, and a digital level. While Branson in *Heist Wind* and Jenna in *Dark Poppy's Demise* find closure toward the end of the novel, Robson's Christian protagonist is left with unanswered questions and is unable to reunite with her Muslim friend. Robson's novel shows that a reconciliation of cultural differences and of what different communities consider "righteous" (cf. Addams 1902) might take much longer than the juvenile protagonist anticipates. An analysis of *Katy of Sky Road* has shown that a rapprochement between the generations is possible, as both father and child learn to appreciate the other's insights. In a similar manner, *Back to Villa Park* promotes a social ethic that asks for kindness toward individual fates, and argues against holding grudges and for treating others with respect despite one's own troubled past. Even though they address different topics and are located in different places, all these novels include the idea of social democracy in Jane Addams's sense. Juvenile characters strive for social acceptance and learn that individual desires must be negotiated alongside communal codes of conduct in order to achieve this kind of democracy.

[96] For an analysis of *Dark Poppy's Demise* from a gender perspective, see Inggs (2016, 76–77).

3.4 A Literary Social Profile

In her 2009 monograph, Swartz posits that "media-mediated moral panics" have come to "shape public consciousness" about a juvenile counternation, but also in "social science literature [...] young people are seldom, if ever, seen as agents" (4). The previous chapter has shown that terms like vulnerability, criminalization, and marginalization dominate both academic and public discussions about youth development in and beyond South Africa. Scholars such as Everatt (2001), White (2008), Swartz (2009), Jolly (2010, 53–81), and Samara (2011) debate the implication of a public discourse which designates youth, but also women and disabled persons, as vulnerable, lost, marginalized, or potential criminals.

In his article "Youth in South Africa 1990–2000" (2001), sociologist David Everatt produces a contextualized social profile of youth by including both quantitative data gained from official statistics on employment rates or housing conditions, and qualitative data gained from interviews conducted with young South Africans about their "Values and Optimism" or "Social Attitudes" (cf. 320–325). His profile puts the alleged marginalization and criminalization of youth up for debate, in fact showing that the very concept of marginalization "was woolly" in the first place (Everatt 301). Everatt's study does not deny the many social, structural, or self-inflicted problems that young South Africans struggle with on a daily basis. His profile speaks of a less politically active but nevertheless "politically aware and engaged" youth who has only minor confidence in government (cf. 323) – notions that reverberate in young adult literature. Everatt moreover found that "[d]espite 'missing' the anti-apartheid struggle, many young people have notably more progressive social views than their elders", including their rejection of the death penalty and support of women's right to abortion (Everatt 324). Being a generation that "mimic[s] the consumerism that marks South African society" (Everatt 325–326), youth has "created its own culture and style, and developed its own particular problems – but they relate to poverty, growing up in a transitional society, and living with the reality of HIV/AIDS. Some they share with adults. Some they do not" (Everatt 325). Everatt's article shows that social profiling benefits from the inclusion of soft data, as his study produces a significantly more balanced, complex, and thus more realistic picture of South African youth at the turn of the millennium than any enumeration of statistical data in documents such as the "Social Profile of Vulnerable Groups" could.

Everatt's social profile of the youth "2000+" (318) resonates with the literary social profile of twenty-first century young adult novels. Contemporary narrative texts for young adults put publically mediated markers of youth development such as vulnerability, marginalization, and criminalization into context. They use prevalent socio-economic hard data, but go beyond mere representation by telling the story of unique sets of characters. Employing distant and close reading techniques to assess literary hard and soft data has helped to conceptualize a literary social profile of South African young adult literature. Close readings of fictional texts have been particularly important as their sum provides a more contextualized image of what shapes adolescent life in contemporary South Africa.

Fictions for young people investigate the present socio-economic situation of a diverse range of juveniles from different backgrounds and give insights into what youths consider meaningful in their lives. Overall, South Africa's literature for youths has been found to be highly heterogeneous and mimetic in its representation and depiction of the country's socio-economic profile (cf. Stadler 2015). Ethnicity and the notion of a "racial subsidy" (Mbembe 2014) feature prominently in young adult novels, such as Robson's *Back to Villa Park*. Novels written in the realist mode address the issue of socio-economic inequalities in relation to race and discuss their consequences for social cohesion in a time in which "public perceptions about race relations have reached a record low", decreasing from 72% in the year 2000 to 39% in 2012 (Chabane 67). According to Collins Chabane, this "could signa[l] an urgent need for sustainable nation-building initiatives aimed at improving social cohesion in the country" (67), especially since considerably fewer people are confident in 2012 that the country is heading in the right direction (46.1%) than in 1994, when almost 80% were convinced of the bright future of the country (cf. 68).

By contrast, Beverley Naidoo observes that contemporary South African children's and young adult literature "can celebrate the loosening of boundaries around subject matter and the diversifying of places and communities in which stories are set" (267). The genre is thus potentially more open-minded than South Africa's society at large as literary texts repeatedly envisage a hopeful future in a transcultural South Africa for their protagonists. The novels in the corpus display representations of a diverse range of belief systems and codes of conduct that correspond to South Africa's diverse cultural landscape. Tolerance of difference, the idea of putting the interests of others before one's own, morality, and personal integrity frequently feature to a greater or lesser extent as topics in the storylines. Laws and legal codes that enforce social ethics, i.e. the human rights written into the country's constitution, are also discussed in recent fictions.[97] Generally, protagonists are depicted as being more open-minded and tolerant than adults (cf. *E Eights*). Often, children perceive their parents' opinions and stereotypes as outdated and far from their own perceptions of reality (cf. *Monday Evening, Thursday Afternoon*). Some of them are depicted as having the courage to stand

[97] See, for instance, Malan's *My "Funny" Brother*, which mentions gay rights, or D'Achada's *Sharkey's Son*, which refers to one's right to earn a living.

up for their beliefs and speak out against their parents, while others remain silent and are shown to obey their parents' wishes. As South Africa is a culture of many silences, books like *This Book Betrays My Brother*, *Untitled*, *A Man Who Is Not a Man*, or *Monday Evening, Thursday Afternoon* deliberately address the predicaments connected to these silences. HIV and AIDS, sexual violence, male circumcision and traditional rites of passage, or physical handicaps, as well as homo- and transsexuality, remain delicate topics in both public and fictional discourse, as do stereotypes related to ethnicity, religion, and gender. Without making their stories sound condescending, the abovementioned novels promote the end of that era of silence and argue for an era of debate and open exchange. In the majority of cases, these arguments for a new era are fought at the cost of the protagonists' individual happiness. Nedi (*This Book Betrays My Brother*) is only able to speak about her silence surrounding her brother's rape of his girlfriend many years later. Mokgheti (*Untitled*) can only write about her being raped but cannot speak about it publically in her community. Lumkile (*A Man Who Is Not a Man*) speaks about his failed circumcision because he wants to make known the real circumstances which led to his having to lead a life in social isolation. It becomes clear that ubuntu is an ideal that many protagonists strive for, but which they cannot attain for themselves in the course of the respective novels. In many cases, the chasms between generations, between ethnic groups, between social spaces, and between the genders are just too deep to be overcome in the course of the storyline. To end the novels hopefully rather than in the form of happy endings is characteristic for narratives written in the realist mode in the new South Africa. Young adult novels are shown to promote new ideas about ethics and communal living, yet must admit that it might take much longer for these ideas to take root.

Ultimately, South African young adult novels display the complexity of juvenile lives in contemporary South Africa. In chapter 1, we saw how the surrounding space influences the coming–of–age of adolescent characters. Chapter 2 discussed the relevance of gender for the formation of a juvenile identity. This chapter has shown that socio-economic resources play a most significant role in the lives of young South Africans. Many teenage characters link social acceptance to the possession of material goods. Hence, money, employment, and material objects such as mobile phones or trendy clothes are elements which are factored into young people's concepts of self and shape their ideas of empowerment and self-fulfilment. Often, teenage characters feel that they are lagging behind their potential because of their financial situation. In those cases in which parental guidance is offered, it is often initially perceived as a nuisance and intrusion. Yet both Katy in *Katy of Sky Road* and Branson in *Heist Wind*, for instance, learn to appreciate the grown-ups' views on communal living over the course of their narratives and show that a reconciliation of parental and juvenile ideas about social norms is possible and desirable.

III The Future of South African Youth Literature

> [C]hildren's literature[98] is a uniquely focused lens through which children and young people are asked to look at the images of themselves made for them by their societies. For this reason, it is important that both children's literature and Children's Literature Studies are alert to changing constructions of childhood and the impact of trends such as commercialization, globalization, and the way the media treat children. (Reynolds 2005, 3)

The previous chapters examined three recurring thematic fields in twenty-first century young adult literature written in the realist mode, namely space, gender, and social economics. Oscillating between distant and close reading in order to provide a first comprehensive assessment of this particular genre, it became apparent that contemporary literary productions from South Africa, when approached as *witness documents*, can give insight into the country's state of transition, and into young people's aspirations and frustrations, their hopes and dilemmas.

Contemporary novels discuss urban, rural, coastal, and school life, pointing to the distinctiveness of South African space and how different sub-spaces influence individual development. The setting of a particular story never only serves the purpose of providing a background but is what makes the story distinctly South African. After all, the country's space – and the histories that have shaped it – are what all characters of whatever descent share and what identifies them as 'South African'. This is also the reason why I have entitled this book *South African Young Adult Literature in English*. Characteristically, adolescent characters are shown to rely predominantly on their surrounding social space, on their peers, and on themselves as educator figures, since parental figures of guidance are not always present to actively guide their children through their formative years. The genre addresses a great variety of characters and concepts of life which are similar to the different social environments teenagers encounter in real life. In the narratives, juvenile characters learn that life can change in an instant due to an unwanted pregnancy, sexual abuse, sudden socio-economic decline, social exclusion, or death. Engaging in new discourses of masculinity and femininity, as well as of hetero-, homo-, and transsexuality, a liberation from gender norms is promoted but seldom achieved within a novel's pages. We have seen that fictional narratives written in the realist mode examine twenty-first century cosmopolitanism, capitalism, and neoliberalism just as they discuss the significance of indigenous

[98] Reynolds uses children's literature as an umbrella term "encompass[ing] everything from the earliest literature such as myths, legends, fold and fairy tales to the latest work for teenage readers" (2005, 2).

languages, cultural rites, and the plurality of societal concepts. South Africa's youth, like youths internationally, find themselves in search of an individual identity. This "ongoing project of the 'self' (constructions of personal identity)" is often complicated by "the importance of specific local contexts (material resources and social histories), and wider global social, economic and cultural processes (globalization)" (White 151; cf. Hagedorn; Short and Hughes; van Gemert, Peterson, and Lien).

In contemporary literary texts for adolescents, childhood is never presented as an ideal or as a time of innocence or purity but rather as a time of struggle. The narratives speak of the youth's impatience to come of age and to change their surrounding social space and concomitant socio-economic constraints. Experiencing the in-between status of their country in their years of character formation, adolescent characters comprehend that the country's turmoil as well as its development are connected to their own. Many fictional characters struggle to find their way of living in the midst of a climate of cultural and socio-economic transformation; yet all of them share a will to fight for their concept of life. While some protagonists come closer to what they consider a 'good life' during the course of a novel, others falter in the attempt. Often, the teenagers' understanding of how to live life differs from that of the adult generation in the sense that juveniles are presented as more open-minded and in favour of diversity. All the novels in the corpus suggest that while South Africa's youth participate in the grand social "test" of the nation to create a "social democracy" (cf. Addams 1902, 2), they are also writing their own master-narrative, one which points beyond the known, toward the future. Hence, young adult novels still indicate the emergence of a 'rainbow nation', while in reality the concept appears to have lost its former appeal, as Sisonke Msimang's article "The End of the Rainbow Nation Myth" (2015) illustrates. Msimang's piece is an acute reading of the current zeitgeist and the younger generation's will to take action in the formation of a new nation. Considering herself part of the juvenile counternation, she argues:

> We have lived with choreographed unity for long enough to know that we now prefer acrimonious and robust disharmony. We see reconciliation as part of a narrative that was constructed on the basis of anxieties that are no longer relevant: Democracy has taught us that raised voices don't have to lead to war. This may not feel good, or even comfortable. And it does not offer the peace many black South Africans imagined 20 years ago. Nonetheless our impatience for justice is a new kind of hope; a sign that green shoots may yet emerge from the ruins of the rainbow nation. (Msimang)

Twenty-first century realist novels depict South Africa's contemporary social spaces as uncompromising. Both the nation's social profiles and literary texts for young adults transport notions that South African children grow up in a divided country where their potential is literally left on the streets, in the small towns, and in rural areas. Nevertheless, the great majority of novels end optimistically. One could even argue that there is a pattern to South African youth novels ending hopefully: The integration of hopefulness follows to a certain extent from the young adult genre's intention to guide its readers on their way to becoming full-fledged members of society. This particular tone has thus been used as a tool to achieve this goal even though such hopefulness sometimes stands in stark contrast to reality, in which many are disillusioned because of the slow and sometimes even stagnant developments of the post-apartheid state. Yet this hopefulness is also tied to an "impatience for justice", with the latter being, if we are to believe Msimang's words, "a sign that green shoots may yet emerge from the ruins of the rainbow nation" (2015). The recurrent invocation of a hopeful ending thus serves a purpose that transcends the mere pages of the realist novel as it tries to instil a message of confidence in the reader that the fictional development might at a future point translate into the emergence of a real(ly) alternative society. Moreover, literature for young adults not only takes part in the effort to nourish children on values that are relevant for the making of a new South Africa, but also intends to make young people understand and see through social hierarchies and confinements (cf. chapter 3).

This study has focused on the analysis of twenty-first century English novels for adolescents which were written in the realist mode as this was the most frequently published type of fiction in this early part of the millennium. However, since the mid-2000s, there have been at least three further rapidly evolving sub-genres in South African adolescent – and also in adult – literature which deserve brief mention: a) the popular, b) the transnational, and c) the digital.

a) Toward the Popular: Speculative Fiction, Crime, and the Romance

Locally produced popular literature has only recently gained more prominence in the South African literary market, especially speculative fiction, crime novels, and the romance. Christopher Warnes explains that

> [d]uring the apartheid years there was a strong critical perception that popular fiction abrogated the social and political mission to document injustice, challenge preconceptions, and conscientize readers. The end of apartheid was interpreted as signalling the lifting of this literary-political injunction to be serious. (2014, 156)

Since then, both new and established voices of the country's literary scene have started to write fiction in the popular mode,[99] and, given the genre's success, literary scholars have also taken up the study of this trend. Examining fourteen

[99] For a theorization of this term see Karin Barber's foreword to Newell and Okome's essay collection *Popular Culture in Africa: The Episteme of the Everyday* (2013).

romances published by Sapphire Press and Nollybooks, Warnes's study shows that although at first sight these

> romances may appear to be the purest examples of a thoroughly commercial mode of writing, free from any but the most superficial engagement with questions of politics or historicity[, o]n closer inspection they reveal themselves to be products of their place and time, implicated by their nature in complex relationships with discourses of gender, race, change, and power. (2014, 155)

Fiona Snyckers's 'chick lit' series about Trinity Luhabe, which was examined in chapter 1.2.3 with regard to its depiction of heterotopian sites, is one example of literature for young adults which appears shallow at first sight but under closer examination touches on "discourses of gender, race, change, and power" (*ibid.*). While Warnes's article (2014) is the first to critically assess South Africa's popular romance genre, locally produced crime fiction has already enjoyed greater critical attention (cf. Davis; Petzold 2009; Schleh; Steinberg). The "explosion of crime fiction in contemporary South Africa" (Warnes 2012: 981, abstract) can be seen, according to the Comaroffs, as a literary response to "the popular obsession with scenes of violent disorder" (2004). In South Africa, they argue,

> criminal violence is taken to be diagnostic of the fragility of civil society; concomitantly, officers of the law become the prime embodiment of a state under pressure. Thus, ironically, in the effort to build a posttotalitarian democracy, South Africans find themselves calling for "MORE POLICE." (Comaroff and Comaroff 2004; emphasis in the original)

The Comaroffs reason that "many ordinary South Africans are drawn to mass-mediated dramas in which men with badges confront, and typically overcome, the most heinous, most violent, most antisocial of felons" because of "a nostalgia for authoritative, even authoritarian government" (2004). This nostalgia is apparently catered to by crime novels. Matzke and Mühleisen add that

> crime fiction increasingly transcends, if not invalidates, national boundaries. More often than not, writings which we deem "postcolonial" now portray a world where "cultures" are no longer seen as separate entities located in particular geographic terrains – and fighting over "domination" – but a world characterized by an increasing interconnectedness in response to what Vera Alexander calls "important phenomena of present-day life." (8)

The present thesis has shown that crime features prominently in contemporary youth novels (cf. close readings of *Young Blood*, *Heist Wind*). Michael Williams's *The Eighth Man* (2002), which won the 2004 Percy FitzPatrick Prize for Children's Literature, is a further case in point for a young adult novel which "challenges the reader to consider critically the difference between how a radio talk-show host and a newspaper journalist with a deep sense of ethics handle a crime story" (Jenkins 2006, 180). *The Eighth Man* differs from *Young Blood* or *Heist Wind* in the sense that it not only focuses on the coming–of–age tale of the protagonist but also includes detailed representations of adult relationships.

Last but not least, since the mid-2000s, speculative fiction has been gaining ever more prominence both locally and globally and has become one of the fastest growing sub-genres in recent years. Lauren Beukes is one of the most prolific South African writers in this area. Starting out with the young adult novel *Moxyland* (2008), she has since written three genre-blending novels for adults (cf. *Zoo City* 2010, *The Shining Girls* 201, *Broken Monster* 2014). *Afro SF* is the first anthology of *Science Fiction by African Writers* (Hartman). Author collaborations like "Sarah Lotz" or "Lily Herne" are another occurrence of this sub-genre. Authors who have so far only written novels in the realist mode, like Sally-Ann Partridge and Edyth Bulbring, have also started to branch out into the science fiction genre. The growing significance of literature written in the fantastical mode has also been recognized by literary critics, leading to a growing number of scholarly publications (cf. Brown 2008a, 2008b; Cloete; Duncan; Inggs 2016, 85–117; Stadler 2014, 17, forthcoming; Stobie).

b) Toward the Transnational

In 2007, Njabulo Ndebele said that "the challenge of the future in South Africa is nation building: no more, no less. It [will be a] massive task [to create] one nation out of the institutional divisions that currently beset it" (24). Ndebele understood the transitional moment that the country is encountering as its chance for change and as a possibility for the making of an alternative national identity. Yet, with more and more South African authors setting their stories beyond their country's borders, critics have started to question whether the aspiration toward a national literature will ever become reality (cf. Chapman 2011a; de Kock 2011; Lenta). According to Chapman, the concept of a national literature which could be classified as "South African" has always been "problematic" given the country's "history of radical heterogeneity" (2011a, 5–6; van der Vlies). Moreover, when the turn of the century marked for many the beginning of the end of the rainbow nation concept, this change in attitude toward the newly formed country could also be traced in South African literary texts regarding the choice of setting. Today, many of what have been called the best publications – "Anne Landsman's *The Rowing Lesson* and Michiel Heyns' *Body Politics*" (de Kock 2009, 31) – no longer have a local, but a transnational setting. This turn toward the transnational is highly significant, given the significance that was formerly placed on the distinctly South African setting as the one unifying aspect in literary texts produced in South Africa. For de Kock, "the 'trans' in transnational creates a cusp between the national and what lies beyond it, not a severance" (2009, 31), and yet he finds the trend of transnational settings to be signifying a moment of "crisis" (de Kock

2014) in the field of English South African literature. In his article "Postcolonial Problematics" Michael Chapman points to another contemporary "orthodoxy", as he calls it: "It is not fashionable today in the South African academy to invoke the concept or the field 'South African Literature.' Prizes still honor South African writing, but academic criticism prefers terms such as postcolonial or transnational" (Chapman 2011b, 60; cf. de Kock 2009). In a paper presented at the "Writing the Rainbow Nation" Conference at Regensburg in 2014, Willie Burger asked in a similar fashion

> What arguments could be adduced to delimit Afrikaans literature (or even South African literature) and to study it in isolation at a time of globalisation when capital flows and communication technology are indifferent to borders of any kind? And how does one assess the status of Afrikaans literature in its own right without losing sight of its position as seen from an international perspective at all levels?

While contemporary scholarship still vacillates between consternation and celebration (cf. Attwell and Attridge; cf. de Kock 2009, footnote 4) in the face of the transnational turn, South African writers have already embarked on a journey to discover new ways of describing the now and to develop new national narratives through radical heterogeneity.

c) Toward the Digital

"In this country of nearly fifty million people, the general book-buying public is numbered between 800 000 and 1 000 000" (Murray 2011, 83). These numbers imply that the overwhelming majority of people are not reached by printed books. Although access to the internet is not yet common in South Africa (cf. "Census 2011: Key Results" 12), digital literature has become a serious alternative to printed books. As the mobile phone is one of the most accessible technological devices in South Africa and many (young) South Africans use it to go online to communicate, local publishers and organizations have started to develop ebooks. Since the mid-2000s, an ever larger number of texts is being published specifically for this medium and sold at a fraction of the cost of printed books.

Change in the structures of South Africa's literary market is presently being brought about most noticeably by non-profit organizations, NGOs, reading trusts such as PRAESA, Nal'ibali, The Little Hands Trust, Biblionef SA, Zama SA, or FunDza, and independent publishers, all of which provide a space for new genres and voices to get published and be read across the country and abroad, both online and offline. These numerous organizations are all working to establish a reading culture in South Africa by providing underprivileged areas with reading material for children and youth in the eleven official languages, by developing new forms of reader participation, and by establishing free online libraries. An example is FunDza's Mobi Library, which was installed in 2010. FunDza presents itself on many social media platforms, such as Facebook, Twitter, MXit, and MyMsta, and aims to connect readers by integrating them in the story writing process, offering reader competitions, or simply providing a space where the teens can give "feedback on the books" (Nevill). Contrary to the conventional South African book market, where the publication and success of a novel are often dependent on whether the book has won a prize in a competition, the success of a mobile phone book or the blog of a fictional character on a social media site such as "The Diary of Zinzi Zwane" on Facebook can be measured immediately by the number of 'likes'. Due to the success that projects like FunDza and PRAESA are achieving, the question arises whether the printed book is actually still an attractive enough purchase option for young South African readers, when it is so much easier and cheaper to download a mobile phone book wherever and whenever they like. Aware of the competition from digital publishers, authors and publishers have taken to two measures to keep the traditional printed book attractive for readers: Firstly, they have made new technologies the topics of their novels (cf. Sally-Ann Partridge's *Dark Poppy's Demise*) and secondly, they have updated the superfice and design of the printed book itself (cf. Fanie Viljoen's *Onderwêreld*; Anker).

According to Joanna Penn (2013), printed books remain the preferred choice of readers in "Nigeria or other African countries", for now. Yet one can guess that the further the digital landscape of African countries evolves, the more texts will be read on mobile devices. Moreover, due to these technological developments a lot more material will be available in the future for both young readers and critics. Evidently, the South African literary market is changing profoundly and the ways of reading and receiving South Africa's literary productions have already begun to change. By branching out into new sub genres, new contents, and new publishing formats, the genre has been updated not only with regard to content, but also concerning accessibility. Although authors have been constantly expanding their topics of discussion and have continuously enlarged the group of addressees both locally and globally, they remain true to their South African origins in the sense that they debate topical local issues. A reading revolution is under way and it will be the task of upcoming analyses to investigate its nature.

IV Works Cited

Primary Sources

Alnam, Biron, 2003. *No Problem, Man!* Claremont: New Africa Books.

Baldwin, May, 1912. *Corah's School Chums*. London: Chambers.

Bauling, Jayne, 2009. *E Eights*. Johannesburg: Pan Macmillan.

Beukes, Lauren, 2008. *Moxyland*. Nottingham: Angry Robot.

Beukes, Lauren, 2010. *Zoo City*. Auckland Park: Jacana.

Beukes, Lauren, 2013. *The Shining Girls*. Cape Town: Random House Struik.

Beukes, Lauren, 2014. *Broken Monster*. Cape Town: Umuzi.

Blacklaws, Troy, 2004. Karoo Boy. London: Duckworth.

Brink, André, 1993. *On the Contrary: Being the Life of a Famous Rebel, Soldier, Traveller, Explorer, Reader, Builder, Scribe, Latinist, Lover and Liar*. London: Secker & Warburg.

Brink, André, 1996. *Imagenings of Sand*. London: Secker & Warburg.

Britten, Sarah, 2002. *Welcome to the Martin Tudhope Show!* Cape Town: Tafelberg.

Bulbring, Edyth, 2007. *The Summer of Toffie and Grummer*. Cape Town: Oxford University Press.

Bulbring, Edyth, 2010. *Melly, Mrs Ho and Me*. Johannesburg: Penguin.

Bulbring, Edyth, 2011. *Melly, Fatty and Me*. Johannesburg: Penguin.

Bulbring, Edyth, 2013. *A Month with April–May*. London: Hot Key Books.

Bulbring, Edyth, 2013. *100 Days with April–May*. London: Hot Key Books.

Bulbring, Edyth, 2014. *I Heart Beat*. London: Hot Key Books.

Case, Dianne, and Yvonne Hart, 2007. *Katy of Sky Road*. Cape Town: Maskew Miller Longman.

Collins, Suzanne, 2009–2011. *Hunger Games* Series. New York: Scholastics.

D'Achada, Gillian, 2008. *Sharkey's Son*. Cape Town: Tafelberg.

"The Diary of Zinzi Zwane", n.d. *FunDza Literary Trust*. Web blog. 02 Jul. 2016. <https://www.facebook.com/zinzizwane>.

De Villier, Leon, 2009. *Shorn*. Trans. By Elsa Silke. Pretoria: LAPA.

Dickens, Charles, 2013. *Oliver Twist (Retold by Margareth Tarner)*. Johannesburg: Pan Macmillan.

Donald, David, 2007. *Call on the Wind*. Auckland Park: Jacana.

Duiker, K. Sello, 2000. *Thirteen Cents*. Cape Town: David Philip.

Dyer, Dorothy, 2012. *Two-Faced Friends*. Cape Town: Cover2Cover Books.

Dyer, Dorothy, 2013. *Friends Forever*. Cape Town: Cover2Cover Books.

Dyer, Dorothy, and Ros Haden, 2011. *Jealous in Jozi*. Cape Town: Cover2Cover Books.

Ford, Janis, 2003. *Drugs Are for Mugs*. Cape Town: NB Publishers.

Gamedze, Londi, and Dorothy Dyer, 2013. *From Boys to Men*. Cape Town: Cover2Cover Books.

Glass, Linzi, 2006. *The Year the Gypsies Came*. Johannesburg: Penguin.

Haden, Ros, 2010. *Broken Promises*. Cape Town: Cover2Cover Books.

Haden, Ros, 2011. *Sugar Daddy*. Cape Town: Cover2Cover Books.

Heyns, Michiel, 2008. *Body Politics*. Cape Town: Jonathan Ball.

Heyns, Michiel, 2009. *The Children's Day*. Portland, OR: TinHouse Books.

Hofmeyr, Dianne, 1988. *When Whales Go Free*. Cape Town: Tafelberg.

Hofmeyr, Dianne, 2012. *Oliver Strange and the Journey to the Swamps*. Cape Town: Tafelberg.

Kaschula. Russell H., 2006. *Take Me to the River*. Glosderry: Ney Africa Books.

Kendal, Charmaine, 2015. *Miscast*. Cape Town: Junkets.

Kenmuir, Dale, 1988. *Son of the Surf*. Cape Town: Maskew Miller Longman.

Kruger, Gavin, and Val Kruger, 2006. *A Story of Hope! For Teens and Adolescents*. Hillcrest: Focus on the Family Africa.

Landsman, Anne, 2007. *The Rowing Lesson*. New York: Soho Press.

Mahapeletsa, Sello, 2005. *When Lions Smile*. [2003]. Cape Town: Kwela.

Mahapeletsa, Sello, 2007. *Tears of an Angel*. [2007]. Cape Town: Kwela.

Malan, Robin, 2012. *My "Funny" Brother*. Mowbray: Junkets.

Maloni, Mbu, n.d. *Becoming Indoba – A Real Man*. FunDza Mobi Library. Web. 16 Oct. 2016. <http://live.fundza.mobi/home/library/non-fiction-short-stories/becoming-indoda-a-real-man/>.

Marsh, Donovan (dir.), 2010. *Spud*. Cape Town: Rogue Star Films, BLM Production.

Marsh, Donovan (dir.), 2013. *Spud 2: The Madness Continues*. Cape Town: Rogue Star Films.

Matlwa, Kopano, 2007. *Coconut*. Auckland Park: Jacana.

Mazantsi, Sivuyile, and Sam Roth, 2012. *Too Young to Die*. Cape Town: Cover2Cover Books.

Mazibuko, Nokuthula, 2007. *In the Fast Lane*. Claremont: New Africa Books.

Memela, Sandile, 2005. *Flowers of the Nation*. Scottsville: University of KwaZulu–Natal Press.

Meyer, Stephenie, 2005–2008. *Twilight* Series. New York: Little, Brown and Company.

Mgqolozana, Thando, 2010. *A Man Who Is Not a Man*. Scottsville: University of KwaZulu–Natal Press.

Mhlongo, Niq, 2004. *Dog Eat Dog*. Cape Town: Kwela Books.

Mhlongo, Niq, 2007. *After Tears*. Cape Town: Kwela.

Moele, Kgebetli, 2006. *Room 207*. Cape Town: Kwela Books.

Moele, Kgebetli, 2009. *The Book of the Dead*. Cape Town: Kwela Books.

Moele, Kgebetli, 2013. *Untitled: A Novel*. Cape Town: Kwela Books.

Molope, Kagiso Lesego, 2004. *Dancing in the Dust*. Cape Town: Oxford University Press.

Molope, Kagiso Lesego, 2005. *The Mending Season*. Cape Town: Oxford University Press.

Molope, Kagiso Lesego, 2009. *Im Schatten des Zitronenbaums*. Basel: Baobab.

Molope, Kagiso Lesego, 2012. *This Book Betrays My Brother*. Cape Town: Oxford University Press.

Mpe, Phaswane, 2001. *Welcome to Our Hillbrow*. Pietermaritzburg: University of Natal Press.

Mzobe, Sifiso, 2010. *Young Blood*. Cape Town: Kwela

Mzongwana, Mteto, Onele Mfeketo, and Lamna Orbin, 2003. *Mom's Taxi.* Claremont: New Africa Books.

Namukasa, Glaydah, 2013. *Voice of a Dream.* Oxford: MacMillan Education.

Ngcowa, Sonwabiso, 2014. *In Search for Happiness.* Cape Town: Cover2Cover Books.

Orford, Margie, 2004. *Dancing Queen.* Oxford: Heinemann Educational Publishers.

Partridge, Sally A., 2009. *Fuse.* Cape Town: Human & Rousseau.

Partridge, Sally-Ann, 2011. *Dark Poppy's Demise.* Cape Town: Human & Rousseau

Phalime, Maria, 2013. *Second Chances.* Cape Town: Maskew Miller Longman.

Pinnock, Patricia Schonstein, 2000. *Skyline.* Cape Town: David Philip.

Raath, George and Lorrie, n.d. *Chums of Meredrift School.* Johannesburg: Afrikaanse Pers-Boekhandel.

Riordan, Rick, 2005–2009. *Percy Jackson* Series. New York: Disney Hyperion.

Robson, Jenny, 2006. *Praise Song.* Cape Town: Tafelberg.

Robson, Jenny, 2013. *Back to Villa Park.* Cape Town: Tafelberg.

Robson, Jenny, 2013. *Monday Evening, Thursday Afternoon.* Cape Town: Tafelberg.

Roth, Veronica, 2011–2013. *Divergent* Trilogy. New York: Katherine Tegen Books.

Rowling, J. K., 1997–2007. *Harry Potter* Series. London: Bloomsbury.

Sara Research Team, 2000. *Sara – The Empty Compound.* Cape Town: Maskew Miller Longman.

Slaughter, Carolyn, 2002. *Before the Knife: Memories of an African Childhood.* London: Doubleday.

Smith, Gail, 2003. *Someone Called Lindiwe.* Oxford: Macmillan Education.

Snyckers, Fiona, 2009. *Trinity Rising.* Cape Town: Jonathan Ball.

Snyckers, Fiona, 2010. *Trinity on Air.* Johannesburg; Cape Town: Jonathan Ball.

Snyckers, Fiona, 2013. *Team Trinity.* Athlone: Modjaji Books.

Stevenson, Robert Louis, 2013. *Treasure Island (Retold by S. Colbourn).* Johannesburg: Pan Macmillan.

Van de Ruit, John, 2005. *Spud.* Johannesburg: Penguin.

Van der Post, Laurens, 1967. *The Hunter and the Whale.* London: Hogarth.

Van der Vyver, Marita, 2007. *The Hidden Life of Hannah Why.* Cape Town: Tafelberg.

Van der Walt, Willem 'Thembalethu', 2003. *Heist Wind.* Roggebaai: Kwela.

Van Dijk, Lutz, 2000. *Stronger than the Storm: A Novel for Young Adults about HIV and AIDS in South Africa.* Cape Town: Maskew Miller Longman.

Van Rooyen, Suzanne, 2013. *The Other Me.* Tallahassee: Harmony Ink Press.

Viljoen, Fanie, 2008. *Onderwêreld.* Cape Town: Tafelberg.

Viljoen, Fanie, 2011. *Scarred Lion.* [Cutting Edge]. Winchester, UK: Ransom Publishing. (A)

Von Meck, Anoeschka, 2011. *My Name Is Vaselinetjie.* Cape Town: Tafelberg.

Watson, Mary, 2004. *Moss.* Cape Town: Kwela.

Wieler, Diana, 1989. *Bad Boy.* Toronto: Groundwood Books.

Williams, Michael, 2002. *The Eighth Man.* Cape Town: Oxford University Press.

Zadok, Rachel, 2005. *Gem Squash Tokoloshe.* Johannesburg: Picador Africa.

Secondary Sources

"Census 2011: Key Result," n.d. *Statistics South Africa*. Web. 29 June 2015. <http://unstats.un.org/unsd/demographic/sources/census/2010_PHC/South_Africa/ZAF07-Census2011.pdf>.

"Commission for Employment Equity Annual Report 2013/2014," 2014. *Pretoria Department of Labour*. Web. 12 May 2015. <http://www.labour.gov.za/DOL/downloads/documents/annual-reports/employment-equity/2013-2014/14ceereport_part5.pdf>.

"Constitution of the Republic of South Africa, 1996," n.d. *Sabinet Online*. Web. 11 June 2015. <http://www.constitutionalcourt.org.za/site/theconstitution/english-2013.pdf>.

"Country Profile South Africa: In-depth PESTLE insights," 2012. *South Africa Country Profile* by *Marketline* [Reference Code: ML00002-025]. *Business Source Premier*, EBSCO*host*. Web. 23 June 2015. <http://web.b.ebscohost.com/ehost/pdfviewer/pdfviewer?sid=3222336e-215f-48a2-8233-6ff37f6527ba%40sessionmgr113&vid=5&hid=124>.

"Definition of Youth," n.d. Factsheet prepared by the United Nations Department of Economic and Social Affairs. Web. 20 June 2015. <http://www.un.org/esa/socdev/documents/youth/fact-sheets/youth-definition.pdf>.

"emo," 2015. *Oxford Learner's Dictionary*. Web. 06 July 2015. <http://www.oxfordlearnersdictionaries.com/definition/english/emo>.

"Gender Statistics in South Africa, 2011," 2012. *Statistics South Africa*. Pretoria: Statistics South Africa.

"Grade 7–9 Catalogue 25 03 2013," 2013. *Government of South Africa* 25 March. Web. 20 June 2015. <http://www.google.de/url?sa=t&rct=j&q=&esrc=s&source=web&cd=1&ved=0CCQQFjAA&url=http%3A%2F%2Fwww.thutong.doe.gov.za%2FResourceDownload.aspx%3Fid%3D47315&ei=uCqFVY3mEYWp7AaIxI6ADA&usg=AFQjCNHkcJW1ra1VbradU-NmyE7DAuICIQ&bvm=bv.96339352,d.ZGU>.

"Kagiso Lesego Molope," 2014. *Africa Junior*. Web. 25 Aug. 2014. <http://www.africa-junior.com/en/youth/authors/kagiso-lesego-molope.html>.

"Macmillan Catalogue," 2015. *Macmillan South Africa*. Web. 14 June 2015. <www.macmillan.co.za/catalogue/seniorphase/grade-9/novels/124>.

"National Spatial Development Perspective 2006," 2007. *The Presidency: Republic of South Africa*. The Presidency, RSA. Web. 23 June 2015. <http://www.thepresidency.gov.za/docs/pcsa/planning/nsdp/intro1.pdf>.

"Native (Urban Areas) Act No. 21 of 1923," n.d. *O'Malley Archive. Nelson Mandela Centre of Memory*. Web. 16 Oct. 2016. <https://www.nelsonmandela.org/omalley/index.php/site/q/03lv01538/04lv01646/05lv01758.htm>.

"Natives Land Act, Act No. 27 of 1913," n.d. *South African History Online*. Web. 27 June 2015. < http://www.sahistory.org.za/archive/natives-land-act-act-no-27-1913>.

"Responses to Becoming Indoba – Chapter 3," n.d. *FunDza Mobile Library*. Web. 11 June 2015. <http://live.fundza.mobi/home/library/non-fiction-short-stories/becoming-indoda-a-real-man/chapter-3/comment-page-1/#comments>.

"Situation Analysis of Children in South Africa: April 2009," 2009. *The Presidency: Republic of South Africa*. The Presidency, RSA. Web. 2 Feb. 2015. <http://www.thepresidency.gov.za/ docs/pcsa/gdch/situation-analysis.pdf>.

"Social Profile of South Africa, 2002–2009," 2010. *Statistics South Africa*. Pretoria: Statistics South Africa. Web. 17 Jan. 2013. <http://www.statssa.gov.za/publications/Report-03-19-00/Report-03-19-002009.pdf>.

"Social Profile of Vulnerable Groups in South Africa 2002–2011," 2012. *Statistics South Africa*. Pretoria: Statistics South Africa. Web. 20 June 2015. <http://www.rmchsa.org/wp-content/resources/resources_by_theme/NewKnowledge/SocialProfileVulnerableGroups_2011.pdf>.

"South African Schools Act, 1960," n.d. *Southern African Legal Information Institute*. Web. 15 June 2015. <http://www.saflii.org/za/legis/num_act/sasa1996228/>.

"Spatial Development Intiative," n.d. Maputo Corridor Logistics Initiative (MCLI). Web. 21 June 2015. <http://www.mcli.co.za/mcli-web/mdc/sdi.htm>.

Addams, Jane, 1902. *Democracy and Social Ethics*. New York; London: Macmillan. Web. 21 June 2015.

Addams, Jane, 2002. *Democracy and Social Ethics*. Introduction by Charlene Haddock Seigfreid. Chicago: University of Illinois Press.

Adichie, Chimamanda Ngozi, 2009. "The Danger of the Single Story." *Ted–Talk*. Web. 22 May 2015. <http://www.ted.com/talks/chimamanda_adichie_the_danger_of_a_single_story>.

Agnew, John, 2011. "Space and Place." *The SAGE Handbook to Geographical Knowledge*. Eds. John Agnew and David N. Livingstone. London: SAGE Publications Ltd. 316–331.

Anker, Johan, 2011. "Fanie Viljoen se *Onderwêreld* as voorbeeld van die gesag- en magstryd in die jeugroman." *LitNet Akademies* 8.3: n. pag. Web. 31 Aug. 2016. <http://www.litnet.co.za/Article/fanie-viljoen-se-onderwereld-as-voorbeeld-van-die-gesag-en-magstryd-in-die-jeugroman>.

Ashcroft, Bill, G. Griffiths, and H. Tiffin, eds., 2000. *Post-colonial Studies: The Key Concepts*. London: Routledge.

Ashman, Sam, Ben Fine, and Susan Newman, 2011. "The Crisis in South Africa: Neoliberalism, Financialization and Uneven and Combined Development." *Socialist Register* 47: 174–195.

Asthana, S., and R. Oostvogels, 2001. "The Social Construction of Male 'Homosexuality' in India: Implications for HIV Transmission and Prevention." *Social Science and Medicine* 52.5: 707–721.

Attebery, Brion, 1992. *Strategies of Fantasy*. Bloomington: Indiana University Press.

Attridge, Derek, and Rosemary Jolly, 1998. *Writing South Africa: Literature, Apartheid, and Democracy, 1970–1995*. Cambridge: Cambridge University Press.

Attwell, David, and Derek Attridge, 2012. *The Cambridge History of South African Literature*. Cambridge: Cambridge University Press.

Baldick, Chris, 2004. *Oxford Concise Dictionary of Literary Terms*. [1990]. Oxford: Oxford University Press.

Bangura, Abdul Karim, 2012. "Post-election Conflict Resolution in Africa: Lessons from African Peace Paradigms." *Managing Conflicts in Africa's Democratic Transitions*. Ed. Akanmu G. Adebayo. Lanham: Lexington Books. 193–232.

Barnard, Rita, 2008. "Tsotsis: On Law, the Outlaw, and the Postcolonial State." *Contemporary Literature* 49.4: 541–72.

Battle, Michael, 1997. *Reconciliation: The Ubuntu Theology of Desmond Tutu*. Cleveland, OH: The Pilgrim Press.

Bauer, Nickolaus, 2011. "South Africa Desperate for Skilled Teachers." *Mail and Guardian* 21 Sept. Web. 2 Feb. 2015. <http://mg.co.za/article/2011-09-21-south-africa-desperate-for-skilled-teachers>.

Belsey, Catherine, 1980. *Critical Practice*. London: Routledge.

Benjamin, Walter, 1997. *Charles Baudelaire: A Lyric Poet in the Era of High Capitalism*. Trans. Harry Zohn. London: Verso.

Benjamin, Walter, 2002. *The Arcades Project*. Transl. by Howard Eiland and Kevin McLaughlin. Cambridge, MA; London: The Bellknap Press of Harvard University Press.

Bhabha, Homi, 2007. *The Location of Culture*. London: Routledge.

Bhana, Deevia, 2005. "Violence and the Gendered Negotiation of Masculinity among Young Black School Boys in South Africa." *African Masculinities: Men in Africa from the Late Nineteenth Century to the Present*. Eds. Lahoucine Ouzgane and Robert Morrell. New York: Palgrave. 205–220.

Bloch, Joanne, and Karen Martin, 2005. "Introduction." *Balancing Act: South African Gay and Lesbian Youth Speak Out*. Eds. Joanne Bloch and Karen Martin. Claremont: New Africa Books. 6–7.

Blume, Svenja, 2005. *Texte ohne Grenzen für Leser jeden Alters. Zur Neustrukturalisierung des Jungendliteraturbegriffs in der literarischen Postmoderne*. Freiburg i. Br.: Rombach.

Bond, Patrick, 2000. *Elite Transition: From Apartheid to Neoliberlism in South Africa*. London: Pluto Press.

Bort, Wolfgang, 2002. "Orte der Kindheit - Orte für Kinder?" *Kindergartenpädagogik. Online–Handbuch*. Ed. Martin R. Textor. Web. 22 May 2012. <http://www.kindergartenpaedagogik.de/759.html>.

Bottomley, Edward-John, 2012. *Poor White*. Cape Town: Tafelberg.

Bourdieu, Pierre, 1998. *Practical Reason: On the Theory of Action*. Stanford: Stanford University Press.

Boyce, Paul, 2007. "'Conceiving *Kothis*': Men Who Have Sex with Men in India and the Cultural Subject of HIV Prevention." *Medical Anthropology* 26.2: 175–203.

Brathwaite, Edward Kamau, 1971. *The Development of Creole Society in Jamaica*. London: Claredon.

Bremner, Lindsay, 1998. "Crime and the Emerging Landscape of Post-apartheid Johannesburg." *Blank____: Apartheid, Architecture and Beyond*. Eds. Hilton Judin and Ivan Vladislavić. Rotterdam: NAI Publishers. B2.

Bremner, Lindsay, 2008. "Reframing Township Space: The Kliptown Project." *Johannesburg: The Elusive Metropolis*. Eds. Sarah Nuttall and Achille Mbembe. Durham and London: Duke University Press. 337–347.

Brouard, Pierre, 2009. "Gender, Same-Sex Sexuality and HIV/AIDS in South Africa: Practical Research Challenges and Solutions." *From Social Silence to Social Science: Same-Sex Sexuality, HIV & AIDS and Gender in South Africa, Conference Proceedings*. Eds. Vasu Reddy, Theo Sandfort, and Laetitia Rispel. Cape Town: HSRC Press. 58–65.

Brown, Molly, 2008a. "Between the Rock and a Hard Place: Hidden Stories and the Hidden Star." *Mousaion* 26.2: 162–173.

Brown, Molly, 2008b. "Why are South Africans Afraid of Tokoloshes?" *The Lion and the Unicorn* 32.3: 260–270.

Budlender, Debbie, ed., 1996. *The Women's Budget*. Cape Town: Institute for Democracy in South Africa.

Budlender, Debbie, ed., 1997. *The Second Women's Budget*. Cape Town: Institute for Democracy in South Africa.

Budlender, Debbie, ed., 1998. *The Third Women's Budget*. Cape Town: Institute for Democracy in South Africa.

Burger, Philippe, 2005. *The Transformation Process in South Africa: What Does Existing Data Tell Us?* [*Berichte aus dem Weltwirtschaftlichen Colloquium der Universität Bremen*, Nr. 97.] Bremen: IWIM – Institut für Weltwirtschaft und Internationales Management.

Burger, Rulof, and Rachel Jafta, 2010. "Affirmative Action in South Africa: An Empirical Assessment of the Impact on Labour Market Outcomes." CRISE Working Paper No. 76. University of Oxford. Web. 6 July 2015. <http://www3.qeh.ox.ac.uk/pdf/crisewps/workingpaper76.pdf>.

Burger, Willie, 2014. "Afrikaans Literature after 20 Years of Democracy." Paper presented at the "Writing the Rainbow Nation" Conference at the University of Regensburg, 4–5 April.

Butler, Judith, 2011. *Das Unbehagen der Geschlechter*. Frankfurt a. M.: Suhrkamp.

bwa Mwesigire, Bwesigye, 2014. "An Open Letter to African Intellectuals." *This Is Africa* 13 Oct. Web. 15 Oct. 2014. <http://thisisafrica.me/open-letter-contemporary-african-intellectuals/ >.

Cáceres, C. F., and A. M. Rosasco, 1999. "The Margin Has Many Sides: Diversity among Gay and Homosexually Active Men in Lima." *Culture, Health and Sexuality* 1.3: 261–275.

Caminero-Santangelo, Byron, and Garth A. Myers, 2011. "Introduction." *Environment at the Margins: Literary and Environmental Studies in Africa*. Eds. Byron Caminero-Santangelo and Garth A. Myers. Athens, OH: Ohio University Press.

Carpenter, Carole, Margot Hillel, and Thomas van der Walt, 2005. "The Same but Different: The Dynamics of Local and Global in Australian, Canadian and South African Children's Literature." *Children's Literature Global and Local: Social and Aesthetic Perspectives*. Eds. Emer O'Sullivan, Kimberley Reynolds, and Rolf Romøren. Oslo: Novus Press. 173–199.

Case, Robbie, 1985. *Intellectual Development: Birth to Adulthood*. New York: Academic Press.

CBN, 2015. "The Jay Heale Collection." *Children's Book Network* 16 Dec. Web. 16 Aug. 2016. <http://www.childrensbook.co.za/news/2015/12/16/jay-heale-collection>.

Chabane, Collins, 2013. "2012 Development Indicators." *The Presidency of South Africa*. Cape Town: The Presidency of South Africa. Web. 30 Nov. 2013. <http://us-cdn.creamermedia.co.za/assets/articles/attachments/45572_development_indicators.pdf>.

Chapman, Michael, 1996. "Writing Literary History in Southern Africa." *Rethinking South African Literary History*. Eds. Johannes A. Smit, Johan van Wyk, and Jean Philippe Wade. Durban: Y–Press. 40–50.

Chapman, Michael, 2011a. "Introduction: SA Lit beyond 2000?" *SA Lit beyond 2000*. Eds. Michael Chapman and Margaret Lenta. Scottsville: University of KwaZulu–Natal Press. 1–18.

Chapman, Michael, 2011b. "Postcolonial Problematics: A South African Case Study." *Research in African Literatures* 42.4: 60–71.

Chapman, Michael, and Margaret Lenta, 2011. "Preface." *SA Lit beyond 2000*. Eds. Michael Chapman and Margaret Lenta. Scottsville: University of KwaZulu–Natal Press.

Chipkin, Ivor, 2009. "Citizenship, Knowledge and the Nationalist State." *Re-imagining the Social in South Africa: Critique, Theory and Post-apartheid Society.* Eds. Heather Jacklin and Peter Vale. Pietermaritzburg: University of KwaZulu–Natal Press. 47–75.

Chris, 2013. "Lindsay Callaghan Interviews Jenny Robson about Her Latest Youth Novel, Back to Villa Park." *NB @ Books LIVE* 23 July. Web. 14 Oct. 2016. <http://nb.bookslive.co.za/blog/2013/07/23/lindsay-callaghan-interviews-jenny-robson-about-her-latest-youth-novel-back-to-villa-park/>.

Cixous, Hélène, 1981a. "The Laugh of the Medusa." Trans. by Keith Cohen and Paula Cohen. *Signs: Journal of Women in Culture and Society* (1976) 1.4: 875–93. Reproduced in *New French Feminism.* Eds. Elaine Marks and Isabelle de Courtivron. Brighton: Harvester. 56–67.

Cixous, Hélène, 1981b. "Castration or Decapitation?" Transl. by Annette Kuhn. *Signs: Journal of Women in Culture and Society* 7.1: 41–55.

Cixous, Hélène, 1991. *"Coming to Writing" and Other Essays.* Translated by Sarah Cornell, et al. Cambridge, MA: Harvard University Press.

Clifton, Nicole, 2005. "The Seven Sages of Rome, Children's Literature, and the Auchinleck Manuscript." *Childhood in the Middle Ages and the Renaissance: The Results of a Paradigm Shift in the History of Mentality.* Ed. Albrecht Classen. Berlin: Walter de Gruyter. 185–202.

Cloete, E., 2009. "Ecofutures in Africa: Jenny Robson's *Savannah 2116 AD.*" *Children's Literature in Education* 40.1: 46–58.

Cloete, Pieter, and Frans Kotze, 2009. "Concept Paper on Social Cohesion/Inclusion in Local Integrated Development Plans." Department of Social Development, Republic of South Africa, 6 July. Web. 19 May 2015. <http://www.presidentsaward.co.za/wp-content/uploads/2013/04/Social-Cohesion-Final-Draftcorrect-IDP-DSD.pdf>.

Coertze, R., 2001. "Ubuntu and Nation Building in South Africa." *South African Journal of Ethnology* 24.4: 113–118.

Comaroff, Jean, and John Comaroff, 2004. "Criminal Obsessions, after Foucault: Postcoloniality, Policing, and the Metaphysics of Disorder." *Critical Inquiry* 30.4: 800–824.

Comaroff, Jean, and John Comaroff, 2012. *Theory from the South: Or, How Euro-America Is Evolving toward Africa.* Boulder; London: Paradigm.

Connell, R. W., 1995. *Masculinities.* Berkeley: University of California Press.

Davies, Shirley, 1992. *Reading Roundabout: A Review of South African Children's Literature.* Pietermaritzburg: Shuter and Shooter.

Davis, Geoffrey V., 2006. "Political Loyalties and the Intricacies of the Criminal Mind: The Detective Fiction of Wessel Ebersohn." *Postcolonial Postmortems: Crime Fiction from a Transcultural Perspective.* Eds. Christine Matzke and Susanne Mühleisen. New York: Rodopi. 181–200.

Dawkins, Cedric, and Faith Wambura Ngunjiri, 2008. "Corporate Social Responsibility Reporting in South Africa: A Descriptive and Comparative Analysis." *International Journal of Business Communication* 45.3: 286–307.

Dawson-Tunik, T. L., K. W. Fischer, and Z. Stein, 2004. "Do Stages Belong at the Center of Developmental Theory? A Commentary on Piaget's Stages." *New Ideas in Psychology* 22: 255–263.

De Beauvoir, Simone, 2000. *Das andere Geschlecht: Sitte und Sexus der Frau.* Reinbek bei Hamburg: Rowohlt–Taschenbuch–Verlag.

De Boeck, Filip, and Alcinda Honwana, 2005. "Introduction: Children and Youth in Africa." *Makers and Breakers: Children and Youth in Postcolonial Africa.* Eds. Alcinda Honwana and Filip de Boeck. Oxford: James Currey. 1–18.

De Certeau, Michel, 1988. *The Practice of Everyday Life.* Transl. Steven Rendeall. Berkeley: University of California Press.

De Certeau, Michel, 2002. "The Practice of Everyday Life." *The Blackwell City Reader.* Eds. Sophie Watson and Gary Bridge. Oxford: Blackwell Publishing. 111–118.

De Kock, Leon, 2005. "Does South African Literature Still Exist? Or: South African Literature is Dead, Long Live Literature in South Africa." *English in Africa* 32.2: 69–83.

De Kock, Leon, 2009. "Judging New 'South African' Fiction in the Transnational Moment." *Current Writing: Text and Reception in South Africa* 21.1–2: 24–58.

De Kock, Leon, 2011. "The End of 'South African' Literary History?" *SA Lit beyond 2000.* Eds. Michael Chapman and Margaret Lenta. Pietermaritzburg: University of KwaZulu–Natal Press. 19–49.

De Kock, Leon, 2014. "The SA Lit Issue Won't Go Away." *Mail and Guardian* 22 Aug. Web. 28 June 2015. <http://mg.co.za/article/2014-08-22-the-sa-lit-issue-wont-go-away>.

De Meyer, Bernard, and Neil ten Kortenaar, eds., 2009. *The Changing Face of African Literature/Les nouveaux visages de la littérature africaine.* Amsterdam; New York: Rodopi.

DeLoughrey, Elizabeth, Renee Gosson, and George Handley, 2005. *Caribbean Literature and the Environment.* Charlottesville: University of Virginia Press.

Dike, Virginia, 2005. "Developing Fiction for Today's Nigerian Youth." *Sankofa: Journal of African Children's and Young Adult Literature* 6: 6–17.

Douglas, M., and B. Isherwood, 1996. *The World of Goods: Towards an Anthropology of Consumption* [1979]. London: Routledge.

Dreier, Annette, 2008. "Zur Bedeutung von Räumen für die Bildung." *Die Grundschulzeitschrift* 217: 26–9.

Dreier, Annette, 2011. "Raum als 3. Erzieher(in)." *Handlexikon der Reggio-Pädagogik* 4. erw. Aufl. Ed. Sabine Lingenauber. Bochum; Freiburg: Projektverlag. 136–144.

Duncan, R., 2014. "Contemporary South African Horror: On Meat, Neo-liberalism and the Postcolonial Politics of a Global Form." *Horror Studies* 5.1: 1–10.

Edigheji, Omano, 2007. "Affirmative Action and State Capacity in a Democratic South Africa." *Policy: Issues and Actors* 20.4: 1–13. Web. 6 July 2015. <http://cps.org.za/cps%20pdf/pia20_4.pdf>.

Edmans, Ursula, 1982. "Writing South Africa: A Survey of South African Fiction, 1960–1980." *English–Amerikanische Studien* 4: 523–536.

Eggert, Dietrich, and Lucien Bertrand, 2002. *RZI – Raum-Zeit-Inventar der Entwicklung der räumlichen und zeitlichen Dimension bei Kindern im Vorschul- und Grundschulalter und deren Bedeutung für den Erwerb der Kulturtechniken Lesen, Schreiben und Rechnen.* Dortmund: Borgmann.

Ekema-Agbaw, Stephen, and Vivian Yenika-Agbaw, 2014. "How African Youth Control Their Identities through Social Media." *African Youth in Contemporary Literature and Popular Culture: Identity Quest.* Eds. Vivian Yenika-Agbaw and Lindah Mhando. New York: Routledge. 184–193.

Elshtain, Jean B., 2002. *Jane Addams and the Dream of American Democracy.* New York: Basic Books.

Erikson, Erik, 1968. *Identity: Youth and Crisis*. Oxford: Norton & Co.

Evans, Ian, 2008. "South Africa Wakes up to Growing White Poor." *The Independent* 1 Aug. Web. 17 Feb. 2015. <http://www.independent.co.uk/news/world/africa/south-africa-wakes-up-to-growing-white-poor-882631.html>.

Everatt, D., 2001. "From Urban Warrior to Market Segment? Youth in South Africa 1990–2000." *Youth Citizenship and Empowerment*. Eds. H. Helve and C. Wallace. Aldershot: Ashgate. 293–327.

Ewers, Hans-Heino, 2000. *Literatur für Kinder und Jugendliche. Eine Einführung in grundlegende Aspekte des Handlungs- und Symbolsystems Kinder- und Jugendliteratur*. Stuttgart: UTB.

Fairclough, Norman, 2010. *Critical Discourse Analysis: The Critical Study of Language*. 2nd ed. London, et al.: Pearson.

Fine, B., and E. Leopold, 1993. *The World of Consumption*. London: Routledge.

Fink, Katharina, 2011. "Beyond the Texts: Further Thoughts on the Need for an On-Going Debate on 'Gender', Knowledge-Production and Silence." *BIGSAS Working Papers 1: Women's Life Worlds 'In-Between'*. 124–134. Web. 18 June 2015. <http://scholar.googleusercontent.com/scholar?q=cache:x-QlJvvfEEkJ:scholar.google.com/+thando+Mgqolozana+masculinity&hl=de&as_sdt=0,5>.

Fletcher, Richard, 1995. "Changing the Lives of Boys." *Boys in Schools*. Eds. Rollo Browne and Richard Fletcher. Sidney: Finch Publishing. 202–211.

Foucault, Michel, 1977. "An Interview Entitled 'Revolutionary Action: Until Now'." *Language, Counter-memory, Practice*. Ed. Donald F. Bouchard. Ithaca, NY: Cornell University Press. 218–233.

Foucault, Michel, 1980. "Questions on Geography." *Power/Knowledge: Selected Interviews and Other Writings 1972–1977*. Ed. Colin Gordon. New York: Pantheon. 63–77.

Foucault, Michel, 1986. "Of Other Spaces." *Diacritics: A Review of Contemporary Criticism* 16: 22–27.

Foucault, Michel, 2002. "Discipline and Punish: The Birth of the Prison." *The Blackwell City Reader*. Eds. Sophie Watson and Gary Bridge. Oxford: Blackwell Publishing. 221–227.

Gartman, D., 1994. *Auto Opium: A Social History of Automobile Design*. London: Routledge.

Glaser, Barney G., and Anselm L. Strauss, 2006. *The Discovery of Grounded Theory: Strategies for Qualitative Research*. [1967]. New Brunswick; London: Adline Transaction.

Glotfelty, Cheryll, and Harnold Fromm, eds., 1996. *The Ecocriticism Reader: Landmarks in Literary Ecology*. Athens, GA: The University of Georgia Press.

Göhlich, Michael, 2001. "'Was ist Reggiopädagogik?' Antwort auf eine problematische Frage." *PÄD Forum* 3: 177–180.

Gray, Keith, 2008. "Eye of the Madcap Storm." *The Guardian* 31 May. Web. 16 June 2015. <http://www.theguardian.com/books/2008/may/31/booksforchildrenandteenagers2>.

Grünkemeier, Ellen, 2013. *Breaking the Silence*. Suffolk: James Curry.

Günzel, Stephan, ed., 2010. *Raum: Ein interdisziplinäres Handbuch*. Stuttgart; Weimar: Metzler.

Hagedorn, J., ed., 2007. *Gangs in the Global City: Alternatives to Traditional Criminology*. Chicago: University of Illinois Press.

Hamann, Ralph, and Paul Kapelus, 2004. "Corporate Social Responsibility in Mining in Southern Africa: Fair Accountability or Just Greenwash?" *Development* 47.3: 85–92.

Hamilton, Lawrence, 2014. *Are South Africans Free?* London, et al.: Bloomsbury.

Haraway, Donna, 1991. *Simians, Cyborgs, and Women: The Reinvention of Nature*. New York: Routledge.

Harrison, David, 2014. "Language Can Reshape Our Country." *City Press* 23 Oct. Web. 20 Jan. 2015. <http://www.citypress.co.za/columnists/language-can-reshape-economy/>.

Hartman, Ivor, 2012. *AfroSF: Science Fiction by African Writers*. Fish Hoek: StoryTime.

Hawtin, Murray, et al., 1994. *Community Profiling: Auditing Social Needs*. Buckingham; Philadelphia: Open University Press.

Heale, Jay, 1991. "South African Children's Literature in English." *Bookchat* 102: 19.

Heiberg, Turid, ed., 2005. "10 Essential Learning Points: Listen and Speak out against Child Sexual Abuse." Save the Children Norway. Web. 14 Jan. 2013 <http://resourcecentre.savethechildren.se/sites/default/files/documents/2673.pdf>.

Hemer, Oscar, 2012. *Fiction and Truth in Transition. Writing the Present Past in South Africa and Argentina*. [Freiburg Studies in Social Anthropology 34]. Berlin; Zürich: Lit Verlag.

Henke-Bockschatz, Gerhard, 2006. "Zeitzeugenbefragung." *Wörterbuch Geschichtsdidaktik*. Eds. Ulrich Mayer, et al. Schwalbach/Ts: Wochenschau Verlag.

Herlitzius, Eva-Marie, 2005. *A Comparative Analysis of the South African and German Reception of Nadine Gordimer's, Andre Brink's and J.M. Coetzee's Works*. Münster: LIT Verlag.

Hickel, Jason, 2014. "'Xenophobia' in South Africa: Order, Chaos, and the Moral Economy of Witchcraft." *Cultural Anthropology* 29.1: 103–127.

Hickson, Joyce, and Susan Kriegler, 1996. *Multicultural Counseling in a Divided and Traumatized Society: The Meaning of Childhood and Adolescence in South Africa*. Westport: Greenwood.

Hillel, Margot, and Thomas van der Walt, 2009. "Where Is the Mother in All This? Representations of Mothers and Mothering in Popular Australian and South African Books for Young Adults." *Mousaion* 28.2: 227–244.

Hlongwane, Gugu, 2006. "'Reader, Be Assured This Narrative Is No Fiction': The City and Its Discontents in Phaswane Mpe's Welcome to Our Hillbrow." *Ariel* 37.4: 69–82.

Hoad, Neville, 2005. "Introduction." *Sex and Politics in South Africa*. Eds. Neville Hoad, Karen Martin, and Greame Reid. Cape Town: Double Story Books. 14–24.

Hoad, Neville, 2007. *African Intimacies: Race, Homosexuality, and Globalization*. Minneapolis: University of Minnesota Press.

Hollindale, Peter, 1988. *Ideology and the Children's Book*. Stround: Thimble Press.

hooks, bell, 1998. "Men: Comrades in Struggle." *Feminism and Men: Reconstructing Gender Relations*. Eds. S. P. Schacht and D. W. Ewing. New York: New York University Press. 265–280.

Huggan, Graham, and Helen Tiffin, 2010. *Postcolonial Ecocriticism: Literature, Animals, Environment*. London: Routledge.

Hunt, Peter, ed., 2004a. *International Companion Encyclopedia of Children's Literature*. 2nd ed. Vol. I. London; New York: Routledge.

Hunt, Peter, ed., 2004b. *International Companion Encyclopedia of Children's Literature*. 2nd ed. Vol. II. London; New York: Routledge.

Inggs, Judith, 2000. "Character, Culture and Identity in a Contemporary South African Youth Novel." *Text, Culture and National Identity in Children's Literature. International Seminar on Children's Literature: Pure and Applied.* Ed. Jean Webb. Helsinki: Nordinfo. 46–55.

Inggs, Judith, 2002. "Grappling with Change: The English Language Youth Novel in South Africa." *CREArTa* 3.1: 22–33.

Inggs, Judith, 2004. "Space and Race in Contemporary South African English Youth Literature." *Change and Renewal in Children's Literature.* Ed. Thomas van der Walt. Westport: Praeger. 25–33.

Inggs, Judith, 2006. "New Frontiers in English-Language Young Adult Fiction in South Africa." *Bookbird* 44.2: 22–29.

Inggs, Judith, 2007. "Effacing Difference? The Multiple Images of South African Adolescents." *English in Africa* 34.2: 35–49.

Inggs, Judith, 2009. "Transgressing Boundaries? Romance, Power and Sexuality in Contemporary South African English Young Adult Fiction." *International Research in Children's Literature* 2.1: 101–114.

Inggs, Judith, 2016. *Transition and Transgression: English Young Adult Fiction in Post-Apartheid South Africa.* Breslau: Springer.

Inhelder, Bärbel, and Jean Piaget, 1958. *The Growth of Logical Thinking from Childhood to Adolescence: An Essay on the Construction of Formal Operational Structures.* Trans. by Anne Parsons and Stanley Milgram. London: Routledge and Kegan Paul.

Irigaray, Luce, 1985a. *Parler n'est jamais neuter.* Paris: Les Éditions de Minuit.

Irigaray, Luce, 1985b. *This Sex Which Is Not One.* Translated by Catherine Porter, with Carolyn Burke. Ithaca: Cornell University Press.

Irigaray, Luce, 1985c. *Speculum of the Other Woman.* Translated by Gillian C. Gill. Ithaca: Cornell University Press.

Jacobs, Johan U., 2013. "Young South Africans and Cultural (Mal)practice: Breaking the Silence in Recent Writing." *Literator* 34.1: Art. #33, 9 pages. Web. 15 Oct. 2016. <http://dx.doi.org/10.4102/lit.v34i1.33>.

Jenkins, Elwyn, 1993. *Children of the Sun: Selected Writers and Themes in South African Children's Literature.* Johannesburg: Ravan Press.

Jenkins, Elwyn, 2002. *South Africa in English Language Children's Literature, 1814–1912.* Jefferson, NC: McFarland & Company.

Jenkins, Elwyn, 2004. "English South African Children's Literature and the Environment." *Literator* 25.3: 107–124.

Jenkins, Elwyn, 2005. "Fictional Paintings and Immigration in a South African Young Adult Novel." *Children's Literature Global and Local: Social and Aesthetic Perspectives.* Eds. Emer O'Sullivan, Kimberley Reynolds, and Rolf Romoren. Oslo: Novus Press. 283-290.

Jenkins, Elwyn, 2006. *National Character in South African English Children's Literature.* New York; London: Routledge.

Jenkins, Elwyn, 2008. "Research into the Multilingual Children's Literature of South Africa." *Children's Literature Association Quarterly* 33.4: 428–440.

Jenkins, Elwyn, 2012. *Seedlings: English Children's Reading & Writers in South Africa.* Pretoria: Unisa Press.

Jenkins, Elwyn, and Elizabeth Muther, 2008. "Cross-Cultural Misreadings: MacCann and Maddy's *Apartheid and Racism* Revisited." *The Lion and the Unicorn* 32.3: 237–259.

Jennifer, 2015. "Award-Winning Mozambican Author Mia Couto's Open Letter to Jacob Zuma on Xenophobia Crisis: 'We Remember You in Maputo'." *BooksLIVE* 20 April. Web. 20 April 2015. <http://bookslive.co.za/blog/2015/04/20/award winning-mozambican-author-mia-coutos-open-letter-to-jacob-zuma-on-xenophobia-crisis-we-remember-you-in-maputo/>.

Jolly, Rosemary, 2010. *Cultured Violence: Narrative, Social Suffering, and Engendering Human Rights in Contemporary South Africa.* Liverpool: Liverpool University Press.

Jolly, Rosemary, and Derek Attridge, 1998. "Introduction." *Writing South Africa: Literature, Apartheid, and Democracy, 1970–1995.* Eds. Rosemary Jolly and Derek Attridge. Cambridge: Cambridge University Press. 1–13.

Jones, Megan, 2013. "Conspicuous Destruction, Aspiration and Motion in the South African Township." *Safundi: The Journal of South African and American Studies* 14.2: 209–224.

Kapp, R., 2004. "Reading on the Line: An Analysis of Literacy Practices in ESL Classes in a South African Township School." *Language and Education* 18.3: 246–263.

Karimi, Faith, 2015. "What's behind Xenophobic Attacks in South Africa?" *CNN* 19 April. Web. 20 April 2015. <http://edition.cnn.com/2015/04/18/africa/south-africa-xenophobia-explainer/>.

Kaschula, Russell, 2007. "Identity in the Siyagruva Series of Novels: Toward an Intercultural Literary Discourse." *Tydskrif vir Letterkunde* 44.2: 74–88.

Khorana, Meena, 1994. *Africa in Literature for Children and Young Adults: An Annotated Bibliography of English-Language Books.* Westport, CT: Greenwood Press.

Killam, D., and R. Rowe, 2000. *The Companion to African Literatures.* Oxford: James Currey.

Kimble, Lisa, and Barbara A. Lehman, 2014. "The Writing of Diane Case: Making Choices and Facing Consequences." *Creating Books for the Young in the New South Africa: Essays on Authors and Illustrators of Children's and Young Adult Literature.* Eds. Barbara A. Lehman, et al. Jefferson: McFarland. 38–46.

Knauf, Tassilo, 2001. "Einführung in das Thema: 100 Sprachen der Kinder zu Wort kommen lassen." *PÄD Forum* 3: 175–176.

Knauf, Tassilo, n.d. "Bildungsräume für Kinder von 0 bis 6: Der Raum als 'dritter Erzieher'." *Kindergartenpädagogik: Online Handbuch.* Ed. Martin R. Trexler. Web. 03 July 2012. <http://www.kindergartenpaedagogik.de/2076.html>.

Knight, Louise, 2005. *Citizen: Jane Addams and the Struggle for Democracy.* Chicago: University of Chicago Press.

Kristeva, Julia, 1990. "The Adolescent Novel." *Abjection, Melancholia and Love.* Eds. John Fletcher and Andrew Benjamin. London; New York: Routledge. 8–23.

Kumo, Wolassa Lawisso, Jan Rieländer, and Babatunde Omilola, 2014. "African Economic Outlook: South Africa 2014." AfDB, OECD, UNDP. Web. 16 June 2015. <http://www.africaneconomicoutlook.org/fileadmin/uploads/aeo/2014/PDF/CN_Long_EN/Afrique_du_Sud_EN.pdf>.

Lane, Tim, 2009. "From Social Silence to Social Science: HIV Research among Township Men Who Have Sex with Men in South Africa." *From Social Silence to Social Science: Same-Sex Sexuality, HIV & AIDS and Gender in South Africa, Conference*

Proceedings. Eds. Vasu Reddy, Theo Sandfort, and Laetitia Rispel. Cape Town: HSRC Press. 66–77.

Le Roux, Elisabeth, 2012. "Does the North Read the South? The International Reception of South African Scholarly Texts." *Postcolonial Audiences: Readers, Viewers and Reception*. Eds. Bethan Benwell, James Procter, and Gemma Robinson. London: Routledge. 73–85.

Lefebvre, Henri, 1994. *The Production of Space*. [1974] Transl. by Donald Nicholson-Smith. Oxford, UK; Cambridge, MA: Blackwell.

Lefebvre, Henri, 1996. *Writings on Cities*. Trans. Eleonore Kofman and Elizabeth Lebas. London: Blackwell.

Lehman, Barbara A., et al., eds., 2014. *Creating Books for the Young in the New South Africa: Essays on Authors and Illustrators of Children's and Young Adult Literature*. Jefferson: McFarland.

Lehohla, Pali, 2012a. "Census 2011: Census in Brief." *Statistics South Africa*. Pretoria: Statistics South Africa. Web. 21 June 2015. <http://www.statssa.gov.za/census/census_2011/census_products/Census_2011_Census_in_brief.pdf >.

Lehohla, Pali, 2012b. "Poverty Profile of South Africa, 2008/2009." *Statistics South Africa*. Pretoria: Statistics South Africa. Web. 03 July 2015. <http://www.statssa.gov.za/publications/Report-03-10-03/Report-03-10-032009.pdf>.

Leibbrandt, M., et al., 2010. "Trends in South African Income Distribution and Poverty since the Fall of Apartheid." *OECD Social, Employment and Migration Working Papers No. 101*. OECD Publishing.

Lenta, Margaret, 2011. "Expanding 'South Africanness'." *SA Lit beyond 2000*. Eds. Michael Chapman and Margaret Lenta. Pietermaritzburg: University of KwaZulu–Natal Press. 50–68.

Levander, Caroline, 2006. *Cradle of Liberty: Race, the Child, and National Belonging from Thomas Jefferson to W. E. B. Du Bois*. Durham: Duke University Press Books.

Lohaus, Arnold, and Marc Vierhaus, 2015. *Entwicklungspsychologie des Kindes- und Jugendalters für Bachelor*. Berlin; Heidelberg: Springer–Verlag.

Lorway, R., 2007. "Breaking a Public Health Silence: HIV Risk and Male-Male Sexual Practices in the Windhoek Urban Area." *Unravelling Taboos: Gender and Sexuality in Namibia*. Eds. S. La Font and D. Hubbard. Windhoek: Ford Foundation. 276–295.

Lukács, Georg, 1962. *Realism in Our Time: Literature and the Class Struggle*. New York; Evanston: Harper & Row.

Lundgren, Berit, and Mathabo Khau, 2015. "*Broken Promises* – A Novel's Impact on Shaping Youth Identity." *Reading & Writing* 6.1: Art. #86, 8 pages. Web. 15 Oct. 2016. <http://www.rw.org.za/index.php/rw/article/view/86/191>.

MacCann, Donnarae, and Yulisa Amadu Maddy, 2001. *Apartheid and Racism in South African Children's Literature 1985–1995*. New York: Routledge.

MacKenzie, Craig, 1990. "Njabulo Ndebele's Fiction and Criticism: Some Observations and Caveats." *Commonwealth Literary Cultures: New Voices, New Approaches: Conference Papers, Lecce, 3–7 April, 1990*. Eds. Giovanna Capone, Claudio Gorlier, and Bernard Hickey. Lecce: Edizioni del Grifo. 121–141.

MacKenzie, Craig, 2010. "More Rebellious than Ever." *Mail and Guardian: Supplement on the M&G Literary Festival, Johannesburg, 3–5 September 2010*. 27 Aug. Web. 11 June 2015. < http://mg.co.za/article/2010-08-27-more-rebellious-than-ever>.

Maddy, Yulisa Amadu, and Donnarae MacCann, 1996. *African Images in Juvenile Literature: Commentaries on Neocolonialist Fiction.* Jefferson, NC: McFarland.

Maddy, Yulisa Amadu, and Donnarae MacCann, 1998. "Ambivalent Signals in South African Young Adult Novels." *Bookbird* 36.1: 27–32.

Mallan, Kerry, 2008. "Space, Power and Knowledge: The Regulatory Fictions of Online Communities." *International Research in Children's Literature* 1: 66–81.

Mann, Susan, 2012. "Out of the Mouths: Voices of Children in Contemporary South African Literature." *Trauma, Memory, and Narrative in the Contemporary South African Novel: Essays.* Eds. Ewald Mengel and Michaela Borzaga. [Cross/Cultures 153]. Amsterdam; New York: Rodopi. 335–348.

Mapadimeng, Mokong Simon, and Sultan Khan, eds., 2011. *Contemporary Social Issues in Africa: Cases in Gaborone, Kampala, and Durban.* Pretoria: Africa Institute of South Africa.

Marais, Hein, 2001. *South Africa: Limits to Change: The Political Economy of Transformation.* London: Zed Books.

Martin, D. C., 2005. "From the Caldron of Coloured Experiences: Liminality and the Elusive Communitas in Four Novels by South African Coloured Writers." A paper presented at the International Conference on Hybridity, Liminality and Boundaries. University of the North-West, Potchefstroom Campus, June 30–July 2.

Martin, Julia, 1994. "New, with Added Ecology? Hippos, Forests, and Environmental Literacy." *Interdisciplinary Studies in Literature and Environment* 2.1: 1–11.

Martin, Michelle H., 2004. "Eco-edu-tainment: The Construction of the Child in Contemporary Environmental Children's Music." *Wild Things: Children's Culture and Ecocriticism.* Eds. Sidney Dobrin and Kenneth Kidd. Detroit: Wayne State University Press. 215–231.

Maserow, Josuah, 2014. "A Dream Deferred? Review of *Are South Africans Free?* by Lawrence Hamilton." *Aerodrome: Words and People,* 29 July. Web. 04 Jan. 2015. <http://aerodrome.co.za/a-dream-deferred/>.

Matebeni, Zethu, 2009. "Sexing Women: Young Black Lesbians' Reflections on Sex and Responses to Safe(r) Sex." *From Social Silence to Social Science: Same-Sex Sexuality, HIV and AIDS and Gender in South Africa, Conference Proceedings.* Eds. Vasu Reddy, Theo Sandfort, and Laetitia Rispel. Cape Town: HSRC Press. 100–116.

Matzke, Christine, and Susanne Mühleisen, ed., 2006. *Postcolonial Postmortems: Crime Fiction from a Transcultural Perspective.* New York: Rodopi.

Maxwell, Simon, 2001. "Negotiations of Car Use in Everyday Life." Ed. Daniel Miller. *Car Cultures.* Oxford: Berg. 203–222.

Mbao, Wamuwi, 2010. "Inscribing Whiteness and Staging Belonging in Contemporary Autobiographies and Life-Writing Forms." *English in Africa* 37.1: 63–75.

Mbembe, Achille, 1992. "The Banality of Power and the Aesthetics of Vulgarity in the Postcolony." Trans. Janet Roitman. *Public Culture* 4.2: 1–30.

Mbembe, Achille, 2008. "Aesthetics of Superfluity." *Johannesburg: The Elusive Metropolis.* Eds. Sarah Nuttall and Achille Mbembe. Johannesburg: Witwatersrand University Press. 37–67.

Mbembe, Achille, 2012. "Theory from the Antipodes Notes on Jean & John Comaroffs' *T[heory] F[rom the] S[outh].*" *The Johannesburg Salon* 5: 18–25.

Mbembe, Achille, 2014. "Class, Race and the New Native." *Mail and Guardian* 26 Sept. Web. 26 June 2015. <http://mg.co.za/article/2014-09-25-class-race-and-the-new-native/>.

Mbembe, Achille, 2015. *On the Postcolony*. Johannesburg: Wits University Press.

Mbembe, Achille, and Sarah Nuttall, 2004. "Writing the World from an African Metropolis." *Public Culture* 16.3: 347–372.

McCallum, Robyn, 2006. "Young Adult Literature." *The Oxford Encyclopedia of Children's Literature*. vol. 4. Ed. Jack Zipes. Oxford: Oxford University Press. 214–219.

McGillis, Roderick, ed., 2000. V*oices of the Other: Children's Literature and the Postcolonial Context*. New York; London: Garland Publishing.

McKinney, Carolyn, 2007. "'If I Speak English, Does It Make Me Less Black Anyway?' 'Race' and English in South African Desegregated Schools." *English Academy Review* 24.2: 6–24.

McWilliams, A., D. S. Siegel, and P. M. Wright, 2006. "Corporate Social Responsibility: Strategic Implications." *Journal of Management Studies* 43: 1–18.

Meintjes, H., et al., 2009. "Child-Headed Households in South Africa: A Statistical Brief." Cape Town: Children's Institute, Univ. of Cape Town. Web. 23 April 2015. <http://childrencount.ci.org.za/uploads/brief_child_headed_households.pdf>.

Meissner, Ortrun, and David L. Buso, 2007. "Traditional Male Circumcision in the Eastern Cape – Scourge or Blessing?" *South African Medical Journal* 97.5: 371–373.

Messner, M., 1997. *Politics of Masculinities: Men in Movements*. Thousand Oaks: Sage.

Metcalfe, Mary, 2008. "Teacher Quality in Southern Africa." *Commonwealth Education Partnership* 93–96. Web. 2 Feb. 2015. <http://www.cedol.org/commonwealth-education-partnerships/articles-from-20089/>.

Meyer-Spacks, Patricia Ann, 1981. *The Adolescent Idea: Myths of Youth and the Adult Imagination*. New York: Basic Books.

Michals, Teresa, 2014a. *Books for Children, Books for Adults: Age and the Novel from Defoe to James*. Cambridge: Cambridge University Press.

Michals, Teresa, 2014b. "Adult Fiction?" *InsideHigherEd* 15 Aug. Web. 17 Aug. 2014. <https://www.insidehighered.com/views/2014/08/15/essay-why-english-departments-should-teach-and-embrace-young-adult-fiction>.

Miller, Daniel, 2001. "Driven Societies." Ed. Daniel Miller. *Car Cultures*. Oxford: Berg. 1–33.

Miller, Patricia, 2011. *Theories of Developmental Psychology*. 5th ed. New York: Worth.

Moffett, Helen, 2006a. *Lovely beyond Any Singing: Landscapes in South African Writing*. Cape Town: Double Story Books.

Moffett, Helen, 2006b. "'These Women, They Force Us to Rape Them': Rape as Narrative of Social Control in Post-Apartheid South Africa." *Journal of Southern African Studies* 32.1: 129–144.

Moretti, Franco, 2013. *Distant Reading*. London: Verso.

Morgan, Ruth, Charl Marais, and Joy Rosemary Wellbeloved, eds., 2009. *TRANS: Transgender Life Stories in South Africa*. Auckland Park: Jacana.

Morrell, Robert, 2001a. "Corporal Punishment in South African Schools: A Neglected Explanation for Its Persistence." *South African Journal of Education* 21.4: 292–299.

Morrell, Robert, 2001b. "Corporal Punishment and Masculinity in South African Schools." *Men and Masculinities* 4.2: 140–157.

Morrell, Robert, 2005. "Men, Movements, and Gender Transformation in South Africa." *African Masculinities: Men in Africa from the Late Nineteenth Century to the Present.* Eds. Lahoucine Ouzgane and Robert Morrell. New York: Palgrave. 271–288.

Msimang, Sisonke, 2015. "The End of the Rainbow Nation Myth." *The New York Times* 12 April. Web. 14 April 2015. <http://www.nytimes.com/2015/04/13/opinion/the-end-of-the-rainbow-nation-myth.html?_r=2&referrer >.

Muholi, Z., 2004. "Thinking through Lesbian Rape." *Agenda* 61: 116–125.

Muños-Laboy, M., 2004. "Beyond 'MSM': Sexual Desire among Bisexually-Active Latino Men in New York City." *Sexualities* 7.1: 55–80.

Munro, Brenna M., 2012. *South Africa and the Dream of Love to Come: Queer Sexuality and the Struggle for Freedom.* Minneapolis: University of Minnesota Press.

Murray, Sally-Ann, 2008. "Indigenous Gardening, Belonging and Bewilderment: On Becoming South African." *Postcolonialism: South/African Perspectives.* Ed. Michael Chapman. Newcastle: Cambridge Scholars Publishing. 40–60.

Murray, Sally-Ann, 2011. "On the Street with Vladislavic, Mhlongo, Moele and Others." *SA Lit beyond 2000.* Eds. Michael Chapman and Margaret Lenta. Pietermaritzburg: University of KwaZulu–Natal Press. 69–96.

Musgrave, P. W., 1985. *From Brown to Bunter: The Life and Death of the School Story.* London: Routledge & Paul.

Mzamane, Mbulelo Vizikhungo, 1996. "Literature for a National Culture in South Africa: Perspectives of Oppressed Groups." *Anglistentag 1995 in Greifswald, Proceedings of the German Association of University Teachers of English.* Tübingen: Max Niemeyer Verlag. 343–360.

Mzamane, Mbulelo Vizikhungo, 1997. "Domestication of a Tradition: Early Trends in South African Literature, 1820–1930." *South African Literary History: Totality and/or Fragment.* Eds. Erhard Reckwitz, Karin Reitner, and Lucia Vennarini. Essen: Die Blaue Eule. 145–161.

Naidoo, Beverley, 2014. "Afterword." *Creating Books for the Young in the New South Africa: Essays on Authors and Illustrators of Children's and Young Adult Literature.* Eds. Barbara A. Lehman, et al. Jefferson: McFarland. 267–270.

Narsiah, Sagie, 2002. "Neoliberalism and Privatisation in South Africa." *GeoJournal* 57: 3–13.

Navarro, Emilia, 1993. "Manual Control: 'Regulatory Fictions' and their Discontents." *Revista Cervantes* 13.2: 17–35.

Ndebele, Njabulo, 1994. *South African Literature and Culture: Rediscovery of the Ordinary.* Manchester: Manchester University Press.

Ndebele, Njabulo, 2007. *Fine Lines from the Box: Further Thoughts about Our Country.* Cape Town: Umuzi.

Ndebele, Thuthukani, 2013. "South Africa Goes with the Urbanisation Flow." *South African Institute of Race Relations*, 22 Jan. Web. 10 June 2015. <http://irr.org.za/reports-and-publications/media-releases/Urbanisation%20-%2022_Jan_2013.pdf/>.

Ndlovu, Sifiso Mxolisi, 2011. "Part 1: Soweto." *The Road to Democracy in South Africa – Volume 2 (1970–1980).* Ed. S. M. Ndlovu. Johannesburg: UNISA Press. 317–350.

Neumann, Birgit, 2005. *Erinnerung – Identität – Narration: Gattungstypologie und Funktionen kanadischer "Fictions of Memory".* Berlin: Walter de Gruyter.

Nevill, Glenda, 2011. "Cover2Cover Takes Mass Youth Market Readers on Mobile Journey." *The Media Online* 4 April. Web. 02 July 2015. <http://themediaonline.co.za/2011/04/cover2cover-takes-mass-youth-market-readers-on-mobile-journey/2147483647/>.

Newell, Stephanie and Onookome Okome, 2013. *Popular Culture in Africa: The Episteme of the Everyday*. New York: Routledge.

Ngcowa, Sonwabiso, 2014. "Black Men: We Have the Power to End an Era of Brutality." *The Daily Maverick* 25 Aug. Web. 27 June 2015. <http://www.dailymaverick.co.za/opinionista/2014-08-25-black-men-we-have-the-power-to-end-an-era-of-brutality/#.U_r2o6Ohv_a>.

Nodelman, Perry, 1992. *The Pleasures of Children's Books*. New York: Longman.

Nodelman, Perry, 2002. "Making Boys Appear: The Masculinity of Children's Fiction." *Ways of Being Male: Representing Masculinities in Children's Literature and Film*. Ed. John Stephens. New York: Routledge. 1–14.

Nuttall, Sarah, 2004. "City Forms and Writing the 'Now' in South Africa." *Journal of South African Studies* 30.4: 731–748.

Nuttall, Sarah, 2009. *Entanglement: Literary and Cultural Reflections on Post-Apartheid*. Johannesburg: Wits University Press.

Nuttall, Sarah, 2011a. "The Way We Read Now." *SLiP: Stellenbosch Literary Project*, 14 March. Web. 12 Jan. 2013. <http://slipnet.co.za/view/blog/sarah-nuttall/the-way-we-read-now/>.

Nuttall, Sarah, 2011b. "Hungry for What?" *SLiP: Stellenbosch Literary Project*, 26 April. Web. 26 Aug. 2014. <http://slipnet.co.za/view/blog/hungry-for-what/>.

Nuttall, Sarah, and Achille Mbembe, eds., 2008. *Johannesburg. The Elusive Metropolis*. Durham; London: Duke University Press.

Nuttall, S., and C. Michael, 2000. "Introduction: Imagining the Past." *Senses of Culture: South African Culture Studies*. Eds. S. Nuttall and C. Michael. Oxford: Oxford University Press. 1–23.

Odiase, J. O. U., 1986. *African Books for Children and Young Adults*. Bening City, Nigeria: Nationwide Publication Bureau in Collaboration with Unique Bookshop.

Oike, Machiko, 2010. "A New African Youth Novel in the Era of HIV/AIDS: An Analysis of Unity Dow's Far & Beyon'." *New Novels in African Literature*. Ed. Ernest N. Emenyonu. [African Literature Today, vol. 27]. Woodbridge: James Currey. 75–84.

Oldenburg, Ray, 1999. *The Great Good Place: Cafés, Coffee Shops, Bookstores, Bars, Hair Salons, and Other Hangouts at the Heart of a Community*. New York: Marlowe.

Osa, Osayimwense, 1995. *African Children's and Youth Literature*. New York, NY: Twayne Publishers.

Parker, Kenneth, ed., 1978. *The South African Novel in English: Essays in Criticism and Society*. London; Basingstoke: Macmillan.

Parker, R., and C. Cáceres, 1999. "Alternative Sexualities and Changing Sexual Culture among Latin American Men." *Culture, Health and Sexuality* 1.3: 201–206.

Partridge, Sally-Ann, 2011. "Youth Lit in South Africa." *SA Partridge @ Books live* 18 April. Web. 31 Aug. 2016. <http://sapartridge.bookslive.co.za/blog/2011/04/18/youth-lit-in-south-africa/>.

Patel, Khadija, 2013. "Analysis: The Ugly Truth behind SA's Xenophobic Violence." *The Daily Maverick* 28 May. Web. 16 Jan. 2015. <http://www.dailymaverick.co.za/article/2013-05-28-analysis-the-ugly-truth-behind-sas-xenophobic-violence/#.VLjtPMkoGzM>.

Pearson, Lucy, and Kimberley Reynolds, 2010. "Realism." *The Routledge Companion to Children's Literature.* Ed. David Rudd. New York: Routledge. 63–74.

Penn, Joanna, 2013. "Are African Writers and Readers Ready for the eBook Revolution?" *The Creative Penn* 23 March. Web. 1 July 2015. <http://www.thecreativepenn.com/2013/03/23/african-ebook-revolution/>.

Pennell, Beverley, 2002. "Redeeming Masculinity at the End of the Second Millennium: Narrative Reconfigurations of Masculinity in Children's Fiction." *Ways of Being Male: Representing Masculinities in Children's Literature and Film.* Ed. John Stephens. New York: Routledge. 55–77.

Perrow, M., 2004. "Youth Development in Transition, 1992–2004." *Changing Class: Education and Social Change in Post-Apartheid South Africa.* Ed. L. Chisholm. Cape Town: Human Sciences Research Council.

Petzold, Jochen, 2002. *Re-imagining White Identity by Exploring the Past: History in South African Novels of the 1990s.* [Studies in English Literary and Cultural Studies 5]. Trier: Wissenschaftlicher Verlag Trier.

Petzold, Jochen, 2005. "Children's Literature after Apartheid: Examining 'Hidden Histories' of South Africa's Past." *Children's Literature Association Quarterly* 30.2: 140–151.

Petzold, Jochen, 2009. "Geschichte als Verbrechen: Zur Verknüpfung von *history* und *crime* in Romanen André Brinks." *Geschichte im Krimi: Beiträge aus den Kulturwissenschaften.* Eds. Barbara Korte and Sylvia Paletschek. Köln: Böhlau Verlag. 227–239.

Phyega, M. V., 2013. "An Analysis of the National Crime Statistics 2012/13." *SAPS Strategic Management* 31 Aug. Web. 20 June 2015. <http://www.issafrica.org/crimehub/uploads/SAPS-crime-analysis-2013.pdf>.

Piaget, Jean, and Bärbel Inhelder, et al., 1971. *Die Entwicklung des räumlichen Denkens beim Kinde.* Stuttgart: Klett.

Pillay, Pundy, 2001. *South Africa in the 21st Century: Some Key Socio-Economic Challenges.* Johannesburg: Friedrich Ebert Stiftung.

Pillay, Verashni, 2015. "Six Things White People Have That Black People Don't." *Mail and Guardian* 23 Feb. Web. 24 Feb. 2015. <http://mg.co.za/article/2015-02-23-six-things-white-people-have-that-black-people-dont >.

Pinsent, Pat, 2005a. "Language, Genres and Issues: The Socially Committed Novel." *Modern Children's Literature: An Introduction.* Ed. Kimberley Reynolds. New York: Palgrave. 191–208.

Pinsent, Pat, 2005b. "Theories of Genre and Gender: Change and Continuity in the School Story." *Modern Children's Literature: An Introduction.* Ed. Kimberley Reynolds. New York: Palgrave. 8–22.

Pucherová, Dobrota, 2011. *The Ethics of Dissident Desire in Southern African Writing.* [Studien zu Literaturen und Kunst Afrikas, Bd. 2]. Trier: Wissenschaftlicher Verlag Trier.

Putter, Anne, 2012. "Reinventing and Reimagining Johannesburg in Three Post-Apartheid South African Texts." Thesis submitted in fulfilment of the requirements for the degree Master of Arts (English) in the Faculty of Humanities, University of Johannesburg. Web. 21 June 2015. <https://ujdigispace.uj.ac.za/bitstream/handle/10210/8143/Putter.pdf?sequence=1>.

Quigly, Isabel, 1982. *The Heirs of Tom Brown: The English School Story.* London: Chatto & Windus.

Rabinow, Paul, 1982. "Space, Knowledge, and Power. Interview: Michel Foucault." *Skyline*. 16–20. (Also in Rabinow, ed., *The Foucault Reader*. New York: Pantheon, 1984. 239–56).

Raborife, Mpho, 2015. "More Cops to Be Deployed to Xenophobic Violence Hotspots." *Mail and Guardian* 18 April. Web. 20 April 2015. <http://mg.co.za/article/2015-04-18-more-cops-to-be-deployed-to-xenophobic-violence-hotspots>.

Radebe, Kentse, 2013. "The Costly Choice between Public and Private Schooling." *MoneyWeb* 7 March. Web. 15 Oct. 2016. <http://www.moneyweb.co.za/moneyweb-south-africa/the-costly-choice-between-public-and-private-schoo>.

Rätzel, Daniela, 2009. "Wie beeinflusst der Raum pädagogische Qualität? – Der Raum als dritter Pädagoge." *Pädagogische Qualität: Einflussfaktoren und Wirkmechanismen*. Ed. Claudia Dehn. [Schriftenreihe für kritische Sozialforschung und Bildungsarbeit, Bd. 15]. Hannover: Expressum–Verlag, 94–107.

Rauch, Marja, 2012. *Jugendliteratur der Gegenwart: Grundlagen, Methoden, Unterrichtsvorschläge*. Seelze–Velber: Kallmeyer.

Reid, Emma, n.d. "*Sharkey's Son* by Gillian D'Achada: A Teacher's Guide and Activity Resource for Grades 5–7." *NB Publishers*. Web. 19 Jan. 2015. <http://www.nb.co.za/assets/downloads/teachers_guides/Sharkeys%20Son%20Teachers%20Guide.pdf>.

Reynolds, Kimberley, 2002. "Come Lads and Ladettes: Gendering Bodies and Gendering Behaviors." *Ways of Being Male: Representing Masculinities in Children's Literature and Film*. Ed. John Stephens. New York: Routledge. 96–115.

Reynolds, Kimberley, 2005. "Introduction." *Modern Children's Literature: An Introduction*. Ed. Kimberley Reynolds. New York: Palgrave. 1–7.

Reynolds, Kimberley, 2014. "Firing the Canon! Geoffrey Trease's Campaign for an Alternative Children's Canon in 1930's Britain." Keynote Lecture at the "Canon Constitution and Canon Change in Children's Literature" Conference at the University of Tübingen, Germany, 11–13 September.

Richter, L. M., 1991. "Street Children in South Africa – General Theoretical Introduction: Society, Family and Childhood." Part 1 of a paper presented at the First National Workshop of Street-Wise. Johannesburg, April 1990.

Robertson, Janice, 2011. "'Hell's View': Van de Ruit's Spud – Changing the Boys' School Story Tradition?" *Literator* 32.2: 33–63.

Robinson, Jennifer, 1998. "(Im)mobilizing Space – Dreaming of Change." *Blank____: Apartheid, Architecture and Beyond*. Eds. H. Judin and I. Vladislavic. Rotterdam: NAI Publishers. D7.

Robinson, Jennifer, 2006. *Ordinary Cities: Between Modernity and Development*. Abingdon: Routledge.

Rogerson, Christian, 2002. "Spatial Development Initiatives in South Africa: Elements, Evolution and Evaluation." *Geography* 87.1: 38–48.

Romero, Patricia W., 1998. *Profiles in Diversity: Women in the New South Africa*. East Lansing, MI: Michigan State University Press.

Romøren, R. and John Stephens, 2002. "Representing Masculinities in Norwegian and Australian Young Adult Fiction: A Comparative Study." *Ways of Being Male: Representing Masculinities in Children's Literature and Film*. Ed. John Stephens. New York: Routledge, 216-233.

Rosenthal, Jane, 2014. "Untitled: Prey to His Decay." *Mail and Guardian* 24 Jan. Web. 9 Dec. 2014. <http://mg.co.za/article/2014-01-23-prey-to-his-decay>.

Rudge, Andrew, 2014. "Key Findings: Ibali Lami National Writing Competition by Mxit Reach." *Slideee* 24 July. Web. 12 Aug. 2014. <http://www.slideee.com/slide/key-findings-ibali-lami-national-writing-competition-by-mxit-reach>.

Rudwick, S., 2004. "Zulu, We Need [It] for Our Culture: Umlazi Adolescents in the Post-Apartheid State." *Southern African Linguistics and Applied Language Studies* 22.3&4: 159–172.

Russell, David L., 2005. *Literature for Children: A Short Introduction*. 5th ed. Boston, et al.: Pearson.

Rutherford, Jonathan, 1990. "The Third Space: Interview with Homi Bhabha." *Identity: Community, Culture and Difference*. Ed. Jonathan Rutherford. London: Lawrence and Wishart. 207–221.

Sachs, Albie, 1998. "Preparing Ourselves for Freedom." *Writing South Africa: Literature, Apartheid, and Democracy, 1970–1995*. Eds. David Attridge and Rosemary Jolly. Cambridge: Cambridge University Press. 239–248.

Said, Edward W., 2010. *Orientalismus*. Frankfurt am Main: Fischer.

Said-Moorhouse, Lauren, 2014. "These Are the African Writers You Should Be Reading Right Now." *CNN* 5 Aug. Web. 6 Aug. 2014. <http://edition.cnn.com/2014/08/05/world/africa/african-writers-take-center-stage/index.html>.

Samara, Tony Roshan, 2011. *Cape Town after Apartheid: Crime and Governance in the Divided City*. Minneapolis: University of Minnesota Press.

Samuelson, Meg, 2007. "The City beyond the Border: The Urban Worlds of Duiker, Mpe and Vera." *African Identities* 5.2: 247–260.

Sandfort, Theo, and Brian Dodge, 2009. "Homosexual and Bisexual Labels: The Need for Clear Conceptualisations, Operationalisation and Appropriate Methodological Designs." *From Social Silence to Social Science: Same-Sex Sexuality, HIV & AIDS and Gender in South Africa, Conference Proceedings*. Eds. Vasu Reddy, Theo Sandfort, and Laetitia Rispel. Cape Town: HSRC Press. 51–57.

Saul, J., 1999. "Magic Market Realism and the South African Transition." *Transformation* 38: 49–67.

Schleh, Eugene, ed., 1991. *Mysteries of Africa*. Bowling Green: Bowling Green State University Popular Press.

Schmidt, Nancy, 1975. *Children's Books on Africa and Their Authors: An Annotated Bibliography*. New York: Africana Publishing.

Schmidt, Nancy, 1979. *Children's Books on Africa and Their Authors: An Annotated Bibliography. Supplement*. New York: Africana Publishing.

Schreckenberger, Susanne, and Erika Brodbeck, 2008. "Der Raum als dritter Erzieher – Innenräume, Außenräume und dazwischen." *Kindergartenpädagogik: Online–Handbuch*. Ed. Martin R. Textor. Web. 22 May 2012 <http://www.kindergartenpaedagogik.de/ 1739.html>.

Seekings, Jeremy, 1996. "The 'Lost Generation': South Africa's 'Youth Problem' in the Early 1990s." *Transformation* 29: 103–125.

Seekings, Jeremy, and Nicoli Nattrass, 2005. *Class, Race, and Inequality in South Africa*. New Haven: Yale University Press.

Seigfried, Charlene Haddock, 1996. *Pragmatism and Feminism: Reweaving the Social Fabric*. Chicago: Chicago University Press.

Selikow, T., B. Zulu, and E. Cedras, 2002. "The Ingagara, the Regte and the Cherry. HIV/AIDS and Youth Culture in Contemporary Urban Townships." *Agenda* 53: 22–32.

Sheffer, Susannah, 1997. "Adolescent Girls and Sexual Desire." *New Moon Network* Fall: 78–80.

Shields, David, 2010. *Reality Hunger: A Manifesto*. New York: Knopf.

Shields, Patricia M., 2006. "Democracy and the Social Feminist Ethics of Jane Addams: A Vision for Public Administration." *Administrative Theory and Praxis* 28.3: 418–443.

Short, J., and L. Hughes, eds., 2006. *Studying Youth Gangs*. Walnut Creek, CA: AltaMira Press.

Shutte, Augustine, 2001. *Ubuntu: An Ethic for a New South Africa*. Pietermaritzburg: Cluster Publications.

Sigler, Carolyn, 1994. "Wonderland to Wasteland: Toward Historicizing Environmental Activism in Children's Literature." *Children's Literature Association Quarterly* 19.4: 148–153.

Simone, Abdoumaliq, 1998. "Globalization and the Identity of African Urban Practices." *Blank____: Apartheid, Architecture and Beyond*. Ed. Hilton Judin and Ivan Vladislavič. Rotterdam: NAI Publishers.

Smith, C., 2001. *Proud of Me: Speaking out against Sexual Violence and HIV*. London: Penguin.

Soja, Edward W., 1989. *Postmodern Geographies: The Reassertion of Space in Critical Social Theory*. London; New York: Verso

Soja, Edward W., 1996. *Thirdspace: Journeys to Los Angeles and Other Real–and–Imagined Places*. Oxford, UK; Malden, MA: Blackwell.

Soja, Edward W., 2008. "Vom Zeitgeist zum Raumgeist. New Twists on the *Spatial Turn*." *Spatial Turn: Das Raumparadigma in den Kultur- und Sozialwissenschaften*. Eds. Jörg Döring and Tristan Thielmann. Bielefeld: transcript. 241–262.

Soja, Edward W., 2009a. "Taking Space Personally." *The Spatial Turn: Interdisciplinary Perspectives*. Ed. Barney Warf and Santa Arias. New York: Routledge. 11–35.

Soja, Edward W., 2009b. "The City and Spatial Justice." *Justice Spatiale Spatial Justice* 1. Web. 18 Aug. 2016. <http://www.jssj.org/wp-content/uploads/2012/12/JSSJ1-1en4.pdf>.

Stadler, Sandra, 2014. "Generation Z und die Revolution der südafrikanischen Lesekultur." *AfrikaSüd* 3: 16–17.

Stadler, Sandra, 2015. "Debating Equal Representation in South African Youth Literature Written in English (2000–2013) – A Statistical Assessment." *Bookbird* 53.2: 47–58.

Stadler, Sandra, forthcoming. "Facing up to Reality: Recent Developments in South Africa's English Literature for the Young." *Routledge Companion to International Children's Literature*. Ed. John Stephens. New York: Routledge.

Steinberg, Jonny, 2008. "Crime." *New South African Keywords*. Eds. Nick Shepherd and Steven Robins. Johannesburg: Jacana; Athens: Ohio University Press. 25–34.

Stephens, John, 1992. *Language and Ideology in Children's Fiction*. London; New York: Longman.

Stephens, John, 1996. "Gender, Genre and Children's Literature." *Signal* 79: 16–30.

Stephens, John, ed., 2002. *Ways of Being Male: Representing Masculinities in Children's Literature and Film*. New York: Routledge.

Stephens, John, forthcoming. *The Routledge Companion to International Children's Literature*. London: Routledge.

Stobie, C., 2012. "Dystopian Dreams from South Africa: Lauren Beukes's *Moxyland* and *Zoo City*." *African Identities* 10.4: 367–380.

Struik, Willem, and Beth le Roux, 2012. "Annual Book Industry Survey Report 2011." Johannesburg: University of Pretoria. Web. 21 June 2015. <http://www.publishsa.co.za/downloads/industry-statistics/PASA_Survey_2011.pdf>.

Swanson, Dena Phillips, Malik Chaka Edwards, and Margaret Beale Spencer, 2010. *Adolescence: Development during a Global Era*. San Diego: Elsevier.

Swartz, Sharlene, 2009. *The Moral Ecology of South African Township Youth*. New York: Palgrave.

Thorpe, Jen, 2014. "Patriarchy Revisited: Alarming Anti-feminist Rhetoric Expressed at Ministry of Women Meeting." *Feminists SA.com* 7 Nov. Web. 10 Nov. 2014. <http://feministssa.com/2014/11/07/patriarchy-revisited-alarming-anti-feminist-rhetoric-expressed-at-ministry-of-women-meeting/>.

Tötemeier, Andrée-Jeanne, 1993. "Trends in Children's Literature at Home and Abroad." Ed. Isabel Chilliers. *Towards More Understanding*. Cape Town: Juta. 159–169.

Trites, Roberta Seelinger, 2000. *Disturbing the Universe: Power and Repression in Adolescent Literature*. Iowa City: University of Iowa Press.

Van de Ruit, John, 2012. "Transcript of 'John van de Ruit on Inspiring New Ways'." *Brand South Africa* 04 July. Youtube. Web. 20 Jan. 2014. <https://www.youtube.com/watch?x-yt-ts=1421914688&v=smf41YXwxdE&x-yt-cl=84503534>.

Van der Berg, Servaas, et al., 2011. "Improving Education Quality in South Africa: Report for the National Planning Commission." *University of Stellenbosch*. Web. 18 June 2015. <http://resep.sun.ac.za/wp-content/uploads/2012/10/2011-Report-for-NPC.pdf>.

Van der Merwe, Chris, and Christopher Saunders, 2001. "Introduction." *Strangely Familiar: South African Narratives on Town and Countryside*. Eds. Chris van der Merwe and Christopher Saunders. Cape Town: Contentlot. 1–16.

Van der Vlies, Andrew, 2007. *South African Textual Cultures: White, Black, Read All Over*. Manchester: Manchester University Press.

Van der Westhuizen, Betsie, 2008. "Guest Editor's Introduction to Cluster: Children's Literature in South Africa." *The Lion and the Unicorn* 32.2: vi.

Van Dijck, José, 2013. *The Culture of Connectivity: A Critical History of Social Media*. Oxford: Oxford University Press.

Van Gemert, F., D. Peterson, and I.-L. Lien, eds., 2008. *Youth Gangs, Migration, and Ethnicity*. Devon: Willan Publishing.

Van Huyssteen, Elsona, and Alize Botha, 2008. "A National Overview of Spatial Trends and Settlement Characteristics 2008." CSIR, Built Environment and EconRise. Web. 20 June 2015. <http://sacitiesnetwork.co.za/wp-content/uploads/2014/06/overview.pdf>.

Van Lierop-Debrauwer, Wilhelmina L., and Neel Bastiaansen-Harks, 2005. *Over grenzen: De adolescentenroman in het literatuuronderwijs*. Delft: Eburon.

Van Zyl, Dorothea, 2006. "'I Am Becoming Someone Completely Different ...': The Utilisation of Liminality in Vaselinetjie (Little Vaseline) by Anoeschka Von Meck / 'Ek Is Besig Om Iemand Heeltemal Anders Te Word ...': Die Ontginning Van Liminaliteit in Vaselinetjie Deur Anoeschka Von Meck." *Literator: Journal of Literary Criticism, Comparative Linguistics and Literary Studies* 27.1: 39–56.

Veriava, Faranaaz, 2013. *The 2012 Limpopo Textbook Crisis: A Study in Rights-Based Advocacy, the Raising of Rights Consciousness and Governance*. Johannesburg: Section 27. Web. 15 Oct. 2016. <http://www.section27.org.za/wp-content/uploads/2013/10/The-2012-Limpopo-Textbook-Crisis1.pdf>.

Vital, Anthony, 2008. "Toward an African Ecocriticism: Postcolonialism, Ecology and *Life & Times of Michael K.*" *Research in African Literatures* 39.1: 87–106.

Vogel, Manuela, 2011. "Raum als 3. Erzieher(in)." *Handlexikon der Reggio–Pädagogik*. Ed. Sabine Lingenauber. Bochum; Freiburg: Projektverlag. 136–144.

Von der Beek, Angelika, 2001. "Der Raum als 3. Erzieher." *PÄD Forum* 3: 197–202.

Vorster, Magdel, 2014. "On a Journey with Leon De Villiers." *Creating Books for the Young in the New South Africa: Essays on Authors and Illustrators of Children's and Young Adult Literature*. Eds. Barbara Lehman, et al. Jefferson, NC: McFarland. 120–127.

Walker, Liz, 2005. "Men Behaving Differently: South African Men since 1994." *Culture, Health and Sexuality* 7.3: 225–238.

Warnes, Chris, 2012. "Writing Crime in the New South Africa: Negotiating Threat in the Novels of Deon Meyer and Margie Orford." *Journal of Southern African Studies* 28.4: 981–991.

Warnes, Chris, 2014. "Desired State: Black Economic Empowerment and the South African Popular Romance." *Popular Culture in Africa: The Episteme of the Everyday*. Eds. Stephanie Newell and Onookome Okome. London: Routledge. 154–173.

Warren, Crystal, 2003. "South Africa." *The Journal of Commonwealth Literature* 38.4: 125–182.

Warren, Crystal, 2004. "South Africa." *The Journal of Commonwealth Literature* 39.4: 113–164.

Warren, Crystal, 2005. "South Africa." *The Journal of Commonwealth Literature* 40.4: 195–234.

Warren, Crystal, 2006. "South Africa." *The Journal of Commonwealth Literature* 41.4: 181–214.

Warren, Crystal, 2007. "South Africa." *The Journal of Commonwealth Literature* 42.4: 167–201.

Warren, Crystal, 2008. "South Africa." *The Journal of Commonwealth Literature* 43.4: 183–217.

Warren, Crystal, 2012. "South Africa and Zimbabwe." *The Journal of Commonwealth Literature* 47.4: 577–606.

Warren, Crystal, 2014. "South Africa and Zimbabwe." *The Journal of Commonwealth Literature* 49.4: 615–645.

Watson, Victor, ed., 2001. *Cambridge Guide to Children's Books in English.* Cambridge: Cambridge University Press.

Webb, Jean, 2000. "Introduction." *Text, Culture and National Identity in Children's Literature. International Seminar on Children's Literature: Pure and Applied.* Ed. Jean Webb. Helsinki: Nordinfo. 7–12.

Weinkauff, Gina, and Gabriele von Glasenapp, 2010. *Kinder- und Jugendliteratur.* Paderborn: Schöningh.

Wells, Gary L., and Elizabeth A. Olson, 2003. "Eyewitness Testimony." *Annual Review of Psychology* 54: 277–295.

Westcott, Lucy, 2015. "Xenophobic Violence in South Africa Exposes Unresolved Tensions." *Newsweek* 17 April. Web. 20 April 2015. <http://www.newsweek.com/xenophobic-violence-south-africa-exposes-unresolved-tensions-323178 >.

White, Rob, 2008. "Disputed Definitions and Fluid Identities: The Limitations of Social Profiling in Relation to Ethnic Youth Gangs." *Youth Justice* 8.2: 149–161.

Wieselberg, Lukas, 2007. "Migration führt zu 'hybrider' Gesellschaft. Interview mit Homi Bhabha." *science.ORF.at* 9 Nov. Web. 23 April 2013. <http://sciencev1.orf.at/science/news/149988.html>.

Wilkie-Stibbs, Christine, 2002. *The Feminine Subject in Children's Literature*. New York; London: Routledge.

Williams, Jenna, 2008. "A Changing Didacticism: The Development of South African Young Adult Fiction from 1985 to 2006." Unpublished Master's Thesis. Rhodes University.

Williams, John, 2014. "The Great Y.A. Debate of 2014." *The New York Times. Sunday Book Review* 20 June. Web. 15 Oct. 2014. <http://www.nytimes.com/2014/06/22/books/review/the-great-ya-debate-of-2014.html>.

Wybenga, Gretel, and Maritha Snyman, eds., 2005. *Van Patrys-hulle tot Hanne Hoekom: 'n Gids tot die Afrikaanse Kinder- en Jeugbook*. Pretoria: LAPA.

Yenika-Agbaw, Vivian, 2008. *Representing Africa in Children's Literature: Old and New Ways of Seeing*. London: Routledge.

Zander, Horst, 1999. *Fact – Fiction – "Faction": A Study of Black South African Literature in English*. Tübingen: Narr.

Zegeye, Abebe, and Richard L. Harris, 2003. "Introduction." *Media, Identity and the Public Sphere in Post-Apartheid South Africa*. Eds. Abebe Zegeye and Richard L. Harris. Leiden: Brill. 1.

Zipes, Jack, ed., 2006. *The Oxford Encyclopedia of Children's Literature*. 4 vols. Oxford: Oxford University Press.

Zulu, N. S., 2007. "Racial Reconciliation and Healing in Russell Kaschula's *Emthonjeni*." *South African Journal of African Languages* 27.1: 1–5.

V Appendix

The annotated corpus was first published in *Bookbird* (cf. Stadler 2015, 56–58). Explanations: (A) Realistic novels; (B) Texts with fantastical elements/science fiction; (C) Memoirs/historical fictions/folklore; (D) Comics/pamphlets/books that provide guidelines/pocket books

Alnam, Biron, pseud., 2003. *No Problem, Man!* Claremont: New Africa Books. (A)

Apteker, Becky, 2007. *Written in Water.* Cape Town: Maskew Miller Longman. (A)

Aronson, Roy, 2011. *Jamie James and the Curse of the Ancestors.* Cape Town: Human & Rousseau. (B)

Baars, Marion, [2009]. *Scapegoat.* [Uitenhage]: The Author. (A)

Barr-Sanders, Amy, 2008. *The Things We Left Unsaid.* Univ. of Cape Town Thesis. (A)

Bauling, Jayne, 2009. *E Eights.* Oxford: Macmillian Education. (A)

Bauling, Jayne, 2011. *Stepping Solo.* Oxford: Maskew Miller Longman. (A)

Bauling, Jayne, 2012. *Dreaming of Light.* Cape Town: Tafelberg. (A)

Beake, Lesley, 2009. *Remembering Green.* London: Frances Lincoln Children's Books. (B)

Beake, Lesley, 2006. *Traveller.* Cape Town: Maskew Miller Longman. (A)

Blacklaws, Troy, 2005. *Karoo Boy.* London: Duckworth. (A)

Blacklaws, Troy, 2009. *Bafana Bafana.* Auckland Park: Jacana. (B)

Bloch, Joanne, illustr. by Lois Neethling, 2009. *A Few Little Lies.* London: Hodder Education. (A)

Bloemhof, Francois, 2009. *City at the End of the World* [2008]. Cape Town: Maskew Miller Longman. (B)

Bohle, Gail, 2009. *The Web of Silence.* [Hatfield]: Crink. (A)

Brain, Helen, 2009. *No More Secrets.* London: Hodder Education. (A)

Brickwood, L. M., 2007. *Children of the Moon.* Johannesburg: Zulu Planet. (B)

Bristow-Bovey, Darrel, 2006. *SuperZero.* Cape Town: Tafelberg. (A)

Britten, Sarah, 2000. *The Worst Year of My Life.* Cape Town: Tafelberg. (A)

Britten, Sarah, 2002. *Welcome to the Martin Tudhope Show!* Cape Town: Tafelberg. (A)

Brodrick, Susan Isabel, 2006. *Gap.* Cape Town: Oxford University Press. (A)

Brodrick, Susan Isabel, 2006. *Rockface.* Cape Town: Oxford University Press. (A)

Brodrick, Susan Isabel, 2006. *Runout.* Cape Town: Oxford University Press. (A)

Brooks, Karen Michelle, 2008. *Emily and the Battle of the Veil.* Cape Town: Ispirato. (B)

Brooks, Karen Michelle, 2009. *Emily and the Spirits of the Light.* Cape Town: Ispirato. (B)

Bulbring, Edyth, 2008. *The Summer of Toffie and Grummer.* Cape Town: Oxford University Press. (A)

Bulbring, Edyth, 2008. *The Club*. Johannesburg; Cape Town: Jonathan Ball. (A)

Bulbring, Edyth, 2010. *Melly, Mrs Ho and Me*. Johannesburg: Penguin. (A)

Bulbring, Edyth, 2010. *Pops & the Nearly Dead*. Johannesburg: Penguin. (A)

Bulbring, Edyth, 2011. *Melly, Fatty and Me*. Johannesburg: Penguin. (A)

Case, Dianne, and Yvonne Hart, 2007. *Katy of Sky Road*. Cape Town: Maskew Miller Longman. (A)

Chikukwa, Charles Chido, 2006. *Echoes of Anguish*. Florida Hills: Vivlia. (A)

Clacherty, Glynis, illustr. by Alzette Prins, 2004. *Love in a Time of Mourning*. Oxford: Heinemann Educational. (A)

Coetzee, John, 2007. *Black Swan Down*. Cape Town: Tafelberg. (A)

Coetzee, John, 2008. *Dance of the Freaky Green Gold*. Cape Town: Tafelberg. (A)

Coetzer, Owen, 2001. *The Secret of St Augustines*. Johannesburg: Covos. (A)

Coman, Carolyn, 2000. *Many Stones*. Asheville, NC: Front Street. (A)

Craig, Colleen, 2008. *Afrika*. Toronto, ON: Tundra Books. (A)

Cross Frances, 2008. *Marty's Diary*. [Cutting Edge]. Winchester, UK: Ransom Publishing. (A)

Cundill, Liam, 2007. *The White Quill*. Johannesburg: Zulu Planet. (A)

D'Achada, Gillian, 2008. *Sharkey's Son*. Cape Town: Tafelberg. (A)

Davids, Mogamat I., 2005. *111 Colleen Court*. Glosderry: New Africa Books. (A)

De Villiers, Leon, 2009. *Shorn*. Pretoria: LAPA. (A)

Delannoie, Johan, 2002. *The Adventures of Themba and Bizza: The Seven Mthombothi Beads*. Vol. 1.1. Southdale: Mthobothi Studios. (D)

Delannoie, Johan, 2002. *The Adventures of Themba and Bizza: The Enchanted Country*. Vol. 1.2. (2000). Southdale: Mthobothi Studios. (D)

Delannoie, Johan, 2003. *The Adventures of Themba and Bizza: Bizza's Revenge*. Vol. 1.3. (2001). Southdale: Mthobothi Studios. (D)

Dlamini, Gcinaphi, 2002. *Love, Chocolate and Shopping*. Claremont: New Africa Books. (A)

Dlanga, Khaya, 2012. *In My Arrogant Opinion*. [The Youngsters Series]. Johannesburg: Picador Africa. (D)

Donald, David, 2007. *Call on the Wind*. Auckland Park: Jacana. (A)

Duiker, K. Sello, 2000. *Thirteen Cents*. Claremont: New Africa Books. (A)

Duiker, K. Sello, 2001. *The Quiet Violence of Dreams*. Cape Town: Kwela. (A)

Duiker, K. Sello, 2006. *The Hidden Star*. Cape Town: Umuzi Books Random House. (C)

Dyer, Dorothy, 2012. *Reading the Wind*. Cape Town: Maskew Miller Longman. (C)

Dyer, Dorothy, 2012. *Two-faced Friends*. Cape Town: Cover2Cover Books. (A)

Dyer, Dorothy, and Ros Haden, 2011. *Jealous in Jozi*. Cape Town: Cover2Cover Books. (A)

Dyer, John B., 2002. *Ingilube: The Wonderful Adventures of a Young Zulu Warrior*. Ballyhalbert: Ajubatus. (C)

Ewing, Deborah, 2009. *Secret Celebrity*. London: Hodder Education. (A)

Ferreira, Anton, 2003. *Sharp Sharp, Zulu Dog*. Bellevue: Jacana. (A)

Fikkert, Maggie, 2003. *Jade and the Serpent's Circle*. Johannesburg: Iziza Publishing. (B)

Fritz, Ian, 2004. *Taking the Rap*. Claremont: New Africa Books. (A)

Ford, Janis, 2003. *Drugs Are for Mugs – The Street Detective Series.* Cape Town: Human & Rousseau. (A)

Ford, Janis, 2005. *It's a Dog's Life – The Street Detective Series.* Cape Town: Human & Rousseau. (A)

Ford, Janis, 2009. *Sink or Swim – The Street Detective Series.* Cape Town: Human & Rousseau. (A)

Froman, Judy, 2011. *Solomon's Story.* Johannesburg: Pan Macmillian. (B)

Gamedze, Londi, and Dorothy Dyer, 2013. *From Boys to Men.* Cape Town: Cover2Cover Books. (A)

George, Shona Evelyn, 2006. *A Kiss between Friends.* Malvern: umSinsi. (A)

Glass, Linzi, 2006. *The Year the Gipsies Came.* Johannesburg: Penguin. (C)

Glass, Linzi, 2007. *Ruby Red.* Johannesburg: Penguin. (C)

Godsell, Gillian, 2011. *Helen Suzman.* [They Fought for Freedom Series]. Cape Town: Maskew Miller Longman. (C)

Gongo, Phakamile, 2007. *The Boy from Selamanzi.* Georgeville: Manx. (A)

Green, Pippa, 2010. *Trevor Manuel.* [They Fought for Freedom Series]. Cape Town: Maskew Miller Longman. (C)

Haden, Rosamund, 2010. *Broken Promises.* Cape Town: Cover2Cover Books. (A)

Haden, Rosamund, 2011. *Sugar Daddy.* Cape Town: Cover2Cover Books. (A)

Halberstam, Gaby, 2009. *The Red Dress.* London: Macmillan Children's Books. (C)

Halberstam, Gaby, 2009. *Blue Sky Freedom.* London: Macmillan Children's Books. (C)

Heale, Jay, 2011. *Hotwire.* Pietermaritzburg: Shuter & Shooter. (A)

Hearn, Heather, 2011. *Trust Njenga.* Pietermaritzburg: Shuter & Shooter. (A)

Herne, Lily, 2011. *Deadlands.* Johannesburg: Penguin. (B)

Herne, Lily, 2012. *Death of a Saint.* London: Puffin. (B)

Hichens, Joanne, 2009. *Stained.* [Cutting Edge]. Winchester, UK: Ransom Publishing. (A)

Hiles, Linda, 2010. *Do I, Don't I? Making Good Decisions about Sex.* Pietermaritzburg: Shuter & Shooter. (D)

Hill, Katherine, 2005. *The Oxwagon List.* Leicester: Matador. (C)

Hlongwane, Sipho, 2013. *Get Me Started.* [The Youngsters Series]. Johannesburg: Picador Africa. (D)

Hofmeyr, Dianne, 2005. *Fish Notes and Star Songs.* London: Simon & Schuster. (B)

Hofmeyr, Dianne, 2012. *Oliver Strange and the Journey to the Swamps.* Cape Town: Tafelberg. (A)

Jaco, Paul, 2008. *The Leopards of Sh'ong.* Cape Town: Human & Rousseau. (A)

Jethro, Duane, 2004. *Weekend Away.* Claremont: New Africa Books. (A)

Jeynes, Karen, 2004. *Jacques Attack.* Claremont: New Africa Books. (A)

Jeynes, Karen, 2007. *Flipside.* Claremont: New Africa Books. (A)

K., Danny, 2012. *Take It from Me.* [The Youngsters Series]. Johannesburg: Picador Africa. (D)

Kaschula, Russell H., 2002. *Divine Dump Dancer.* Claremont: New Africa Books. (A)

Kaschula, Russell H., 2003. *Flying High.* Claremont: New Africa Books. (A)

Kaschula, Russell H., 2006. *Mama, I Sing to You.* Cape Town: Bateleur Books. (A)

Kaschula, Russell H., 2006. *Take Me to the River.* Glosderry: New Africa Books. (A)

Kent, Trilby, 2011. *Stones for My Father.* Toronto, ON: Tundra Books. (C)

Kitching, Garth, 2001. *Bracelet 12–005–35700.* Malvern: umSinsi. (A)

Kramer, Ann, 2005. *Mandela: The Rebel Who Led His Nation to Freedom.* [World History Biographies]. Washington, DC: National Geographic. (C)

Kruger, Gavin, and Val Kruger, 2006. *A Story of Hope! For Teens and Adolescents.* Hillcrest: Focus on the Family Africa. (A)

Laird, Christa, 2010. *The Dangerous Dream of Ben Maludzi.* Pietermaritzburg: Shuter & Shooter. (A)

Lancaster, Graham Vivian, 2010. *The Adventurous Life of Rory Flint.* Pietermaritzburg: Alexander House. (A)

Lancaster, Graham Vivian, 2010. *When the Earth Thunders.* Pietermaritzburg: Alexander House. (A)

Leggat, Gillian, 2001. *Setting up Shop.* Cape Town: Maskew Miller Longman. (A)

Lotter, Elbie, 2005. *It's Me, Anna.* Cape Town: Kwela. (A)

Louw, Wynand, 2004. *Mr Humberdinck's Wonderful Whatsit.* Cape Town: Human & Rousseau. (B)

Lucouw, Pierre, 2006. *A Maze Zing.* Vanderbijlpark: Corals. (A)

Macgregor, Fiona, 2008. *Jesse's Story.* Cape Town: Maskew Miller Longman. (A)

Macgregor, Joanne, 2011. *Turtle Walk.* Pretoria: Protea Book House. (A)

Macgregor, Joanne, 2013. *Rock Steady.* Pretoria: Protea Book House. (A)

Magona, Sindiwe, 2005. *Life Is a Hard but Beautiful Thing.* Lansdowne: Juta Gariep. (A)

Magubane, Khulekani, 2005. *Angels Anointing.* Malvern: umSinsi. (A)

Magubane, Khulekani, 2006. *Angels Redemption.* Malvern: umSinsi. (A)

Magubane, Khulekani, 2007. *Angels Salvation.* Malvern: umSinsi. (A)

Mahapeletsa, Sello, 2005. *When Lions Smile.* [2003]. Cape Town: Kwela. (A)

Mahapeletsa, Sello, 2008. *Tears of an Angel.* [2007]. Cape Town: Kwela. (A)

Malan, Robin, 2005. *The Story of Lucky Simelane: A Novel.* Bellevue: Jacana. (A)

Malan, Robin, 2012. *My "Funny" Brother.* Mowbray: Junkets. (A)

Malbusch, Rusleen, 2003. *Boy in da City.* Claremont: New Africa Books. (A)

Malherbe, Neil, 2012. *The Magyar Conspiracy.* Cape Town: Tafelberg. (A)

Maphosankala, Gerald, 2006. *Foggy Road.* Florida Hills: Vivlia. (A)

Mathabane, Mark, and Miriam Mathabane, 2001. *Miriam's Song: A Memoir (Africa Junior).* (2000). New York, et al.: Simon & Schuster. (C)

Maunder, Catherine, 2006. *Umlilo's Treasure.* Cape Town: Struik. (A)

Maunder, Catherine, 2010. *Danger Point: When the Ghost Lion Roars.* Johannesburg: Hope Press. (A)

Mazantsi, Sivuyile, and Sam Roth, 2012. *Too Young to Die.* Cape Town: Cover2Cover Books. (A)

Mazibuko, Nokuthula, 2003. *In the Fast Lane.* Claremont: New Africa Books. (A)

Mazibuko, Nokuthula, 2009. *Freedom Song.* Cape Town: Maskew Miller Longman. (C)

McNamara, Bevinn, 2006. *Thadi's Fate and Other Stories.* (2005). Cape Town: Kagiso Education. (D)

Mdoda, Anele, 2012. *It Feels Wrong to Laugh, but...* [The Youngsters Series]. Johannesburg: Picador Africa. (D)

Mhlongo, Niq, 2004. *Dog Eat Dog.* Cape Town: Kwela. (A)

Mhlongo, Niq, 2007. *After Tears.* Cape Town: Kwela. (A)

Molope, Kagiso Lesego, 2004. *Dancing in the Dust.* Cape Town: Oxford University Press. (C)

Molope, Kagiso Lesego, 2006. *The Mending Season.* (2005). Cape Town: Oxford University Press. (A)

Molope, Kagiso Lesego, 2012. *This Book Betrays My Brother.* Cape Town: Oxford University Press. (A)

Monsoon, Moni, 2010. *Fire & Ice.* Cape Town: New Voices. (B)

MoonPony, 2009. *G.A.T. Universtiy (Guardian Angel Training): What Happens If Heaven Fails?* Bloomington, IN: iUniverse. (B)

Moroukian, Colleen, 2002. *Breaking Out.* Claremont: New Africa Books. (A)

Morsbach, Jill, 2011. *Capture the Light.* Pietermaritzburg: Shuter & Shooter. (A)

Morton, Carolyn, 2013. *Hearing Helen.* Cape Town: Human & Rousseau. (A)

Motimele, Mobonchi Goodwill, 2007. *The Boy with the Guitar.* Cape Town: Maskew Miller Longman. (A)

Mzobe, Sifiso, 2010. *Young Blood.* Cape Town: Kwela. (A)

Mzongwana, Mteto, Onele Mfeketo, and Lamna Orbin, 2003. *Mom's Taxi.* Claremont: New Africa Books. (A)

Nalam, Nibor, 2002. *High Heels and Hijack.* Claremont: New Africa Books. (A)

Ndlovu, Zama, 2013. *A Bad Black's Manifesto.* [The Youngsters Series]. Johannesburg: Picador Africa. (D)

Nemutanzhela, Thiathu, 2007. *Bua, Comrade!* Cape Town: Maskew Miller Longman. (C)

Neser, Cristien, 2013. *Amper Einstein.* Cape Town: Tafelberg. (A)

Newsome, Julia M., 2008. *Nelson's Dream.* Cambridge: Cambridge University Press. (A)

Nicholson, Pamela, 2013. *Space Station Venetia.* Cape Town: Cambridge University Press. (B)

Nkosi, Lewis, 2006. *Mandela's Ego.* Cape Town: Umuzi Books Random House. (A)

Noble, Leslie Hyla Winton, 2009. *Regina.* Durban: Just Done Productions. (B)

Nomsa, Justine, 2006. *Kidz 2 Kidz: A Diary with a Difference.* Braamfontein: Macmillan South Africa. (D)

Nyembezi, C. L. S., 2010. *My Child! My Child!* Cape Town: Maskew Miller Longman. (A)

Olielo, Justus, 2000. *Sara – The Trap.* Cape Town: Maskew Miller Longman. (D)

Oppel, Martin, 2007. *I Loved That Place Tdjouboegas.* Cape Town: Kwela. (C)

Orford, Margie, 2004. *Dancing Queen.* Oxford: Heinemann Educational. (A)

Partridge, Sally A., 2007. *The Goblet Club.* Cape Town: Human & Rousseau. (A)

Partridge, Sally A., 2009. *Fuse.* Cape Town: Human & Rousseau. (A)

Partridge, Sally A., 2011. *Dark Poppy's Demise.* Cape Town: Human & Rousseau. (A)

Partridge, Sally A., 2013. *Sharp Edges.* Cape Town: Human & Rousseau. (A)

Pender-Smith, Andrew, 2008. *Hunting Zanga.* Malvern: umSinsi. (B)

Pender-Smith, Andrew, 2009. *Dream a River.* (2008). Malvern: umSinsi. (A)

Pieper, Jens Ulrich, 2007. *Arbormoss.* Cape Town: Struik. (B)

Pinnock, Patricia Schonstein, 2000. *Skyline.* Cape Town: David Philip. (A)

Pryde, Shelley, 2008. *Secrets.* Cape Town: New Voices. (A)

Rabinowitz, Nik, and Gillian Breslin, 2012. *South Africa: A Long Walk to a Free Ride*. [The Youngsters Series]. Johannesburg: Picador Africa. (D)

Radloff, Adeline L., 2010. *Side Kick*. Cape Town: Tafelberg. (B)

Ramashau, Rudzani, 2005. *Make Choices in Life*. Malvern: umSinsi. (A)

Rapola, Zachariah, 2006. *Stanza on the Edge*. (2001). Cape Town: Maskew Miller Longman. (A)

Rapola, Zachariah, 2007. *Stanza and the Jive Mission*. (2005). Cape Town: Maskew Miller Longman. (A)

Rapola, Zachariah, 2009. *Stanza's Soccer World Cup*. Cape Town: Maskew Miller Longman. (A)

Reid, Chris Ntombemhlophe, 2008. *Nomtombomsa and the Sacred Pool*. Cape Town: Juta. (B)

Rhys, Nichola, 2001. *Road to Nowhere*. Malvern: umSinsi. (A)

Richardson, Dick, 2005. *The Oglin: A Hero's Journey across Africa…towards the Tomorrow*. Monte Vista, CO; Vryburg: Savannah Press. (B)

Robson, Jenny, 2004. *Savannah 2116 AD*. Cape Town: Tafelberg. (B)

Robson, Jenny, 2005. *Breaking the Silence*. [HIV/AIDS Action Readers Level 2]. Oxford: Macmillan Education. (A)

Robson, Jenny, 2005. *A Letter to Pearl*. [HIV/AIDS Action Readers Level 2]. Oxford: Macmillan Education. (A)

Robson, Jenny, 2006. *Praise Song*. Cape Town: Tafelberg. (A)

Robson, Jenny, 2006. *Mopati's Story*. [HIV/AIDS Action Readers Level 3]. Oxford: Macmillan Education. (A)

Robson, Jenny, 2013. *Back to Villa Park*. Cape Town: Tafelberg. (A)

Robson, Jenny, 2013. *Monday Morning, Thursday Afternoon*. Cape Town: Tafelberg. (A)

Rose-Innes, Henrietta, 2000. *Shark's Egg*. Cape Town: Kwela. (A)

Roth, Sam, 2012. *Time Twisters: Cape of Slaves*. London: Puffin. (B)

Sara Research Team, 2008. *Sara – The Tight Spot*. Cape Town: Maskew Miller Longman. (D)

Schermbrucker, Reviva, 2003. *Lucky Fish*. Bellevue: Jacana. (C)

Schlebusch, Anne, 2002. *Troubles, Taxis and Toilets*. Claremont: New Africa Books. (A)

Schlebusch, Anne, 2003. *Dance Idols*. Claremont: New Africa Books. (A)

Scholtz, A. H. M., 2001. *A Place Called Vatmaar*. Cape Town: Kwela. (C)

Scholtz, Pieter, 2006. *The Demon of the Curry Powders*. Cape Town: Struik. (B)

Scholtz, Pieter, 2009. *Milo & the Sunflower: A Journey beyond the Sunset*. Durban: Horus Publications. (B)

Scholtz, Pieter, 2011. *The Tree Whisperer*. Durban: Horus Publications. (B)

Silver, Norman, 2000. *A Monkey's Wedding*. London: Faber and Faber. (A)

Sisulu, Shaka, 2012. *Becoming*. [The Youngsters Series]. Johannesburg: Picador Africa. (D)

Slingsby, Peter, 2001. *Leopard Boy*. Cape Town: Tafelberg. (A)

Slingsby, Peter, 2002. *Jedro's Bane*. Cape Town: Tafelberg. (A)

Smith, Alex, 2010. *Agency Blue*. Cape Town: Tafelberg. (B)

Smith, Clive E., 2003. *Girl Goes Missing*. Claremont: New Africa Books. (A)

Smith, Clive E., 2007. *From Belhar to Bollywood*. Claremont: New Africa Books. (A)

Smith, Gail, 2003. *Someone Called Lindiwe.* Oxford: Macmillan Education. (A)

Smith, Gail, 2010. *Bongani's Secret.* Oxford: Macmillan Education. (B)

Snyckers, Fiona, 2009. *Trinity Rising.* Johannesburg; Cape Town: Jonathan Ball. (A)

Snyckers, Fiona, 2010. *Trinity on Air.* Johannesburg; Cape Town: Jonathan Ball. (A)

Snyckers, Fiona, 2013. *Team Trinity.* Athlone: Modjaji Books. (A)

Sooknanan, Nalini, 2004. *Storm & Skye: The Lost Island of Magicon.* Victoria, BC: Trafford. (B)

St John, Lauren, 2007. *The White Giraffe.* New York: Dial Books for Young Readers. (B)

St John, Lauren, 2010. *The Elephant's Tale.* New York: Dial Books for Young Readers; Burlington, MA: Walden Media. (B)

Tlhankana, Ipeleng, 2010. *A Girl's Life: A Woman's Journey.* (2008). Johannesburg: Manx. (D)

Turkington, Nola, 2004. *Secrets, Secrets.* Oxford: Heinemann Educational Publishers. (A)

Van der Ruit, John, 2005. *Spud.* Johannesburg, et al.: Penguin. (A)

Van der Ruit, John, 2009. *Spud – The Madness Continues.* Johannesburg, et al.: Penguin. (A)

Van der Ruit, John, 2011. *Spud – Learning to Fly.* Johannesburg, et al.: Penguin. (A)

Van der Ruit, John, 2012. *Spud – Exit, Pursued by a Bear.* Johannesburg, et al.: Penguin. (A)

Van der Vyver, Marita, 2007. *The Hidden Life of Hanna Why.* Cape Town: Tafelberg. (A)

Van der Walt, Willem 'Thembalethu', 2005. *Heist Wind.* (2003). Roggebaai: Kwela. (A)

Van Dijk, Lutz, 2000. *Stronger than the Strom: A Novel for Young Adults about HIV and AIDS in South Africa.* Cape Town: Maskew Miller Longman. (A)

Van Dijk, Lutz, 2006. *Crossing the Line.* Pietermaritzburg: Shuter & Shooter. (A)

Van Dijk, Lutz, 2010. *Themba: A Boy Called Hope.* Pietermaritzburg: Shuter & Shooter. (A)

Van Dijk, Lutz, 2010. *Romeo and Jabulile.* Cape Town: Maskew Miller Longman. (A)

Van Oudtshoorn, Mandy, 2008. *The Pink Prison.* Durban: Just Done Productions. (C)

Van Tonder, Jan, 2006. *Ongenagama, the Child with No Name.* Cape Town: Maskew Miller Longman. (A)

Vegter, Onne, 2004. *Whitney's Kiss.* Bellville: Voices in Africa. (A)

Viljoen, Fanie, 2010. *Mindf**k.* Winchester, UK: Ransom Publishing. (A)

Viljoen, Fanie, 2011. *Scarred Lion.* Winchester, UK: Ransom Publishing. (A)

Vlaming, Morag, 2003. *Gogo's Magic: An African Fable.* Benmore: Writers Inc. (A)

Von Meck, Anoeschka, 2011. *My Name is Vaselinetije.* Cape Town: Tafelberg. (A)

Williams, Michael, 2002. *The Eighth Man: A Jake Mulligan Mystery.* Cape Town: Oxford University Press. (A)

Williams, Michael, 2009. *The Billion Dollar Soccer Ball.* Cape Town: Maskew Miller Longman. (A)

Wood, Nicholas, 2004. *The Stone Chameleon.* Cape Town: Maskew Miller Longman. (B)

Younghusband, Peter, 2006. *The Timbavati Patrol.* Stanford, CA: Capricorn. (A)